Zululan

Dr. Ian Player was with the Natal Parks Board from 1952 to 1974. He initiated wilderness trails and was senior ranger in charge of Operation Rhino, the most successful translocation in conservation history. He was the founder of the Wilderness Leadership School, the Wilderness Trust (U.K.), the International Wilderness Leadership Foundation (U.S.A), the World Wilderness Congress, the Magqubu Ntombela Memorial Foundation and the Msunduzi-Mgeni Canoe Marathon. He was honoured as Knight in the Order of the Golden Ark by Prince Bernhard of the Netherlands and has received many other honours and awards.

Other books written by the author are *Men, Rivers and Canoes* (Simondium, 1963), *White Rhino Saga* (Collins, 1973), *Big Game*, in collaboration with T.C. Robertson (Caltex, 1973).

"This book is Ian Player's tribute to Makhubu Ntombela and the remarkable friendship which grew in the wild. Their relationship and their commitment not only to each other but also to the conservation of wilderness is a shining example of the spirit of the people of this country."

— President Nelson Mandela

ZULULAND WILDERNESS

Shadow and Soul

IAN PLAYER

Chris

I saw this and thought of you!
My brother went on safari with
Ian Player and described it [illegible]
[illegible] as a pivotal moment
in his life.

Enjoy!

Buzz

LINE DRAWINGS BY NOLA STEELE

DAVID PHILIP PUBLISHERS CAPE TOWN

Zululand Wilderness

Sixth Impression published in 2013
by David Philip Publishers
6 Spin Street
Cape Town 8001
South Africa

First published in 1997 by David Philip Publishers

ISBN: 978-0-86486-340-9
e-ISBN: 978-1-86486-891-3

Cover design by Abdul Amien
Front Cover photograph by Jane Campbell

Printed by Pinetown Printers

David Philip is committed to a sustainable future for our business, our readers and our planet.

Contents

This book is dedicated to Dr. Mangosuthu Buthelezi
and the late Nick Steele
Together they led the way to a new understanding
of conservation in KwaZulu-Natal

Foreword

To make a great friend at first meeting is a rare occurrence, but when Ian Player and I came together, at the instigation of a mutual friend, famous for her intuitive understanding, the trick worked to her satisfaction. We both knew of each other's work and had indeed been journeying roughly in the same direction but down different rivers. Our meeting was the confluence. I already knew, of course, of his crucial role in the saving of the white rhino and had read his book *The White Rhino Saga* some twenty-odd years before, which recorded so graphically the trials, twists and tribulations that accompanied that great feat – the work of an intrepid band of men under his leadership.

In this study of Magqubu Ntombela, his lifelong friend and companion, the author, inevitably perhaps, lays bare a portion of his own soul for interpretation. Magqubu becomes the catalyst for this revealing introspection. Though the readers can only glimpse into the opaque depths of Magqubu's unencumbered Zuluness and decipher for themselves a few of the codes that unlock the secrets of the wilderness, they can see clearer, if not further, into the troubled psyche of the author. In the end we know more of Ian Player than we do of Magqubu. In attempting so painstakingly to locate the inner spirit of his great, uncomplicated but mysterious friend he exposes to view the anguish and self-doubt that pervade his own nature, thus throwing into relief its strengths and weaknesses.

I would safely say that few *umlungu* have ever got so near to the traditional Zulu mind as the author has done. How many thousand nights did they spend together over the camp fire, mostly silent and alone, words quenched by the exertions of the day? Magqubu's common sense, vast applicative knowledge of the world around him, his firmness of character and calmness of temperament eventually forced a cultural, racial and hierarchical equipoise between these two men – a rare phenomenon in Africa.

As one is carried along by the momentum of the author's narrative style it is impossible not to marvel at the insight of both these naturalists into the complexities of the pristine wilderness that surrounded them. They hear, see and feel what would pass largely unnoticed by the uninitiated. Sounds seem to echo through the work – the soughing of the morning wind through the bush willows, the 'churring' of the oxpeckers; the soft clatter of acacia pods falling; and so on. He often likens these concerts of sounds to symphonies, rhapsodies and even nocturnes. One can almost hear his prose, feel his sentiment, and scent with him the warm earth after the rainstorm.

I have been days in Umfolozi, Hluhluwe and Ndumu with the author and he would, after a pause, identify each bird by its song, and each mammal by its cry; but however great, however profound, Ian Player's knowledge of and familiarity with these wild lands, that he had lived for and in thirty years or more, it could not measure up to that of Magqubu Ntombela, originally his aide and then his mentor. The Zulu tracker and hunter could call, not only on his own vast experience, but on the cumulative wisdom and inherited instincts of a thousand ancestors.

We alien Europeans are enthralled by the strangeness and wonder at the beauty and variety of wild nature. To the old Zulu the wilderness was part of his life – part of his diet – part of his soul. The wild was his womb as well as his grave. Its untamed denizens were his second kindred, his familiars. He imbued them with his own capacity for language and conversed with them. No greater compliment could a Zulu pay his chiefs and kings than to compare them to lions, elephant, rhino or buffalo.

Ian Players admits to being a romantic – so do I. What choice have we but the gateway to romance? What other paths but the paths of legend and of mystery? They are the only roads we know that lead to that peace of mind that becalmed Magqubu's soul. The old Zulu's empathy with his wild world was bequeathed to him, was his natural inheritance. Ian Player had to seek and find it, blinkered by a European education, half-blinded by "civilized" values, hamstrung by uncomprehending superiors, waylaid by misfortunes, nonetheless he found his way to Magqubu's hearth and shared the warmth of his friendship, his experience, his philosophy and his wisdom.

We can imagine them squatting silently by the dying embers after a strenuous day – silently talking to each other with glance of eye and shift of limb, accompanied only by the chorus of the night.

The gods were generous when they apportioned their gifts and attributes to Ian Player and his companion Magqubu – to Ian Player, romance, the capacity to dream when awake, an earthy practicality, an insight into the mind of animal and man, a tenacity of purpose which has never left him. To Magqubu was given an ability to understand and imitate the language of wild creaures; the stamina of one of Shaka's foot soldiers; the capacity to interpret the signs, sounds and scents of wild animals to a degree hopelessly beyond the reach of any modern ethologist; an acceptance of a subordinate status without any loss of pride or self-esteem, typical of his warrior ancestors; a compendious tribal memory, itself the godchild of an oral culture, with its sister skill the ability to tell a tale and animate it with mime and dance. For this the haunting beauty of the Zulu language was his perfect tool – he used it well.

In this book, that is so close to Ian Player's heart, Magqubu Ntombela's spirit lives again, a noble ornament to a noble race – the lives of both men expended to exhaustion in, for them, the greatest cause of all – the protection of some of the last few, relict scraps of untrammelled widerness that have, to date, survived the human cataclysm.

JOHN ASPINALL

Acknowledgements

This book owes its existence to the help of many people, and to acknowledge each one would require a book in itself.

Without my wife, Ann, this book could never have been written. She has been a continual source of inspiration and constructive encouragement, and I have relied heavily on her intuitive advice.

My initiation into the world of books, came from my mother, Muriel Player. She was always saying, "Now, read this book," and slowly I developed a love for books of all kinds, and became an author myself.

My father, Harry Player, born in the Hela-hela valley, grew up in the world of the Zulu people, speaking their language before he spoke English. He instilled in me my first appreciation of the wonderful qualities of the old Zulu order.

My dear friend the late Nick Steele gave technical help and constant encouragement. His wife Nola Steele has enhanced the book and given life to many pages with her creative illustrations.

Dr. Mangosuthu Buthelezi as Chief Minister of KwaZulu was a staunch advocate of the retention and expansion of the Zululand game reserves, and this had a most beneficial impact on the morale of the poorly paid men who guarded the reserves with their lives.

John Aspinall, a man deeply devoted to the care and propagation of endangered species and a great admirer of the Zulu people, kindly wrote the foreword. He has poured millions of pounds into his private zoos and his efforts to save the gorilla in central Africa. He is a great admirer of the Zulu people and understood at a deep level Magqubu Ntombela's contribution to his people and the animal world.

The late Sir Laurens van der Post, a friend for over thirty years, was a constant source of advice, always most generously given.

Nora Kreher continually prodded me, asking, "Where is the book?" She walked on the trails with Magqubu and saw and understood the interaction between us.

Vance Martin, a friend since 1980, was extremely helpful in his critical appraisal of the first draft and in persuading Bob Baron of Fulcrum to publish the book in America.

David Philip made a decision to publish based on his reading of a rough and unfinished draft, boosting my morale enormously.

Jane Taylor of the United Kingdom attended Zulu classes in London, spent many days with us on trail and later sat recording Magqubu as he told his life story.

Dr. Gloria Gearing of Mariannhill gave me psychological insights into my friendship with Magqubu and repeatedly reminded me to beware of projections, and to look at the man realistically. She trekked with us into the wilderness of Mfolozi and interpreted many dreams of mine that had important bearing on my friendship with this remarkable man.

Maurice Mackenzie, now a member of the KwaZulu-Natal Provincial Parliament and an expert Zulu linguist, was enormously helpful in translating and interpreting what Laurens van der Post used to call Magqubu's Shakespearian Zulu. With his ability to speak Zulu and English, Maurice Mackenzie was able to grasp nuances which were beyond most people.

Africa Khanyile, David Zondi, Mark Astrup, Stan Upfold and Brian Stevens were all helpful at various times with translation.

Gqakaza Ntombela and Mdiceni Gumede, old game-ranger colleagues, provided valuable historical information about Magqubu's early life.

Bongani Ngubane formerly of the KwaZulu Bureau for Natural Resources, accompanied Magqubu and me to Brecon in Wales and to the 4th World Wilderness Congress in America. His diplomatic and interpretative skills and his care for Magqubu's needs were a major contribution to the success of our journey.

Wayne Elliott and Vincent Ngcobo of the Department of Nature Conservation went out of their way to help Magqubu Ntombela's family, and they assisted in bringing the Magqubu Ntombela Memorial Foundation to fruition with historical information from old game guards.

My colleagues in the Wilderness Leadership School – Bruce Dell, Paul Cryer and Ian Read along with Gqakaza Ntombela and Mdiceni Gumede – continue to lead trails in a tradition Magqubu greatly approved, of respect for the land, the ancestral spirits and the wildlife. I am extremely grateful to all the women, past and present, who served the Wilderness Leadership School, for their help and understanding of what Magqubu stood for. They appreciated his real worth.

Andrew Muir, National Director of the Wilderness Leadership School, and his wife Margot, draw on the spirit of Ubuntu that Magqubu exuded and help to keep alive the special ethos that Magqubu exemplified in his years of devotion to the school after leaving the Natal Parks Board.

Andrew Ewing, chairman of the Magqubu Ntombela Memorial Foundation, has expended much time and effort to ensure that the Foundation fulfils its obligations and the promises I made to Magqubu.

My secretary, Hildah McAllen, has devoted many hours to the Magqubu Ntombela Memorial Foundation and to ensuring that Magqubu's family needs are attended to at Macibini in Zululand.

Jennifer Rayner was very helpful in capturing much of the early material of this book on a computer donated by Tom Worrell of America.

I shall always be indebted to Colonel Jack Vincent, MBE, my director at the Natal Parks Board for eleven years. Without his help the wilderness concept could never have become a reality. As a trained staff officer he gave me excellent administrative training which has carried me through life in the organizations and many causes I have served.

I wish to thank Paul and Sheila Dutton for the many years of friendship they extended to Magqubu and myself. Their devotion to conservation and Sheila's psychological understanding helped me to grasp facets I had overlooked.

This book concentrates on the relationship between Magqubu and myself, but while this was developing there was constant interaction with many other Natal Parks Board game rangers in Zululand, and head office personnel in Pietermaritzburg. Space prevents me from mentioning them all by name and I apologize for not being able to do so.

In America, a host of people and organizations supported our cause of conservation in KwaZulu-Natal. Harry Tennison, Bob Cleaves, Ray Arnett and Bob Dill, are some who come immediately to mind.

Thanks are due to Ed Posey, Peter Hitchins, the *Natal Mercury*, the *Daily News*, and the *Natal Witness* for the use of some of the photographs.

I have tried to capture an essence of the political antipathies of the 1950s, 1960s and 1970s. Everything has changed dramatically since 1994 with the national franchise. The lack of bitterness from President Mandela and black people generally, and the acceptance by the Afrikaans-speaking people of majority rule, give all the people of this great country a chance to work together towards a common future.

In the twenty-first century I am certain that the environment will play an ever-increasingly important role. I hope this story is an example of what individuals can do.

The house at Mpila

Introduction

This is the story of my friendship with Qumbu Magqubu Ntombela, a Zulu game guard who spent nearly all his life in the service of wildlife conservation. Magqubu had a profound influence upon my life. We knew each other for close to forty years, first as game rangers in the Mfolozi game reserve with the Natal Parks Board, then later as trail leaders with the Wilderness Leadership School. Magqubu and I first met at Masinda camp in Mfolozi game reserve in 1952, and our lives became inextricably linked. I had gone to Masinda camp to meet old Willie Foster, who was about to take on the post of game supervisor. Willie and I were talking, and he called out to a short, thickset Zulu wearing an old army overcoat and a floppy Australian-type hat who was sitting under a marula tree. The day was hot, and I wondered how he could stand the heavy coat. He came forward, his movements quick and his eyes unwavering when he looked into mine. The dappled light of the big marula tree enhanced his stature.

"This is Magqubu Ntombela, a good man," Willie Foster said slowly. He praised few people.

Magqubu and I greeted each other, and there was an unconscious recognition of our respective inner beings, a connection that went beyond the normal greeting. Magqubu had the bearing of a warrior, and every movement he made emphasized his independence. He was five feet six, yet his presence demanded attention. He was respectful, attentive, and obedient to Willie Foster, but he was his own man. I thought to myself that this was as it had been at the time of the old Zulu order. Our meeting was brief, but he had made a deep impression upon me. Magqubu was fifty-two and had already worked in the game reserves for thirty-eight years. I was twenty-five and had just begun my career. Something stirred within me. I had an intuitive flash and knew that this man would be important in my life. A friendship began that eventually superseded colour, culture, religion, and every other barrier that can exist between men, but the journey was not without its difficulties. Our friendship was one of the most important in my life, and Magqubu seemed an ageless person to me. He was always there, waiting to impart knowledge or tell a new story. His energy was boundless, and his ability to deal with life and all its problems was enviable. He was a guide and mentor on my long and continuous journey toward self-understanding.

This is also the story of the important struggle to protect wild nature. It mostly occurs in a region of South Africa referred to as Zululand, the ancestral and contemporary home of the Zulu people. For those not familiar with my country, some background may be helpful.

The history of the Republic of South Africa is, like many histories, long and involved. The modern history of my province, KwaZulu-Natal, began on Christmas Day 1497, when the Portuguese navigator Vasco da Gama sailed up the east coast of Africa on his expedition to India. As day dawned and he saw the green land in the distance, he named it Natal to mark the day of the birth of Christ. Historians argue that it was probably farther south of the present city of Durban where he saw and named the land, but this is unimportant. What is certain is that he saw a land that would in the future become significant, and the land was beautiful.

Natal, as Vasco da Gama saw it in 1497, had long been inhabited by the San Bushmen and the black Nguni people. Some of the latter had been drifting in from the great lakes of central Africa for centuries.

In the early 1820s a group of traders and sailors arrived at Port Natal (Durban) from the Cape Colony. They built mud huts, then set about hunting elephants and trading goods for ivory with the local black people. They soon learned that the land was under the control of the great King Shaka Zulu, with whom they would have to establish their bona fides. His capital, Bulawayo (The Place of Killing), lay to the north of the Thukela River, so it was to the north that they trekked. What had started as an elephant, rhino, or hippo path had been linked with human footpaths, and these became well worn and known as the *izindhlela enkulu,* or *izindhlela encane* – "big path" and "little path." Animal hooves and pads and human feet beat the earth hard.

Among the traders there were many rugged individualists, men like Nathaniel Isaacs, Thomas Halstead, and John Ross. Each left his mark on the land of Natal. Isaacs wrote a two-volume autobiographical diary full of fascinating details of the early Port Natal. Thomas Halstead mingled his blood with that of the Voortrekkers of Piet Retief's commando who were killed by King Dingane at Mgungundhlovu (Dinganeskraal), near the present capital of KwaZulu at Ulundi. John Ross (Rawdon Maclean) left his nautical journal articles. He trekked through Zululand and across the plains of Tongaland to fetch medicine for his sick companions at the bay in Durban. He was only thirteen years old. He became a friend and confidant of Shaka and a devoted admirer of the Zulu people.

Then there were the Zulu, loyal to new masters and ready to pick up arms to fight whoever might be an enemy. Shaka Zulu held sway. His word was law. A nod of his head or the lifting of a finger could mean a death sentence. He brought the Zulu nation into prominence as the best- disciplined and most powerful black nation in Africa. He is revered by the Zulu people, who every year commemorate his name on a special day. He tolerated the white presence at the bay and liked various white men who came to see him, but John Ross was his favourite.

Acculturation in Durban began with the taking of Zulu wives, and the whites had *imizi* (homesteads) like minor Zulu chiefs. White blood and an Anglo-Saxon desire for land and possessions and a lust to kill animals injected a new awareness into the native people. The whites' stories of the great King George across the sea in England; their trinkets, mirrors, and blankets; their medicines; and above all their muskets brought change to the ancient rhythm of this part of Africa. Another epoch was in the making. Both the Zulu and the white men were dynamic. It was the beginning of a great transformation and the land was to suffer as a result.

Time passed, and King Shaka Zulu was killed at Duguza by his half-brothers Dingane and Mbopa not far from the present village of Stanger. As he lay dying, Shaka made a prophetic statement. He said that they may have killed him, but the swallows (the term was used to describe the whites because they built their huts of mud) would soon come and eat up all the land. Shaka was right, but the wheel would continue to turn – the Zulus would fight valiantly for their land, and time and numbers would in the end be on their side.

Dingane became king, and in 1837 the Boers (Afrikaners) trekking from the Cape Colony came over the Drakensberg (Dragon mountains) into the green lands of Natal. They too followed the animal and the Nguni footpaths until the wagon tracks became a more permanent feature.

The Boers and the Zulus met at the Battle of Blood River in 1838. They fought over land, for both were cattle people continually seeking to increase the size of their herds. The Boers defeated the Zulus at this battle, but it was only the beginning of a struggle for land that would repeat itself in the long and blood-soaked history of South Africa.

In 1850, when there were still elephant within an hour's ride of Durban, my great-grandfather, James Player, arrived from the United Kingdom. He married a fourteen-year-old Afrikaner girl in Pietermaritzburg. She was Sarah Elizabeth van Niekerk, a stepdaughter of the trekker Gert Maritz. It was the first marriage between an Englishman and an Afrikaner in what had become the British Colony of Natal, and it created a stir at the time. They had eleven children.

Dingane was by then long dead, and King Mpande ruled Zululand. More and more traders and hunters were going up the north coast road, men like Baldwin, who had been lured to southern Africa by the stories of Gordon Cumming and other hunters. Game was still plentiful in all the thorn country and in the lower altitudes, where malaria and the tsetse fly kept people away. Natal had become a British colony and Zululand remained an independent black kingdom. The Thukela River was the boundary between the two states.

In 1856 a great battle took place between Cetshwayo and Mbulazi, sons of King Mpande who were vying for the Zulu throne. They fought on the north side of the Thukela River on a raw December day. There is a story of a critical moment in the battle when a gust of wind blew a feather from Mbulazi's hair, causing his men to lose heart and, subsequently, the battle. A terrible massacre of Mbulazi's forces followed. The banks of the Thukela River were strewn with bodies. When Mpande died, Cetshwayo became king, and it was he who stood up against the British in 1879, rallying the Zulu people to fight with great courage for the old Zulu order.

In late 1878 the road to the north from Durban was filled with wagon traffic. The British Army was on the move to Fort Pearson, one of the sites from which the planned invasion of Zululand would take place. A young corporal in the Natal Hussars trotted his horse up the north coast track to Fort Pearson. He was Frank Player, my grandfather, the second-born son of the original Player pioneer who married the young Afrikaner girl in 1852.

The Zulu War was one of the most unjust wars ever perpetrated by Great Britain. The British, who expected a walkover by their soldiers, armed with all the modern weapons of war, received a devastating shock at Isandlwana on January 22, 1879. Some twenty-five thousand Zulus under the command of Mnyaman Buthelezi poured over the Nqutu hills, then swept relentlessly across an open plain to fall with assegai, knobkierie, and shield upon Britain's finest troops in Africa, men who had fought their way through the Transkei against the Xhosa people. The British commanders underestimated the Zulu warriors, and within a few hours some 812 men of Britain's army lay dead, more than at the Battle of Waterloo. Lord Chelmsford, the British commander-in-chief, had been outwitted by the Zulu generals. It was a battle that reverberated around the Western world, and the word Zulu became synonymous with bravery. Benjamin Disraeli, the British prime minister, would later say, "A remarkable people the Zulu. They defeat our generals;

convert our bishops; and put an end to a great European dynasty." He was referring to Lord Chelmsford, the commander of the British forces in South Africa in 1879; Bishop Colenso, "Sobantu," who befriended the Zulu people; and Prince Louis Napoleon, the last of the Napoleonic line, killed by the Zulu in the campaign of 1879.

On the same day another furious battle was taking place north of Fort Pearson on the Inyezane (African willow) hills. The Zulu had attacked Colonel Pearson's column, but the combined imperial and colonial forces beat them off. This victory was forgotten, but the memory of Isandlwana has lived with succeeding generations and been the source of countless books, documentaries, and films. The battle has been fought and refought in dining rooms, lounges, and staff colleges, but the fact remains: it was a disastrous defeat for the British. Only the stubborn resistance of a handful of men at the mission station of Rorke's Drift saved the honour of the imperial army, and a grateful government bestowed on them a record eleven Victoria Crosses.

The Zulu king Cetshwayo knew that, despite the great victory at Isandlwana, he was facing defeat, and he tried to sue for peace, but Lord Chelmsford had to salvage his reputation, and by July 4 his troops were fighting the final battle of the Zulu War. Massed rifles, Gatling guns, cannons, and cavalry were too much for the poorly armed but unbelievably brave Zulu. A small white marble tablet at the Ulundi war memorial says it all: "To the brave Zulu warriors who fell here in defence of the old Zulu order."

It was the end of the Shakan era. After their defeat, the Zulu were prepared to be taken over by the British, whom the Zulu liked despite Britain's appalling treatment of the people, their king, and their customs. Sir Garnet Wolseley, who succeeded Lord Chelmsford, divided Zululand into thirteen kinglets, and the result was probably what was intended: chaos, bloodshed, and civil war reigned. It was divide-and-rule at its worst.

No one was concerned about the wildlife of the territory. Rifles captured by the Zulus at Isandlwana and other battles were used to kill game. It was one means of getting food. Men in times of desperation had always had to rely on wild ungulates for survival. Yet even though they were *in extremis*, the Zulu people still made sure that wildlife survived. A respect for it ran deep in their psyche. Nevertheless, wild animal skins, horns, bones, and ivory were valuable, and an increasing number of whites poured into the territory, some shooting for sport but most to make money. By 1895 the situation was serious.

The discovery of a pocket of surviving white rhino, a species considered extinct, was the final stimulus for the proclamation of the reserves. In terms of a contractual obligation to the land, it was the only positive move the British colonial government had made since taking over. The step was due to a small group of people, among whom Sir Charles Saunders stood out like a bright star. He led a small gathering of white men who were appalled at the decimation of wildlife and wanted to see at least some land set aside where game might have sanctuary. It took courage and resilience to persevere, but in April 1897 the proclamation became law.

The reserves came into being in spite of the political problems and the general apathy and lack of interest by the colonial government and the people. The discovery of white rhino sparked an outcry that led to the proclamation of four reserves, Mfolozi, Mdhletshe, Hluhluwe, and Lake St. Lucia. Mdhletshe did not last long.

Two years later, the Anglo-Boer War, another unjust imperial war, erupted, and white Afrikaner was pitted against white British and colonial. The discovery of gold and diamonds had long heralded the death knell of the Boer Republics. In the Zulu War it was Sir Bartle Frere who forced the issue. In the Anglo-Boer War it was Lord Milner, and even today his memory is cursed by the Afrikaner. Once again members of my own family took up their rifles and rode off to war. But life went on, and my father was born at a trading store on the Umkomaas River on the day of the battle of Spioenkop, January 24, 1899. The Boers, like the Zulu, fought back savagely and inflicted heavy defeats on the British and colonial forces. However, in the end and despite a brilliant guerrilla war campaign led by generals such as Smuts, De la Rey, and Botha, the mass of men and materials from the British Empire proved too much, and the Boers were forced to surrender. Again arms and ammunition flowed into Zululand and freebooters killed more game.

In 1906 Chief Bambatha led a rebellion of the Zulu. It was quickly and ruthlessly crushed, and the cruelty of some of the white troops was beyond comprehension. The rebellion, too, was an excuse for whites to move into Zululand and take over some of the best low-lying and fertile plains.

The Zulu could and would in one way or another be able to look after themselves. The wildlife was helpless. Large tracts of indigenous forest and bush were cleared for the planting of sugarcane. Without habitat, no wildlife survives. So it was not long before little game except ordinary reedbuck, the ubiquitous grey duiker, and bushbuck were left in the sugar-growing areas. In the Zulu tribal reserves set aside after the Bambatha rebellion, game was relatively plentiful despite the introduction of the wire snare and modern guns. Land was handed out to cattle farmers in the drier thornveld areas.

Some farms were allocated along the edges of Mfolozi and Hluhluwe and Mkuze game reserves against the warnings of knowledgeable veterinarians, who knew that *nagana*, a disease carried by the tsetse fly, was a constant danger to cattle.

At the end of the 1914–18 war, returning soldiers were allocated more farms and within a few months cattle were dying of *nagana*. Many farmers had for long eyed the game reserves, and those closest to them hoped to profit by their deproclamation. Other farmers wanted all the game eradicated because they thought this measure would remove the tsetse fly danger. Zulus in adjoining tribal lands also suffered from the depredations of *nagana*, and many of them hoped to have additional land, and the game reserves were the nearest. The whites, however, had the political power. Protest meetings were held, pressure was put on politicians, and in the 1920s a massacre that was euphemistically described as game control took place on the edges of Mfolozi and Hluhluwe game reserves.

Major Vaughan Kirby, who had been appointed chief game conservator in 1912, fought hard to save the wild animals of Zululand. He used the white rhino as a cause and aroused public opinion in Natal. But he was fighting a losing battle and by 1929, when he retired, an unrelenting slaughter of game in the buffer zones adjoining the reserves had become official policy. In 1921, one game drive went into the heart of Mfolozi game reserve, and everything that moved was shot, including some white rhino. All predators were killed on sight. The leopard survived because it was able to take cover in the rougher areas of the reserve. The lions were helpless and were exterminated, although a few were said to survive in the Mpila area of the Mfolozi game reserve. Vaughan Kirby's courage and integrity have become examples to succeeding generations of game rangers, but without the Zulu game guards who stood at his side, men like Mali and Mankenke Mdhletshe and Magqubu Ntombela, he could never have achieved what he did.

Captain H.B. Potter became chief game conservator in 1931, and he fought a skilful diplomatic battle to save the tiny remnants of game in the reserves, and he, too, depended on the game guards.

At the end of the Second World War, *nagana* again broke out among cattle near the Mfolozi game reserve. Once more, ranchers with political clout forced the authorities to take action, and this time everything except the white and the black rhino inside Mfolozi was wiped out. It was a planned and systematic removal of all animals within that reserve. Such was official stupidity that the game guards who did the shooting were not allowed to take the meat. It rotted on the ground.

It is interesting that at the end of a long campaign of planned annihilation, two species, bushbuck and grey duiker, were more numerous than at the beginning. The white rhino (which were not killed) also increased, probably due to the lack of competitive grazers. The white rhino seemed to know they were safe because there were many instances where warthog were shot within a few feet of grazing rhino who took no notice of the shooting, hardly bothering to look up. Many years later in the 1960s, when capture and translocation began in earnest, it was astonishing to see how quickly the rhino learned they were being hunted. Within a few weeks all the rhino became much more alert, and in areas where there was a lot of capture they would run at the sound of a vehicle. Collectively, they sensed that they had become prey. "Operation Rhino" saved the white rhino, but there was a new awareness among the white rhino within the Mfolozi game reserve. Their world was changing. This was also true for all of us who worked in the game reserves. Human populations surrounding the parks were increasing dramatically, and the radio was becoming commonplace. The growing movement called nature conservation was now being passed from one generation to the next. Each generation had to fight to ensure that the game reserves survived.

I began writing the first pages of this book on a cold grey day at the University of Idaho, with snow drifting gently onto the roof of our wooden cabin. Outside was a landscape vastly different from the world where my story takes place. This was a silent world when it snowed. No birds or animals cried out, but it allowed introspection. In contrast, Magqubu's country, where we worked together in Zululand, was always pulsating with life. Even in the middle of winter there were birds that sang, and eagles like the bateleur and the martial soared overhead. I searched the skies in this cold winter and only one red-tailed hawk and a raven flew above the crown of snow-laden fir trees. Yet the quietness of the surroundings enabled me to look deep into the recesses of my memory and bring back some of the most important days and experiences of my life. My time in Zululand with Magqubu had brought a slow but dramatic change to my attitude and feeling for landscape and to my relationship with the black people of my native land. He helped me to begin to overcome a darkness inside me. I was unaware of the psychological term at that time, but he helped me to deal with my shadow.

It is, I believe, not without significance that on the night of January 22, 1993, my first night in Idaho, I had an unusually long dream. In it I was back in Africa, and Magqubu and my father featured vividly. It was as though I had two fathers, one white and one black. For days previously I had had intermittent dreams of Magqubu and of rhino paths clearly marked on the Zululand game reserves' hills and carefully following the contours. The wild animals of Africa have an innate pattern enabling them to walk across the land without doing damage, unless there are too many in a confined space. It was on January 22, 1879, that the battles of Isandlwana and Inyezane were fought, which were two critical encounters in the Anglo-Zulu war.

That my dream should take place on the eve of starting the writing of this book and on such an important day was surely synchronistic, because Magqubu's father and my grandfather both fought in the war, but on opposite sides. Magqubu's father was in the Ngobamakosi regiment at Isandlwana, and Frank Player, my grandfather, was with the Natal Hussars at Inyezane. This had been an important factor in our friendship.

In the midst of the Idaho world of snow and ice I carried in my memory the sight of Magqubu and his Shembe congregation of worshippers dressed in white robes and traditional Zulu headdresses. I could hear their beautiful voices raised in rhythmic hymns, the sound floating across the surrounding hills. During a lull in the singing I heard the birds – sombre bulbuls, mousebirds, cisticola – and bellows from the cattle kraal, or the bleat of a tethered goat. I could smell the air, the mixture of maizemeal porridge, woodsmoke, and cattle dung, and the dark red and black earth of my native Africa.

Magqubu always maintained that if you are going to tell a story you must never leave anything out. This is the Zulu way, and it makes them natural orators. A ten-year-old herd boy can stand up in any company and give a speech that equals any adult. Magqubu, although suffering from a slight stammer, could tell a story in Zulu to people who spoke no word of the language and yet make them understand because of his ability to mimic. This talent of his, together with our close intuitive association, prevented me from learning Zulu properly. Sometimes when we were on patrols together, hours or even a day would pass and we would not speak. Then he would say something, and it was the very thing I was thinking about at that moment – so close had our association become.

Magqubu and I grew up in the same country, but we lived in different worlds. He never had the opportunity of going to school and learning to read and write. "My ears are my books and my lips my pen," he would say with a wide smile, perfect teeth flashing even at the age of ninety-two.

Magqubu began working for the first chief game conservator of Zululand, Major Vaughan Kirby, at the age of fourteen in 1914. The Mfolozi game reserve and surrounding areas were the homeland of the Ntombela clan.

Magqubu knew the country intimately. At the age of ten he had already accompanied white hunters, guiding them for sixpence a day into the adjoining hunting zones of the small game reserves of Zululand. Wild animals lived a precarious existence, and the survival of the parks was constantly at risk. This has been the case since they were first proclaimed in 1895.

I began my schooling at the age of seven, first at a small primary government school in the depression years, then at an expensive private school, a huge financial burden to my parents.

I left school when I was sixteen, and at seventeen I joined the South African Army to serve with the 6th South African Armoured Division in Italy. When I returned from the war I was, like so many ex-servicemen, a lost soul. I had no qualifications and work was scarce. My journey to find work that would become a way of life was long and tortuous. First it was working as a statistician in the Chamber of Mines. Figures were never my strong point, so that did not last long. Then it was working underground in the gold mines in Stygian darkness six thousand feet below the surface. My great-grandfather, James Player, had died on the Kimberley diamond diggings in 1873. My grandfather, Frank Player, worked in the diamond fields in the latter part of his life, and my father spent thirty years working underground in various gold mines. It seemed a natural way for me to follow. I was born near a mine, and my first memories were of mining machinery and men coming up from the bowels of the earth. I became a learner miner on Crown Mines, then a sampler, gathering pieces of gold-bearing rock and bringing them to the surface for assaying. Finally I became an official learner, which would have put me on a career path to a senior position.

This was my rite of passage, and I travelled it with the black and the white Africans from all over the continent, but inwardly I rebelled at not being able to see the sun. So I left mining.

I went to Natal, the original province of my family, and tried many jobs: working on the docks in Durban harbour, as an accountant's clerk, then fishing for a living with rod and reel in the surf. After the Nationalist government came into power in South Africa in 1948, I went to Rhodesia to try to join the permanent army. I knew that the wrath of the Nationalist Afrikaners, which had been building up since their defeat in the Anglo-Boer War, would be unleashed on other South Africans. My worst fears were realized within a few years. Instead of the army I worked as a shift man in a factory. I took the night shift as an option and managed to read many books. When I returned to South Africa to work in an aluminium factory, the frustrations of factory work made me turn to a promise I had made myself in the Apennines in the winter of 1944 – to canoe down the Msunduzi and Mgeni rivers from Pietermaritzburg to Durban. I pioneered this journey in December 1950. It became an annual race and today is one of the big sporting events of the year in South Africa. My book *Men, Rivers and Canoes* tells this story.

The canoes I used in those years were in fact one-man kayaks, frail and made of wood and canvas. It seemed madness to pit them against the might of the rivers. My understanding of the power of wilderness began with the expeditions into the valleys and being alone on much of my first journey. Canoe trips inevitably took place in the summer months, the time of year when the rivers flow. In the storms, thunder rolled overhead, crashing and echoing about the krantzes (cliffs), reverberating from hill to hill. Lightning flickered and lit up dark skies, striking trees and the ironstone in cliffs. It was not possible to carry more than a small backpack with a jacket to sleep in at night, a spare shirt, and long trousers. Sleeping on the hard African earth, wet and cold and with only a fire for warmth, introduced me to wild country. Africa had awakened in my soul. I returned late for work after taking part in the first race in 1951 and was fired. Fate had other paths for me to follow.

The canoe journeys had considerable press coverage, and I became friendly with journalists. One of them, Ken Brokensha, told me about the Natal Parks Board and Jack Vincent, known as the Colonel, who was the secretary of the organization. I decided to apply for a position, and after many interviews with this dynamic man, I was offered a post as relief ranger in Zululand. The gods had smiled upon me. There seemed to be no other explanation. I had a feeling that forces beyond my control and only dimly understood were having a hand in my destiny. A few months before being offered the position by Colonel Vincent, I had spent seven nights in total darkness except for a flickering candle. Someone had told me, or I probably read, that if I did this my life would undergo a dramatic change. From being a lost soul I would be ensouled. Everything I had ever done was a preparation for this time. Psychologically, the aspects of *puer aeternus* (the eternal youth) in my make-up would revel in the constant movement of travelling to the various game reserves.

In 1952 I joined the Natal Parks Game and Fish Preservation Board. With a salary of twenty pounds a month, and, at that time, provided with no vehicle or uniform, I began my career at Lake St. Lucia, the forty-mile-long estuary with crocodile, hippo, flamingo, pelican, and all the wading birds in the summer. My work was to patrol the coastline for illegal stripping of mussels and oysters from the rocks, and to patrol the lake to protect the crocodile, hippo, and the few reedbuck that survived on the great forest-covered dunes. From St. Lucia I went to Richards Bay, then a small village of no more than a few hundred people. Today it is a big harbour and one of the fastest-growing industrial areas in South Africa.

It was meeting and working with the Zulu game guards, beginning with Samuel Mtetwa at St. Lucia estuary, that made the biggest impact upon me. They led me and taught me about the wild animals and wild country, about spoor, dung, animal calls, dangerous snakes, and the need to acknowledge Nkulunkulu – the great god, the creator – and about how to live in the animal world: to kill for food and yet respect the spirit of the animal one was killing, to talk to it before your finger squeezed the trigger. To be afraid was natural and not cowardice: it kept one alive in the bush and on the lakes. The guards seldom, if ever, gambled with their lives. They had too much respect for themselves and the environment they lived in. All life was precious, and you had to *hlonipa* (respect) it. To challenge wild animals out of bravado was neither heroic nor wise, only insulting. They were not only excellent naturalists with powers of observation beyond the understanding of most white people because it was an intuitive way of listening and seeing, but they were also professional guards with an *esprit de corps* that sprang from their warrior past.

My game-conservator predecessors – Major Vaughan Kirby, Roden Symons, Captain Harold Potter, and Peter Potter – and I taught them the rudiments of military drill. However, this was largely a gloss added to their Zulu warrior past initiated by Shaka Zulu, who turned his Nguni people into the finest fighting force in Africa. They wore our uniforms, carried the spears or guns we issued them, but this was an extension of their own military dress and arms, which changed and evolved with every king. Their bravery and loyalty were present no matter who was their master, but if you were sympathetic and cared for their welfare and showed them that you appreciated them as human beings, they gave you much more in return.

The Zulus have a way of instantly seeing the inner person. The old Boers used to say that you could not know a man until you had eaten a bag of salt with him. For the Zulu, a few minutes or even a glance revealed what a person was like. They frequently seem to know well in advance what someone is going to do. They are quick to name people, and it is always an apt name. I have a bad knee from an accident in my youth and in the Second World War I fell off a tank, adding to the problem. The Zulu called me Madolo, The Knee. When I was in a bad mood they said I was like a wounded buffalo, dangerous and prone to ambush when you least expected it. When Ann Farrer and I married in 1957, we were stationed on Lake St. Lucia, where a group of bachelors lived. Before she arrived we used to eat together and, as young men will always do, we told lots of stories, many of a salacious kind, leading to roars of laughter. Once Ann joined us, dirty jokes were of course no longer told. The Zulu were quick to notice the difference, and they named her Bulala ihlega, The One Who Kills the Laugh – in this case, the dirty laugh.

Although I did not know it, I was on an inward journey led outwardly by Magqubu Ntombela. He began to change my view of the natural world through patient instruction in the mysteries and the history of this important landscape. Apartheid under the Nationalist government was affecting the lives of all South Africans. It was Magqubu Ntombela who made me realize my own prejudice and face up to it after a dramatic encounter with a black mamba, the most venomous snake in Africa, and my life changed. Mythologically, the snake has been viewed in most cultures as a symbol of change and healing.

The friendship that Magqubu and I enjoyed was not always smooth. We could both be stubborn, but his patience and understanding of human behaviour enabled him to defuse our disagreements so that they became building blocks for an even better friendship. Our work together through Operation Rhino and the wilderness treks became known in South Africa, and many people saw it as a symbol of hope for unity. South Africa did not have television until the 1970s, so our work together was better known through films in America, Britain, and Europe.

In 1964 I became the chief conservator for all the parks in Zululand, and Ann and our children went with me to live in Hluhluwe game reserve, where the local headquarters were located. In September 1969 I was transferred to the headquarters of the Natal Parks Board in Pietermaritzburg. My brother, Gary Player, the golfer, generously helped us to buy a small farm in the Karkloof valley, and I commuted each day to the office. I spent a lot of time away, and Magqubu appeared one day and announced he was going to live on the farm to take care of my family when I went away.

Magqubu served the cause of wildlife conservation as a game guard from 1914 to 1964. Long before we met, he was known among the early game guards and conservators as a man of courage and integrity. Magqubu had no formal schooling but he was a highly intelligent, dignified, and deeply religious man, and he absorbed knowledge in the traditional oral way of the Zulu people. He had the most incredible memory and could remember praise songs of Zulu kings and praise names of early conservators. Knowledge of animal and bird behavior came naturally to him because he had spent so much time in the veld, first as a young boy looking after cattle and goats, then as a game guard learning his craft from the older men.

In this world we are always searching for heroes, only to find that they have feet of clay. We then miss the essential contribution such people have made and concentrate on their dark side. Magqubu had his shadow, his dark side, and periodically I bore the full brunt of it. There is a danger that I could romanticize aspects of Magqubu's life. This is not my intention. I have tried to write about and record my time with him, what he taught me, and his influence on my life. To Westerners, Magqubu's life and our friendship in the wilderness of Zululand might evoke such exotic images as *Treasure Island*, but this book is not imaginary musings – it is real.

This book is my tribute to Magqubu, but it is also a tribute to the many other game guards or game scouts who have been the front-line men in protecting parks in Africa. There have been other partnerships like the one Magqubu and I enjoyed, but for me, Magqubu was special because he was prepared to share his knowledge and experience.

Indigenous knowledge is very important to our modern society. Eugene Linden, in a cover story of *Time* magazine, wrote on September 23, 1991:

> Today, with little notice, more vast archives of knowledge and expertise are spilling into oblivion, leaving humanity in danger of losing its past and perhaps jeopardizing its future as well. Stored in the memories of elders, healers, midwives, farmers, fishermen and hunters in the estimated 15,000 cultures remaining on earth is an enormous trove of wisdom.

English poet and novelist D.H. Lawrence said the same thing more poetically when he wrote, "In the dust where we have buried the silent races and their abominations, we have buried so much of the delicate magic of life."

It is true that we are losing the greatest living library. The Wilderness Leadership School has always used indigenous people as guides for wilderness trails in South Africa. A senior field officer in the Cape Province tells a story about them. He said that although the Bushmen who grew up in the desert had never seen an otter, when they saw otter spoor in the sand on a riverbank they were able to imagine and describe the animal. Later, our field officer, thinking to impress the Bushmen, pointed out the spoor of a leopard. The Bushmen looked at it and said, "Yes, it is a leopard, but do you know that it is a female and she is carrying a cub?"

I have often sat in the semi-darkness of the caves once inhabited by the Bushmen in the Drakensberg and looked at their exquisite, numinous paintings of the animals, the birds, the snakes, and the people, and in my imagination I heard their voices above the sound of the rapids in nearby streams. There I found a great peace, and the only disturbance was the sickness I felt at the modern graffiti scratched or painted on the ancient walls by persons unfit to be described as human.

In the Drakensberg there are a hundred miles of Bushmen caves, among the greatest art galleries in the world. There are similar caves in the Matopos in Zimbabwe, and in the Brandberg and Waterberg of Namibia. Far from being a poor relation to the world, Africa's riches lie at our feet in wildlands and rock paintings, manna for the sick soul of the industrialized world. Indigenous peoples, who are being assailed from all angles, have a tremendous amount of wisdom and knowledge about animals, birds, plants, and trees that they can pass on to all humankind.

T.S. Eliot once said that modern material civilization is a form of living death. Marie-Louise von Franz, a pupil of Carl Jung and a Jungian psychologist, wrote: "The Western world is in an inner state of crisis. It is so crushed by the mass-mindedness of our civilization due largely to the problem of over-population that many people feel superfluous." Robert Johnson, another Jungian psychologist, said that "people feel too wounded to live but unable to die." He continues: "We see a world anaesthetizing itself with alcohol and drugs. Ironically, in other times and places, these substances were used as divine sacraments to bring visions of God. With no sacred means of expression we can express our need only symptomatically through substance abuse, domestic violence, child abuse, terrorism and wars, and finally, madness." Marie-Louise von Franz said that "Western civilization is in danger of building a wall of rationality in its society, which feeling cannot penetrate. Everything has to be rational, and emotion is frowned upon."

As a result of this growing alienation in modern humans from that which is natural and instinctive, there is an insistent desire to reconnect with the inner world. In Africa, most people are better related to their instinctive lives than are people in the rest of the world.

In the Western world, which I believe Africa would imitate at its peril, there is a continuing need to dominate and subdue nature and all wild things. It represents an acting-out of the dark part of the psyche, and we have seen it in the elimination of 60 million bison in the United States and in the decimation of Native Americans, the Aborigines in Australia, the Polynesians in Hawaii, and wherever else the hand of Western man has rested. The destruction of nature in Africa is visible. All we have left in South Africa are the national parks and game reserves, and even they are only witness areas, but they are, I think, of immense importance for Africa and for the rest of the world. As Jung said of the West, "We have lost a world that once pulsed with our blood and breathed with our breath."

On frequent visits to Europe, the United States, and the Far East, I have noticed that among people there is a weariness caused by travel without purpose: instead of pilgrimages there are escapes. Africa can reintroduce this pilgrimage and give a new dimension to travel linked to our new age of exploration, not only of outer space but also of the inner dimension of humanness.

In the national parks and game reserves of Africa that ancient spirit, described by General Smuts as "older than the spirit of man," still survives in the brooding lowveld, in our remote mountain areas and wild coastlines. What we have in these places is the most precious of worldly gifts, a sense of the spiritual connection between human beings and the land. But the places are vulnerable, protected by a thin membrane, a caul that can be torn and rendered useless. If we protect and nurture this wilderness it could be our greatest contribution to the modern world, and, sensitively managed, it could provide enormous benefits for us because it is a renewable natural resource.

It was to help protect these wild places that I initiated Natal Parks Board trails in 1959. In 1974 I resigned from the Natal Parks Board to become more involved with the Wilderness Leadership School which I founded in 1957. Magqubu Ntombela was a guiding presence and willingly gave his knowledge and wisdom to the many people who walked with us through the Zululand wilderness.

In early 1994 I handed over the Wilderness Leadership School to Andrew Muir, and I revived the Wilderness Foundation. It was the momentous year of South Africa's first free and democratic election. A new South Africa was born, and in 1995 I established the Magqubu Ntombela Foundation in honour of his memory.

1

The Last Days

In February 1992, one of the hottest months of the year, I travelled with my wife to Macibini in Zululand to see Magqubu. It was a nostalgic journey, and I was conscious of the history of the land. This was a landscape of early San Bushmen, and of the Nguni, who under the powerful leadership of Shaka became the Zulu people; a land too of hunters, traders, missionaries, and the soldiers of the Anglo-Zulu War, and latterly of sugarcane and cattle farmers.

The road had changed since I had first gone north in 1947. At that time the tar ended at Stanger, and it stayed that way into the 1960s. Then, as Richards Bay grew, the road was continually upgraded and bridges were improved. Sugarcane, eucalypt, and pine trees now dominated the coastal flats and stretched drearily into the distance. Once there had been pans, and flocks of thousands of geese and ducks.

The road turned west at Mtubatuba into the acacia-clad hills scattered with the Zulu huts and homesteads. The scent of woodsmoke and cattle mingled with the smell of the earth itself, drowning the foreign smell of the eucalypt and pines. Heat waves bounced off the road ahead, creating mirages, and the distant hills had a hazy look.

I turned off the road shortly before the entrance to Mfolozi game reserve, and we made our way past Magqubu's maize field to the entrance of his *muzi*. The track passed erythrina trees where a circle of white stones marked Magqubu's Shembe church site.

I stopped near the cattle kraal and called out Magqubu's name. He emerged from the main hut, more stooped now and his hair going grey. He complained that his legs did not work properly and he could not run uphill any more. To hear Magqubu Ntombela speak the only language he knew – Zulu – was like listening to and watching a Shakespearian actor speaking English. The intonations, phrases, and lilting voice accompanied by facial expressions and movements of his body and hands, were always an experience.

"Good God, Magqubu, you are ninety-two. What do you expect? You still move quicker than an old cripple like me," I said.

He laughed, pointed at my knee, and walked, limping. His imitation had lost none of its subtlety.

Magqubu was recovering from a mild stroke, and for the first time since 1940 he had been persuaded to visit a doctor. He was an unwilling patient. I gently teased him about his reluctance to go anywhere near white medicine. Magqubu smiled, not rising to the bait. His wife Tabete, a fine-looking Zulu woman and a descendant of Dingiswayo, an early Mtetwa king, said that the visit was long overdue. She reminded me that when Magqubu had cholera his family had to wait until he was unconscious before being able to take him to the local clinic. Soon after this traumatic experience he had severe gastro-enteritis, and the combination of the two illnesses weakened his resolve not to see a white doctor.

Magqubu said he had been very ill and that he had gone to see the white doctor in Mtubatuba, who had injected him and given him pills that had relieved his pain. He saw my incredulous look when he spoke about the doctor. He grinned and said he had been to the Shembe church and got dispensation. I knew he must have been in a bad way to have succumbed but surrender to modern medicine was also a tribute to his common sense and his ability to accept and simply to be, rare in our modern age.

We walked from his main hut to the shade of the erythrina trees, then to a huge marula tree near his Shembe religious site. The hot northwesterly

wind roared overhead, creating dust devils. There was the smell of drought, so familiar to those of us who have lived close to the land, anticipating the seasons and looking for the clouds of hope, the dark rain clouds. In 1992 South Africa was in crisis, and the threat of civil war hovered like a hawk waiting to swoop. A few wrong political moves and all the different factions would have been at one another's throats. I reflected on the darkness in the human soul and the dangerous threats to our country. I thought how ironic it was that black clouds brought relief from the relentless sun. So it was with politics. The current dark events could paradoxically be pregnant with great possibilities of renewal.

For far too long political complacency had blinded us to the cruel world of inequality of opportunity. In the same way as we had to go through a drought to make us appreciate the sound, scent, and benefit of rain, so it was with politics. We had to undergo the pain to know the pleasure, and be renewed. If the relationship that Magqubu and I had established, despite the usual human stresses and strains, could be taken as an example of black and white co-operation, then all the peoples of southern Africa could live together. We complemented each other in a multitude of ways, as indeed do all the cultural groups in South Africa if they would only recognize it. South Africa is the one country in Africa where Eurocentric and Afrocentric cultures could meld and become an example of philosophic understanding for the rest of the world. The ideal has always been there, but the historical baggage will take some overcoming. The Indian and coloured people could be the mediators and provide the necessary balance. I had recently heard an old Cape coloured man say, "Ons moet die verlede vergeet and na die toekoms kyk met 'n glimlag" (We must forget the past and look at the future with a smile). He had just been returned to land he and his family had been forcibly removed from in the 1950s. There was little reason for him to smile, but a big heart enabled him to forgive.

Magqubu and I sat talking in a language we had always communicated in, my poor Zulu and his Shakespearian Zulu, repeated with infinite patience. We had a telepathic understanding, too, of the nonspoken word. Our meeting had an air of sadness because both of us knew how age had suddenly caught up. His incredibly strong body, forged as a boy on the misty hills of Ongeni, then tempered as an *udibi* (carrier) to Vaughan Kirby, then as messenger, paymaster, and game guard to Captain Potter, was now ailing.

The old man's face was drawn, and his eyes were beginning to cloud with the bluish tinge of age. He sensed my concern for him, for he knew how much we had been through together and how deeply I loved him. He smiled and patted me on the hand. His teeth were still so strong and white.

Magqubu had once told me that when he was about six years old he had been sent by his father with a shilling to buy a spear. He said that Mpika Manqele, the spearmaker, was close on a hundred years old at that time. He had been a favored spearmaker for kings Cetshwayo and Dinuzulu.

"Mpika was eating a mielie," Magqubu said, and he described the firmness of the old man's teeth, then imitated the crunching of the corn. "His teeth were perfect," he said.

"Why?" I asked.

"Because he cleaned his teeth after every meal with wood ash and massaged his gums. I have done the same," Magqubu said, showing his white teeth and healthy gums.

Apart from two back molars I once insisted be taken out because they were bad and causing him terrible pain, he had all his teeth. His description of his first visit to a dentist was priceless.

"The doctor put the needle in here," and he pointed to his gum. "Then it came out at the back of my neck." He showed how his gum went numb, his lips slack and saliva dripping uncontrollably. He spoke with a lip hanging loose and a perplexed look on his face, which changed to one of horror as the dentist advanced with a pair of forceps. "Vula mlomo" (Open your mouth), the dentist says. Magqubu reluctantly lets his jaw sag. "Vula," the dentist repeats. Magqubu shuts his eyes, then opens them wide with consternation when the dentist thrusts the forceps in. Magqubu imitated the crunch of the forceps on the molar and his strangled cry while he tries to push the dentist's hand away. He play-acted the whole scene, with the water swilling down, the menacing drill hanging overhead, and the sting of the antiseptics. Once he got going nothing could stop him, and the more I laughed the greater and more exaggerated his actions became, ending with a plea to the dentist to let him go and urinate. He acted his fumbling with buttons, saliva running down his chin, and the sounds of urination.

We were silent for a while. The hot wind blew across the dry veld, and I heard the *Cisticola chiniana* singing persistently from the top of an acacia karoo tree. This tiny drab-colored bird has a powerful song. It is not a sound of great beauty, but it personified my time as a game ranger, the hot dry days and the long treks in the stifling valleys and acacia-dotted plains of Mfolozi game reserve. It symbolized the heat, dust, drought, and the rain that inevitably followed.

I was overcome with grief at the thought that Magqubu's time was limited. He had always seemed so indestructible. I tried again to choke back the tears. He saw my grief, held my hand, and began talking to make me laugh. He made a joke of his ailments and imitated his laborious moves in the night to get to the door in time to pass water. He did not tell me not to weep, because he knew and understood the reasons, but by his jokes and laughter he defused my tension. To distract me he spoke a little of politics, for he had listened to news on Radio Zulu. He said that the Zulu people had to remember their history, and he recited the lengthy royal lineage and his own antecedents.

His pride in being Zulu and following Zulu traditions had sustained him all his life. He knew that in the emerging South Africa the Zulu people had to be accommodated or else there would be no peace in the country. As always, he cut to the heart of our nation's problems, made clear statements, but accepted everything that was happening as a natural course of events, even the violence. "Men have always fought," he said. "But we have to work together and believe in Nkulunkulu."

The enervating hot wind blew in fierce gusts, creating more dust devils in the mielie field with the dry yellowing leaves and stalks. It was going to be a poor crop this year. He followed my look and said that in his grain pit he had enough mielies stored to keep his people in the *muzi* in grain for six months.

I had always been impressed with his grain pit in the middle of the cattle kraal. It was as deep as a tall man and covered with a heavy slab of rock and the dung of the cattle. The dung covering hermetically sealed all the openings. Whenever there was a good year he added shelled mielies to the pit. I had been with him when maize had to be brought up from the hole. The dung was scraped away, the stone removed, and a branch that attracted flies was thrown in. Magqubu watched the flies settle and at once die. Methane gas was killing them, and he added branches until the flies did not die. He then sent one of the young grandchildren down to pass up the mielies in a basin.

The grain pit had been part of the Nguni tradition for centuries. The stored grain was used only in times of desperate drought. It was the last resource. Throughout Mfolozi game reserve there were many old kraal and *muzi* sites. The ground had been trodden hard by human feet and cattle hooves, but in some places the old grain pits had collapsed, water had gathered, and in the last ninety years the rhino had turned them into wallows, an example of the interlinkage between man and wild animals that Magqubu was always so graphically describing.

Thoughts and memories flashed into my mind, and I wondered what, more than anything else, I had learned in our long years of association, service, and friendship. Some words of Jung seemed appropriate:

Our ancient contact with nature has gone and with it has gone a profound mental energy that this symbolic action supplied. Thunder is no longer the voice of an angry god, nor is lightning his avenging missile. No river contains a spirit, no tree is the life principle of a man, no snake the embodiment of wisdom, no mountain cave the home of a great demon. No voices now speak to man from stones, plants and animals, nor does he speak to them believing they can hear.

Magqubu was always involved in the natural world. He had really known no other and so had become part of it and in constant harmony with the ebb and flow of the days and the seasons. When the hyena called beyond the fire, Magqubu would answer, so too with the lion, the rhino, the zebra, and wildebeest.

It was the same with the trees: each one was different and alive, and for him an extension of ourselves. He talked with the waving themeda grass or the bateleur eagle, the vulture, or the Natal robin singing from a quiet *kloof* (valley). There was a constant dialogue with the wild world about him, as well as with his cattle, sheep, and goats. This unashamed and natural reaction to all that he saw and heard had over the years made a deep, if not the deepest, impression upon me. It made me realize how with our ubiquitous technology we had become separated from the world, forgetting, as Hermann Hesse so beautifully put it, that "a thousand forgotten years ago, the bird and the blowing wind were like me, and were my brothers." It is only the poets now and the natural people like Magqubu who see and hear the world as it really is. For most of us the world is a place to be used, and everything other than human life has no value beyond its material use.

I heard the flapping of canvas in the hot wind. Magqubu, ever observant, saw me cock my ear.

"*Ganda-ganda*: it is the tractor's covering," he said, and giggled. He remembered the disputes we had had when he first asked me for a tractor. For over four years we had a running argument about a tractor. He wanted one at his *muzi*. I told him he would simply be buying trouble.

"You don't even know how to drive one," I said.

"My sons do," he replied with a steady gaze.

"Look, Magqubu," I said, "you really know about cattle. You have ploughed with them all your life. You understand them and furthermore you can eat them when they are too old to plough."

The old man nodded his head. "Yes, what you say is true, but I want a tractor."

I thought I had a trump card: the expense.

"How much will one be?" he asked.

"At least three thousand rand, and it will be secondhand," I replied.

He was silent. "I will save the money," he said.

It did not matter where we were or with whom, he would raise the subject of the tractor. On one occasion while we were on trail and hiding behind a tree from a snorting black rhino, he suddenly said, "Have you looked for that tractor for me?" Again, in the early hours of the morning when I was doing my watch on trail he joined me, stared into the fire, and talked about the tractor.

I thought I had another trump card: I did not have a tractor on our smallholding in the Karkloof. Then an old friend of mine, John Sterling, gave me a *Vaaljapie*, one of the early Ferguson tractors, and a wonderful machine. It gave Magqubu an opening.

"You see, you have a *ganda-ganda* now. It is a secondhand one. It is like the first tractors we had at Mfolozi. This one of yours is still going. I have saved money. Now I can't ask you any more. I am telling you."

The battle was over, but I tried once more and spoke about spares, breakdowns, servicing, tyres, cost of fuel. They were wasted words. Magqubu had made up his mind and nothing would change it.

We looked around Pietermaritzburg and found some secondhand ones, but the old man was not satisfied. It had to be made by the Insingisi – the English. They made the best. Then he heard that Mafeet (John Tinley) was selling tractors.

John Tinley was six feet six inches tall and the brother of Ken Tinley, who had joined me at Ndumu game reserve in 1954 as a learner ranger. John joined the Natal Parks Board too and we worked together on Operation Rhino. He left after many years of dedicated service and for a time sold tractors for a living. He had enormous feet, which the Zulus were quick to spot, and they named him Mafeet. Magqubu had worked closely with John and trusted him. Magqubu's ability to read the character of a person was infallible. When I was in charge of Mfolozi game reserve in 1958 I used to send new, young, white potential game rangers with Magqubu for a two-week trek around the reserve with a donkey to carry their kit and provisions. When they returned, Magqubu would comment to me in private: either the man was good or he was not. Once I disagreed with him. A young man who was the son of a parson and who had been to one of the best private schools in South Africa did the trek with Magqubu. The man had perfect credentials, and I even wondered if it was necessary to send him with Magqubu, but when they returned Magqubu was adamant that the man was no good. I argued with Magqubu and told him about the man's background, his parson father, and everything else. Magqubu firmly shook his head.

"You have to be wrong sometime. You can't always be right," I said.

Magqubu was emphatic. "This man is not a good man. He will give you trouble and disrupt the staff. I know him because I have slept on the ground next to him, listened to him speak, and watched him when he was not looking. You must not employ him. I have spoken."

"No, Magqubu. You can't be right this time."

Magqubu looked at me and said nothing. I overruled him and employed the young man. He lasted two weeks and caused an immense amount of trouble. Magqubu just smiled when I apologized to him. "You were right. But how did you know?" I asked.

Magqubu smiled again and said, "I know."

When John Tinley came to work in the game reserve he and Magqubu at once became friends and were able to laugh and joke together. The many long hours they worked on Operation Rhino created a special bond.

"Tell Mafeet that we know each other. We have worked together. Tell him he must find my tractor." He knew he could rely on John Tinley.

Two months later I was with a trail party going to Mfolozi game reserve. We stopped at Magqubu's *muzi*, and John Tinley arrived at the same moment to say the tractor was on its way. Magqubu was calm and composed until the red diesel-powered Massey Ferguson swept up the track and stopped where we were standing.

"The tractor has come," I said and put my hand on his shoulder.

The old man turned, put his arm around me, and hugged me. He had tears in his eyes. "Yes, my tractor has come."

We followed the path past the cattle kraal and the strong scent of fresh dung, then carefully stepping over the traces of two old forge sites, we walked to the open clearing on the east side of the *muzi*. Layard bulbuls, or *toppies*, called from above us in the marula tree and there was the soft whistle of a flight of mouse birds.

Magqubu led me to the tractor and pulled off the canvas covering that had caught my attention when it flapped in the wind. He ran his hand over the brightly shining, well-worn steering wheel. "I never learned to drive it, but Ikonamangele [his son] understands this machine." He looked at the tractor with great affection and for a few moments expounded on its virtues, describing how it annually ploughed the heavy soils that his cattle once struggled with. "Ikonamangele can talk to this machine like I talk to cattle," he said.

He now led me to the red trailer I had bought later. "Once the women had to walk to the Nyalazi River and back for days carrying water. Now we can fill our tank in a morning. I carry manure to the fields and cane stalks for the cattle." Magqubu laughed gently because I had also resisted getting the trailer. I patted him on the shoulder and told him that he had been right and that I was glad he had persisted. The tractor had given excellent service with relatively few problems.

The sun was fiercely hot, so we walked back to the Shembe site and sat in the shade. The northeast wind roared through the branches above us, sounding like the repetitive grunts of a lion.

We talked of old times and of the men we had worked with, a fortunate band upon whom the gods had smiled. There were many people, too, who had walked with us on the wilderness trails, and they had been touched by this wonderful man when he spoke about the spirit of the land and shared his deep knowledge of history and the interconnectedness of the natural world and ourselves. His ecopoetic descriptions of birds, animals, plants, and trees, drawn together and presented holistically, were a story of how people and the earth were rooted in each other.

We talked about the dryness, the shrinking of pools in the Nyalazi, the shortage of grass and how the cattle were suffering. He pointed to the mielies, withering under the bitter sun. "We need rain," the old man said, then smiled and shrugged his shoulders. "It will come eventually," he said.

A drunken man staggered up the track. He stopped, swayed, and stood talking loudly and aggressively to Magqubu. I bristled, but Magqubu chided him gently and turned what could have been an ugly scene into comedy. I had seen this happen many times. The old man was so sure of his inner strength that he could defuse potentially disruptive and violent situations. The incident animated him, and he gesticulated and sang a little. He reminded me of the Japanese paper flowers we had in my youth. Placed in water, they bloomed before one's eyes. So it was with Magqubu.

When the drunk had gone Magqubu was quiet for a while, then he spoke again of all the individuals who had worked in Mfolozi game reserve. His own people he knew intimately, and the white game rangers were able to hide little from him.

"Do you remember Bocozi?" he asked.

"Yes," I answered.

"It was up there at Ongeni that you and he caught the butcher poaching. We were glad because that man gave us a lot of trouble. The mist helped you that day because he got lost and Bocozi knew Ongeni from the days of the *nagana* when he was killing out the game."

Magqubu talked about Bocozi, Hendrik van Schoor, remembering the smallest detail of experiences they had together. His stories awakened in me a memory of my first real encounter with Mfolozi. Hendrik and I had crossed the White Mfolozi River together. We are always vulnerable when we cross rivers, both psychologically and physically, and they often appear in our dreams.

2

Crossing the White Mfolozi River

I had paid brief visits to Mfolozi game reserve in 1952, seen the white rhino, and fallen in love with this great grey rejected pachyderm. I loved the country despite the absence of other game in any large numbers, but I had not walked on the land in a way that made me conscious of it. This was to happen in 1953, when I walked with Ranger Hendrik van Schoor. Hendrik was stationed at the small Gome outpost, situated in what was then known as the southern Crown lands, an area of land once heavily populated but at that time uninhabited, with only the few wild animals that had survived the tsetse-fly slaughter campaigns. Hendrik had built a house of wood and iron salvaged from tsetse-fly traps.

Gome outpost was a very special place and was later to be my home in 1955, along with my game-ranger companions Ken Tinley and Jim Feely. Then Jim and Molly Feely lived there during the early days of their marriage in 1956. It became the beloved home of Ranger Nick Steele in 1957, where at first he lived alone, then later with his wife Nola. Gome had played a vital part in all our initial relationships with Mfolozi game reserve. Magqubu had been stationed there in 1940 and lived in a cave with other game guards engaged to shoot game during one of the tsetse-fly campaigns. It was here that Magqubu had been bitten on the head by a boomslang. He fell into a coma and, while unconscious, underwent a journey that parallels Dante's visions. Four days later he regained consciousness, but remembered in detail the journey, which was to lead to a dramatic change in his life, from ancient beliefs to a Christian sect led by the Zulu prophet Shembe.

The word *uGome*, according to Magqubu, meant an open place for conference, but not always a conference to talk about how to rule the country. Trackers used to have a meeting before they went out in advance of the warriors who were to hunt, and the chiefs remained behind to talk and confer on tribal matters. When game was killed, the hunters brought it back to Gome, where it was eaten by the chiefs, trackers, and warriors. But it could have another meaning, too: a gathering about someone suspected of practising witchcraft. Men would be summoned to bring the suspect to Gome, and they would kill the person, then go back to the people and say he had been eaten by a lion or some other wild animal, or had died under strange circumstances.

My first introduction to Gome was through meeting Hendrik van Schoor at Mdindini (Winding) drift on the White Mfolozi River. Hendrik had recently been employed by the Natal Parks Board after working for the veterinary department. We met on the north bank and sat on the rocks opposite a reed island, taking off our shoes and socks and pants in preparation for the crossing. Hendrik was a most impressive man physically: tall, powerfully built, with huge hands and strong, well-muscled calves and thighs. He had the reputation – and later I saw him do it – of being able to lift a full forty-four-gallon petrol drum onto a truck unaided. He was a deadly shot with a rifle and probably killed more game than any other white man in the *nagana* campaigns of the 1940s. If anything needed fixing, Hendrik knew how to do it. As a practical all-rounder with fencing, building, vehicles, and household gadgets he had no equal in my experience. The Zulus called him Bocozi, after a small stream that ran into the White Mfolozi. It related to an incident involving the game guards at the stream when they were nearly injured by rhino that were being driven into the game reserve.

Hendrik was an Afrikaner in the style of the Voortrekkers, who moved out of the Cape in covered wagons and fought their way against the black nations of southern Africa. He was extremely hard on his black staff, and only a man like Magqubu was capable of standing up to him. Magqubu would obey Hendrik's orders to the last letter, but without a trace of submissiveness. The old Boer in Hendrik and the old Zulu in Magqubu met in the modern age with the political and technological advantage being with Hendrik, yet below the surface of words and manoeuvring there was a mutual, if sometimes hostile, respect. Their forefathers had fought at the Battle of Blood River, where the Zulus under Dingane had been defeated by the Boers grouped in a laager behind the locked wheels of their wagons. The bravery on both sides was awe-inspiring: the Zulus with their frontal assault armed with shield and spear against the witheringly accurate firearms of the Boers, and the Boers who at a crucial moment rode out on their horses and fearlessly plunged into the Zulu mass.

Hendrik had been brought up on these tales and the story of the massacre of Piet Retief and his men at Mgungundhlovu. Retief and his men were tricked by Dingane into leaving their weapons outside the *muzi* and then, at a given moment and at the cry of "Bulala abathakathi!" (Kill the wizards!), Dingane's warriors fell upon the Boers and dragged them to Matiwane hill to be beaten to death with knobkieries, then splayed out for the vultures to feed on. Re-examination of the history leading to this massacre brings to light more mysterious facets, and perhaps the full truth will one day be revealed. But for Hendrik van Schoor this killing at Mgungundhlovu was a terrible outrage, and it was seared on his psyche, erupting with an explosive cry of "Remember the day" whenever he was angry with his labourers.

Magqubu once told me a story of how Hendrik had some work to do in the Mgungundhlovu area. He was visiting a Dutch Reformed mission station and had a group of game guards and labourers with him. When he passed the Matiwane hill where Piet Retief and his men were executed, he stopped the vehicle, got out, and with his face suffused with rage ordered the guards and labourers to get off the vehicle and walk home, a good fifty miles away. He said repeatedly, "Remember the day," and nothing anyone said had any effect on him. Magqubu laughed when he told the story, and there was a hint of admiration in his laughter.

"Bocozi was a Boer. He never forgave Dingane because the king was treacherous in making the commando leave their guns behind. Bocozi loved his people and that is good," Magqubu said.

"What did you do?" I asked.

"We walked home, but we took our time. Bocozi could say nothing because he had ordered us to walk. We understood him."

Hendrik seldom discussed the massacre with me, because in his eyes I was an Englishman and therefore by definition a liberal. There was some softening when he heard that my great-grandmother was the stepdaughter of a Voortrekker leader, but it was insufficient to convince him that I was not a liberal, which I was. This subject of Boers and Zulus was a barrier between us, and it made him ill at ease when I queried the historical accuracy of anything he said. For him it was gospel and unquestionable. His strong jaw would jut forward whenever the subject came up, and God help anyone who joked about it.

In the early 1950s Hendrik had many difficulties in his life. He was working for the Natal Parks Board and owed them his loyalty, and he gave it, but there were neighbouring Afrikaners who, like him, supported the National Party and expected favours from him: grazing for cattle on the Crown lands, *biltong* (dried meat), and some hunting if they could get away with it. We later did anti-poaching patrols together, and he was given a very hard time by farmers in the Mkuze district, where he had grown up. He was also unhappy when we caught policemen shooting illegally. Life improved for Hendrik later in his Parks Board career, when magistrates took firmer action against poachers and when locals accepted that the old days of doing what they wanted were over.

It was significant for me that my first real contact with the Mfolozi earth, the deep brooding atmosphere of the hills, rivers, and valleys, was with Hendrik van Schoor. I felt that I was seeing the landscape through two eyes. One was the eye within, which knew the place from a very long time back. This eye communicated to something inside me the splendour and isolation of this land. It was a steady state, simply there, and it had always been so. With the other eye there was a wonderful relationship to all that I was seeing, but the feeling was one of conquest.

Hendrik's ancestors, the Boers, had been in and out of Zululand since the 1830s, first as interested explorers, then as land-grabbers and conquerors. A part of my blood was associated with that time, in the form of my great-grandmother on the Boer side and Frank Player in the Zulu War of 1879. There were my other, English-speaking relatives, the Esserys and the Ashes, who had moved in to get land after the Bambatha rebellion, the final spasm of the Zulu War. There was another form of conquest, too: the game, which, except for the white rhino, had been wiped out during various *nagana* campaigns.

Hendrik was employed as one of the hunters. It was a role he performed to perfection. He was not a killer like some men I had seen who called themselves hunters. They had a joy in killing wild animals, a continuous *bokkoors,* or buck fever. Whatever feeling they had was directed in an orgasmic way solely to killing. With Hendrik it was very different. From the time he was a small boy he had had a gun in his hand, hunting birds, hares, and rats first and progressing to bigger game as he grew up, in a pattern his forefathers had followed for generations. *Die boer en sy roer* (The farmer and his gun). It was part of life, of living in an Africa that was still wild. Hunting provided food, clothing and money.

Hendrik was an uncomplicated man, but determined to improve his lot in life. When hunters had to be recruited, Hendrik was a natural choice. One bullet, one animal, and no suffering. That is what Willie Foster, the game supervisor, wanted, and he got it from Hendrik. Groups of Zulu hunters were responsible to Hendrik, who doled out cartridges and expected a *doppie* (spent cartridge) and a tail back. I think Hendrik was a man who simply blocked off feeling when he had to hunt. He was like a surgeon operating on an anaesthetized body. He was not the romantic hunter of fiction but simply epitomized *die boer en sy roer.*

When Hendrik stripped and I saw the full extent of his body I could understand why he was so strong. The size of his thighs and the depth of his chest put him in an almost superhuman bracket. I was for a moment reminded of my father, who had a similar build. This kind of body came from hard physical work. My father had been a miner; Hendrik had been a farmer, doing everything this entailed: ploughing, carrying bags, handling cattle, and all the other farming chores. It was a natural body, where muscles were developed at a natural tension.

"We must cross now," he said. "My huis is mos ver en dit is nou laat" (My house is far away and it is late).

He seldom spoke Afrikaans to me. It was always a compliment when he did, but it was as though he was speaking to himself. I sensed he wanted to learn as much English as possible: it was the conquerors' language, and the better he knew it the less power they would have over him. The Anglo-Boer War still rankled, and he had never forgiven the English. Not being a swimmer, he was no lover of deep water, so speaking Afrikaans to me this late afternoon was an appeal to the water spirits too, although he would have been perplexed and probably angry if I had told him so. He knew I loved water and was a good swimmer, so he relied on me if we should get into trouble, not that I fancied holding up his huge frame in a raging torrent. He had given a lift to an old African, not a Zulu, who had appealed to him for a job. This man shambled down to the water's edge and stripped, wrapped his clothes in a torn old brown jacket, and put them on his head and walked into the river. We followed, holding our clothes in both hands. The water was waist deep and flowing swiftly, and sand shifted under our feet. To stumble and fall would make it difficult to regain equilibrium. I had a stick that I held out to Hendrik, and we made our way slowly over. The old African splashed ahead, making good progress despite his frailness.

The clouds had been gathering all day, and by the time we began our crossing the sky was dark and threatening. Thunder was rolling in the west, and flashes of sheet and forked lightning illuminated the sky.

"Dit sal reen" (It will rain), Hendrik said, glancing upward.

He had barely spoken when the first drops began falling. I saw them and could hear them plopping into the river. I looked about me, enthralled at the sky, the thunder and lightning, hearing it and feeling it, and the steady swish of the water against our bodies. Waves passed us, carrying debris and foam. I knew from my canoeing experience that this was a sign that the river was rising. We had only a short distance to go before reaching the reeds on the other bank. I could see them waving in the storm, and the big sycamore fig trees were shaking in a strong wind that swept down the valley. The krantz downstream below Dengezeni hill (Hill of Broken Pots) was visible, with its long line of dark-green fig trees marking the river. Behind me were the bush-clad ravines of the Mpila cliffs. Swallows flew low, gliding overhead, a definite indication of rain to come. I heard a baboon bark faintly in the direction of Momfu, and a mountain reedbuck whistled. My outer eyes and ears were absorbing everything, and there was the excitement in myself at the sheer adventure of it all, but it was a purposeful adventure too. I was part of the protective team that would look after and care for this wild nature all around me.

For a moment the thought of crocodiles occurred to me. I shouted to Hendrik, "Crocodiles, are there any crocodiles?"

He looked at me, startled. "Waar?" (Where?) Then he laughed. "No, not here. Very few."

The old African heard the word 'crocodile', and he turned too, saw Hendrik's smile, and, reassured, plodded on.

The smell of the rain on the wind was strong, and with it came the fragrant scent of the *Acacia robusta* mixed with the heavy musty smell of the muddy water. This was a different river from all the others I had been associated with in Natal. The wildness forced itself upon the imagination. The inner eye knew this world and surveyed it with calm understanding. Rain was splattering down, and I could hear it on the leaves of the giant fig tree. Drops formed on the tassles of the reeds, and peals of thunder shook the earth, a sensation caused by echoes from the surrounding cliffs. Hadeda ibis flew downstream, calling loudly, disturbed by continuous rolling thunder, and lightning burst with jagged forks across the sky.

We reached the sandbank on the south side and pulled ourselves out using the reeds, wiping off the mud that collected near the edge of the bank.

The wilderness area

A flock of green pigeons, illuminated for a split moment in a flash of lingering lightning, took off and flew past us with their unmistakable whistling call. I watched them appearing and disappearing as the lightning caught their sheen, then they vanished into the leaves of another fig tree. We sat on the coarse sand wiping our feet before putting on socks and *velskoene* (bush shoes). This was always a moment to take breath and savour the relief of crossing safely. I looked back. The river was rising steadily, and in another hour we would have been swimming.

My pioneering canoe days down the Msunduzi, Mgeni, Mkomaas, and part of the Mzimkulu had taught me a lot about rivers, initiating me into their moods and characteristics. They were all wild rivers in the early 1950s, but people inhabited the valleys. One was never too far from human habitation, nothing near as pronounced as it is today, but one was aware of people – dogs barking in the distance, smoke from huts, cattle tracks, and wooden sled marks on the banks. A sense of use. This early evening on the White Mfolozi was radically different. Not a sign of human beings or their habitation, only wild Africa all around, baboons barking on their way to the krantzes, and a solitary vulture in a stoop to a night roost. I later found that there were some *nagana* cattle camps, but they were so remote that they made no visible or audible impact on this vast river basin.

Hendrik, putting on his shoes, looked fondly across the river to his Chevy pickup truck. He told me that in the dry season he cut reeds and laid a corduroy road across the river. With a little shoving and pushing and wheel spinning the vehicle could cross. All this was to change with the arrival of the four-wheel-drive Jeep and Land-Rovers. But Hendrik's truck was like the Boers' horses, and he looked after it with great feeling. I could see by the look in his eye that he was just making sure no rising river would wash it away. I never had any emotional attachment to vehicles, knew almost nothing about them, and considered anything mechanical a problem. Hendrik's affection for his truck made me look and think differently. To Hendrik his truck was not only horse but wagon too. There was always a blanket roll, food, water, petrol and canvas to protect the truck from sun or dew. With a last look at the brown truck, Hendrik led us up the bank.

Rain fell steadily for the first half-mile. The road was deeply rutted and crisscrossed with white rhino and small-game tracks. We walked through a shallow depression with *umThombothi* trees on either side. Then the road began to rise gently and the vegetation changed to big acacia trees dotted about in tall themeda grassland. We stopped to scrape thick, heavy black mud from our boots. Boulders were lying close to the road; some of them had been used by the rhino as rubbing posts and there was the strong fresh smell of rhino and mud. The themeda redgrass was bending beneath the force of the wind and rain, and I could smell its freshness too. A rhino path wound through the grass going toward the river and the krantzes at Esiwasamanqe (Cliffs of the Vultures). Piles of fresh dung lay steaming on the path. "Net verby" (Just passed), Hendrik commented with a glance. The old African heard Hendrik, and he shuffled up a little faster. A grey duiker startled us as it leapt out of a patch of grass and ran with the diving weaving run that gave it its name into a thicket of bush.

Hendrik began to stride out, I walked wearily behind him, and the old African soon lagged a long way back. I'd had a tiring week and wanted to rest, but Hendrik would not have it. We were now almost opposite Ncoki hill and had a view of the country stretching to Nqoloti and the back of Nqabaneni (Little Fort) hill, with the expansive basin of bush in between. He pointed to the west and I could see another huge storm sweeping downriver. Intermittent rain and drizzle fell as we walked, but the storm that was coming was ferocious in its dark clouds, vivid forked lightning, and heavy rolling thunder.

"Ons sal baie nat kry" (We will get very wet), Hendrik murmured to himself. He stopped for an instant, brushed the rain off his bush hat, and stared at the coming storm. "Kos is vorentoe. Kom ons loop" (Food is ahead. Come let us walk), he said, walking off with his long, loping stride.

The noise of thunder grew louder and louder, and I could hear the wind that precedes the storm rising in a whistling frenzy. It would be minutes before it was upon us. Jagged lightning lit up the sky near us, so bright that I was left with an impression like a negative print. Then the rain came in a dark deluge, a blinding rain whipping around and stinging any exposed parts of the skin. Hendrik disappeared from sight, and the old African was now so far behind it would be a long time before he caught up with us. I plodded on, the water running down my neck and rivulets appearing on the road. Soon water was rushing down the hill slopes through the themeda grass and cascading over the rocks. Thunder crashed and reverberated about the surrounding hills. Lightning struck, and I saw the burning fierce bluish light at the point of contact among some rocks on a hill. I stopped to see what had happened and smelled burning metal. The lightning struck again, this time in a clump of trees, and one burst instantly into flame at its base. The fire glowed, and there were some flames that were fanned by the howling wind, but the heavy rain soon put them out. I could smell the strong scent of woodsmoke with the smell of fresh rain, an exhilarating contact with the earth and air of Africa. It reminded me of my first canoe journey and being caught in a raging storm in the deep gorge near the Mfula trading store where the Mgeni River bursts out. I saw lightning strikes and smelled the burnt air in the rain for the first time. It was a form of fusion between the body and the earth, but here in the hills of Mfolozi the rawness of the experience pierced me more deeply.

I heard a faint shouting and in a flash of lightning that lit up the whole landscape I saw Hendrik sheltering under a rock. He beckoned to me and went on shouting. I jogged to where he was sitting and got under the rock next to him. He said we were at great risk from the lightning and should wait awhile for the storm to pass over. The old African had obviously decided to wait it out lower down the track. The wind ripped overhead, lightning shot across the darkening sky, and the thunder rolled down the valley. Rain came down in a deluge, and above the noise of the thunder and the splattering rain I could hear the sound of water pouring over the rocks and forming a torrent in every depression. We sat in silence. The sounds of the storm made conversation impossible, not that I wanted to talk.

On the way up I had noticed many Stone Age artefacts, and I thought to myself as we sat watching the storm pass that we were part of the continuous evolution of hominids who had known this landscape. Life could not have been too tough for our early forebears in this land. Water, plants, game, and wood were plentiful. I wondered what went on in the minds of those early men as they walked through the patches of savannah, companion to the rhino, baboons, eagles, vultures, and hyena. It was a symbiotic life, stealing from the lion kills before the hyena got the leftovers. Were they not, like me, caught up for moments in the sheer music, the symphony of land, sky, water, and other life? Even the baboons perched on overhanging rocks stared as though transfixed by some distant vista. At times, too, they looked as though they were contemplating: just sitting, watching, heads drooping on hunched shoulders. If they did this, then surely early humans were at special moments gripped by the glowing morning sun shining on the golden sands of the river.

Hendrik stood up, looked around, and announced that the main eye of the storm had passed. "Laat ons loop" (Let us walk), he said, and began climbing up a steep bend in the road just ahead of us. I was stiff and cold, and to get going again was not easy, but gradually the warmth came back to my limbs and I was able to take bigger steps. I heard the thunder growing fainter in the east as the storm continued downstream toward the junction of the two rivers, for me a remote place yet to be explored. There is always something mysterious about the junction of rivers: a meeting place of forces that rise in the hills and flow to join each other and become a greater force that eventually reaches the sea.

I had learned that the origin of the larger game reserves of Zululand began as a result of rhino being shot on a hunting expedition at the meeting point of the two Mfolozi rivers. What were thought to be black rhino turned out to be white rhino, then considered to be extinct. No greater impulse for the proclamation of a game reserve existed in Africa at that time, 1895. From 1820 to 1893 the white rhino had been hunted nearly to extinction, first by the sport hunters, then by the commercial men who sold the horns and the skin. The governor of Natal was besieged by people who knew the significance of saving this species. From the dense bush of the Mfolozi rivers' junction emerged a preservation plan that ultimately would enhance the lives of hundreds of thousands of people. At the last second before midnight a cosmic force intervened to save a species from extinction and led many humans in a quest to know themselves and the land in which they lived. Even those who scoff at forces greater than ourselves would find it difficult to explain the phenomenon of the saving of the white rhino and all that followed in the wake of that action.

In the distance through a gap in the hills I saw the lightning splash like a gigantic hand across the sky above where the two rivers met, symbolically a sign of the confirmation of the thoughts that were going through my mind. I looked around and, as I had done on my canoe journeys, raised my hand in salutation to the universe that had given birth to our planet and to us as a species in order to experience it. Thunder rolled continuously and more light split across the dark clouds, illuminating the landscape, bathing it in a numinous light that I held in my mind's eye, fixed like a developed photograph.

I walked on, following the fast-moving figure of Hendrik van Schoor, wondering if he and the old African still far behind us were experiencing this enormous surge of energy that was coming from all around. I turned periodically, looking in a 360° arc, my inner eye and ear catching sights and sounds: a sparkling drop of water on the wind-beaten and drooping themeda grass glowing red, the dark bark of a marula tree shining in the twilight of the day. Water in pools on the road, black ants scurrying to avoid having to swim. The splayed footprints of a white rhino that had passed in the storm, slipping in the mud. A land monitor lizard lying still beneath a tree, its body shining in the last rays of the sun. The hush of the veld after the storm. The anticipatory silence of less than a minute, waiting for the first frog or bird to call. Then a chorus of frogs in a paean of praise for the rain. From down at the river and in the kloofs different frogs called, each group or individual giving space to the others. A soft soughing of the last of the storm wind carried with it the sounds of the white-browed scrub robin and the black-crowned tchagra shrike, a soft whistle from the tchagra that rose and fell with extraordinary clarity, like a soprano holding a lilting trill. Each song complemented the other – the frogs, the birds, then the deep bass of a baboon troop leader in the direction of Nqabaneni.

Hendrik had stopped some way ahead and was staring at a ledge on the krantz overlooking the great bend in the river. As I walked to catch up and see what he was looking at, I was filled with the emotion of the storm and the symphony of bird, frog, wind, and all the things I had seen. Some unknown part of me had been touched. It went far beyond ordinary human emotion. Somewhere there was this ancient core that had understood all I had experienced. A thought crossed my mind: Had I not been here before? Before I could rationalize it, a voice within me said, "Look upon your home."

I caught up with Hendrik and looked where he was pointing his finger in Zulu fashion. Two hyenas and some tiny pups were playing under a ledge.

"Kyk, kyk" (Look, look), Hendrik said urgently. I peered again, not sure why he was so intense.

"It's the brown hyena," he said. "I've never seen them here before."

We sat down quietly to watch the family scene in front of us. The light was going fast, and the pups shot out, ran a few feet toward us, and stood staring until the female made a sound and they ran back. The male knew we were there but he took little notice, seeming to sense that we intended no harm. The female stood up, stretched herself, and the pups moved underneath her. Now I could see the difference between this animal and its closest relative, the spotted hyena. The brown hyena was much more shaggy. It had a ghostly air to it.

"We were lucky," Hendrik said quietly, indicating we should now leave the animals.

I was surprised at Hendrik's sensitivity and saw a hidden side of this man who was the epitome of the Boer hunter. Behind that rough exterior, the killer of thousands of animals, there was a deep respect for the privacy of another predator. Emotionally he was linked with this beast, and after years of association he understood its role in nature. His eyes had shone with excitement when he first saw it, and he watched the animals with approval. It might have been a flight of my imagination, but both the man and the animals were so aware of each other that there was some telepathic communication. These hunters knew each other and there was mutual respect.

We walked away and I kicked a stone. It clinked. The hyena swivelled in our direction but made no move. Hendrik turned at the noise of the stone rolling. He raised his finger to his lips, another gesture of respect for the animals. I glanced back as we walked up the hill. Five heads stared at us. It had been an intimate encounter never to be repeated with brown hyena, because they disappeared or died out in the Mfolozi game reserve. The experience cemented a bond between Hendrik and me, and he often referred to the hyena.

Darkness had spread out across the valley and only the river glowed in the last light of the day. Crickets were beginning to sing, and the warm, wet red earth of Africa, the rocks and trees, gave off a strong heady scent. There can be no comparison with those few moments in the southern African bushveld after a big summer thunderstorm. The rawness and the power of the responding earth assailed the senses, and the chirruping of the crickets rose in a deafening crescendo. I followed Hendrik with renewed energy, and he turned and said we did not have far to go. The road rose steeply and Hendrik turned right along a rhino path partially covered in themeda. I felt the seeds penetrating my socks, and in the dampness they quickly worked their way in until they were pricking and irritating my skin. I stopped to pull some out and saw that I had walked through a nest of tiny pepper ticks, accurately named because where they had fed there was a continuous burning and itching sensation. Some had already dug deep into my skin. I began to scratch them out when Hendrik shouted, "Los dit, ons is hier" (Leave that, we are here).

I looked up and saw the house, a small wood-and-iron building. A lantern was shining and Hendrik's wife and two children were standing outside. The children ran to greet him, and I saw the smile of pleasure on his wife's face.

We washed in an old hand basin outside. I got rid of my socks and the themeda seeds, and Hendrik handed me a rag saturated with paraffin to wipe over the ticks. The paraffin smothered them and they let go. Only the aftermath of itching and scratching and the possibility of the bites going septic remained to be dealt with, but I was too tired to care. Mrs. van Schoor handed me a glass of ice-cold fresh milk. They had their own cows and a paraffin-run refrigerator. Never before or since have I drunk milk with such relish, and I took small sips at a time, savouring every drop. The children looked at me, wondering why I was taking such a long time.

"Drink, oom" (Drink, uncle), they said, using the word *oom* as a term of respect and staring at me with big eyes.

How could I explain to them that it was not only the taste of the milk and the slaking of the thirst, but that in the last few hours I had gone on a journey in the inner and the outer wilderness. A rush of emotion had threatened to overwhelm me when the first drops of cold milk had rested on my tongue. In one flash I had been transported from the wild world back to the world of comparative civilization, from a hunter-gatherer to an agriculturist. The taste of milk took me back to my youth in the rural area where I had seen Jersey and Friesland cows being milked and had tasted the milk still warm from the udders. I remembered the heavy smell of cows, the dung and the sound of the milk being squirted into the pail, and the lowing in the early morning and late afternoon when the cows were separated from their calves and driven to the wooden sheds for milking by hand. Gum trees, kikuyu grass, poplar trees, Cape sparrows, and fiscal shrikes, the muddy dams where the cattle drank, and as they sucked and splashed in the water the bishop birds rose out of the reeds, the scarlet and yellow brilliance of the neck contrasting with the black feathers. A domesticated world, tamed by humans. It could have been another hemisphere compared with the last hour's walk.

That first sip brought back rural memories. The second sip took me back to our semi-detached mine house in Booysens. Electric trams rattled past, the driver's bell clanging a warning to cars and pedestrians and drowning out the sounds of even the chattering Cape sparrows. My mother would send me to the local café owned by Greek Cypriots to buy a quart bottle of milk. Moving from the rural area to a suburb had been a great shock. I walked to the café, remembering the cows and their body scent and their breath misting on the cold Transvaal winter mornings. Now we were surrounded by concrete pavements, tarred roads, and the smell of diesel from the heavy lorries. Only the Turffontein golf course contained an element of wildness. On moonlit nights I sometimes heard the crowned plovers calling in the lull of traffic and when the trams had stopped running for the night. This would remind me of the plovers running in quick jerky steps across the kikuyu grass fields of the cattle paddocks.

The first two sips of milk brought it all back, the rural and the civilized, detached urban world. For what seemed hours, although in reality it was seconds, I had been separated by a chasm of emotion from the crossing of the White Mfolozi and the walk to Hendrik's house. My thirst had been assuaged and there was relish in the relief, but the memories had removed me from the wild and wonderful world we had experienced on this storm-driven African afternoon and evening.

Slowly I drank and finished the cold milk and came back to the Africa of the afternoon. I smelt the earth, the warmth of the rocks, strong wafts of grass, blossoming *Acacia karoo* and *gerardii*, the mingled scent of the yellow and the white blossoms touching some primordial memories in my psyche. The rain was the first heavy rain of spring, a time our early hominid ancestors knew would bring the fruits of the earth, the sweet red ivory berries and everything that bloomed and blossomed. Thus the psyche became conditioned to the seasons that created a flow of living, and the memory was carried by countless generations. I stood for a few moments, the glass in my hand, savouring the night. With my thirst gone and the other memories receding I could enter once again the wild world that lay beyond the light of the lantern. The crickets' high-pitched song reverberated in my ears, blotting out all the other sounds but bringing a resonance and deep connection with the surrounding darkness. Then suddenly they would stop, and I could hear the frog calls rising in waves from the gullies, and way below on the banks of the White Mfolozi the deep repetitive bullfrog voices took over the night. The biological function of the frogs had been known for a long time, but I wondered as I was transported on the waves of sound how their song had touched early humans. In the quiet of the cave and other rough shelters, how many men, women and children had lain beside the small fire listening and absorbing the music of the spring nights.

Hendrik called out, "Kom binne" (Come inside).

I walked reluctantly into the small room where we were going to eat. Mrs. van Schoor put thin slices of fried bushbuck meat, some mieliepap (stiff porridge), and pumpkin on my plate. She had cooked everything perfectly. Hendrik said grace, holding the hands of his family. The light on the faces of this little group in the wilderness asking for blessing on the food was a scene I was never to forget.

That night I slept on a bed with clean white sheets and pillow slips and the luxury of a mattress. Just before fading into sleep I heard Hendrik telling his wife to give the old African food. He had stumbled into the light, wet, exhausted, and frightened by the contact with wild animals. I heard him say, "Dankie, baas" (Thank you, master), then I slept, overcome with the physical and emotional fatigue of a day and evening burnt into the memory by the branding-iron of thunder and lightning and the multiple impressions of scents, trees, grass, insects, animals, and sounds.

We rested the next day. I walked to the long-drop toilet on the edge of the cliff that looked over the expanse of the White Mfolozi River. I doubt if any privy in the world had a view to equal this glimpse into an Africa that was imprinted on the soul of man. As I sat on the wooden seat contemplating the magnificence of the river and the landscape, I could hear baboons barking down below and the faint rumble of a mating white rhino bull. Natal robins sang in the fig trees, imitating the calls of the black-crowned tchagra shrikes and the four-colored bush shrike – *kok-kok-viet*. Hadeda ibis, disturbed by some animal, cried in alarm as they flew out of the reeds. To my right was the krantz where we had observed the brown hyenas in the storm last night. I looked hard, hoping to see if they were still there, but there was nothing. I only heard the high-pitched whistle of the mountain reedbuck echoing from the Utelezi hills. Behind me at the house a cow was lowing, one of the five that Hendrik was allowed to keep. Someone shouted, and I knew the beast was being milked. I could hear the radio, too, on the Afrikaans programme playing boeremusiek: piano accordion, guitar, and mouth organ: "tickeydraai" music we used to call it, when I was at school. It was not unpleasant in these surroundings, and I knew it was needed by the Van Schoors not only as music to listen to but as a reinforcement of their culture and sense of community. They lived in the past and the present, and Hendrik told me how the music reminded them of the Great Trek, when men and women would sing and dance near the wagons after a day's journey. The juxtaposition of past and present was there all the time, and I listened with interest when he spoke about his forebears in the Orange Free State and how they had come to Zululand to get a government farm.

Mrs. van Schoor called my name, and I left the view. Looking into it I felt as though I were discovering myself. Human emotion swept over me in waves: fear, love, awe, inspiration, but above all a deep connectedness.

"Kom, meneer Player," Mrs. van Schoor called out. "Boere beskuit en koffie" (rusks and coffee).

I walked up the path to the veranda and sat drinking the coffee. Red-winged starlings rattled on the corrugated-iron roof, and the metal expanded with the increasing heat.

So the day passed in the bosom of this little Afrikaner family. They constantly reminded me of my youth among similar people on the highveld of the Transvaal outside Johannesburg, where we lived in a mixed community of Afrikaans- and English-speaking people. I was, even at a young age, constantly aware, or made aware, of the difference between us. The Anglo-Boer War had driven a rift and caused a deep resentment that would perhaps never be healed. I felt for the Afrikaners, because part of my blood and history was locked into theirs, but the English name Player branded us, and the division was always there. It had been hard when I had gone to the local government school at Lyndhurst. The young Afrikaners taunted me because I wore shoes. They were incredibly tough physically and used their fists at the slightest excuse. I was a rooinek, a derogatory term for Englishmen whose necks were burnt red by the sun, and that was enough to attack me. Were we not the perpetrators of the Boer War?

Life became really unpleasant shortly before the Second World War, when I was at an English-speaking private school but had to pass many houses to reach ours on a ten-acre plot of land. The roads had not been tarred, long grass grew on the verges, and the children waited to attack me. Some of them drew swastikas on the sand and others hung out the vierkleur, the four-coloured flag of the old Transvaal Republic. Interspersed with the antagonistic households were Afrikaners who followed General Jan Smuts, and they were my allies. It was a divided neighbourhood, but everyone knew where they stood.

The young Van Schoor children played in the sand, shouting and drawing figures, half listening to the boeremusiek and the boy glancing up when birds of prey flew overhead. They called me *oom* and were not in any way antagonistic, but they knew I was different because I was an *Engelsman*.

The hours of the day passed, and soon the afternoon shadows fell on the surrounding glades of acacia trees, then on the house itself, and within a few hours the crickets began to call and in the distance a hyena whooped. Night came and the Southern Cross shone out of a clear sky.

After a dinner of more bushbuck steaks, mieliepap, and pumpkin, Hendrik took the hissing paraffin lamp to the kitchen, and, like an old Boer general plotting a raid, drew a plan of where we were going the next day. Colonel Vincent, the director of the Parks Board, had received an application from a local magistrate for permission to hunt on the western Crown lands. It was refused, but the Colonel's suspicions had been aroused and he wanted Hendrik and me to patrol the area.

Hendrik completed his map, and pointing at one place, said, "Ons sal hier wag en hulle vang" (We will wait here and catch them).

I suspected that through his own grapevine or that of some of the game guards, for he spoke Zulu well, he knew that poaching was going to take place. He had many friends and relatives in the district, and there was little they did not know. Hendrik had to be careful not to fall out with them, because even though he was a ranger, friends and relatives were to be respected. With me present it was different: all the responsibility could be placed upon me. I was happy to accept it and looked forward with pleasure to action. Anyone who interfered with or opposed game conservation was my enemy.

We walked back the next morning, following the track that led to the Mdindini drift we had crossed in the gathering storm. The air was still fresh after the rain, and yellow-billed hornbills called like zebras from all parts of the acacia woodlands. The trail had dried out, and walking was easy and pleasurable. We did not speak. There was no need for conversation, for we were either preoccupied with our own thoughts or immersed in the natural world about us. Hendrik stopped once and pointed out five white rhino grouped together beneath a large shady schotia tree, red flowers hanging like a brilliant necklace among the dark green leaves. The wind was in our favour and the rhino took no notice of us, and we walked quietly on, glad not to have disturbed them. We reached the river and I drank copiously. The dry heat of the Mfolozi valley always made me thirsty. We stripped and crossed over with the water knee-deep, the river having receded since the storm. Hendrik drove the truck to Masinda, where Will Foster, the game supervisor, allocated four game guards to help us, among whom was a fine man named Nkomo, a Zulu gentleman of the old school, and Hosias Mtetwa, a tall, light-skinned man. Both these men were longtime employees.

We drove along the track back into the game reserve over the concrete causeway on the Black Mfolozi, where hamerkop birds (*Scopus umbretta*) waited patiently to catch frogs and small fish. The track wound up Mpila hill and headed west to Mtunzini, where it petered out at Ntaba-amanina hill. Game guards took it in turn to walk in front of the truck to guide it through the long grass on the rhino path heading west toward Nkonjane (Swallow) hill, which jutted up above the White Mfolozi River. We drove slowly through some lovely waist-high themeda grassland and over small streams of clear water until we reached the Hlungwana River. Using spades and moving boulders we edged our way down; then, with cut branches serving as a corduroy, Hendrik skilfully drove the truck up the bank. Early in the afternoon we reached the spot Hendrik had marked on the map the previous evening. A track came from Ulundi and Mahlabatini, turned at the bottom of a rocky hill and wandered over the bushveld country toward Nkonjane hill and the White Mfolozi River on the south. We carefully obliterated our wheel marks and hid ourselves and the vehicle in an acacia thicket. The trap was set. There was no other road either in or out of the area where the game lived.

We settled down to wait. I recalled Colonel Vincent's words. "You must catch some of these poachers and show them that we mean business," he wrote in an official memo.

Hendrik surveyed the elimination of the tracks and our hidden vantage point and said with some satisfaction, "Dis mooi" (That's good). He laughed and clapped his hands. "Ons het hulle" (We've got them).

All that night, while we lay next to our umThombothi fire and ate meat and *pap* from the three-legged pot, we heard the shooting. "Mooi skoot" (Good shot), Hendrik said grimly when a bullet thumped home into some unfortunate animal. Torch lights waved the vehicle to the animal, and we could hear the men loading up and the curses as a horn pierced someone in the leg.

In the early hours of the morning Hendrik said, "Hulle skiet die hele wêreld" (They are shooting everything). He made coffee and we sat and waited.

Late in the afternoon we heard the loaded truck groaning along the bush track. We stamped out our fire and hurried to where the road crossed a deep donga; here we hid behind some boulders. The truck began its descent into the donga, and we ran and jumped onto the running boards, shouting "Stop!" The driver in his fright stalled the engine.

In the back were half a dozen sacks. While I asked the stuttering driver for his game licences, which we knew he didn't have, our guards urged a man into action and made him open up the sacks. They were full of grey duiker and reedbuck. We had everything we wanted: rifles, game, torches – no evidence was lacking.

We drove the thirty kilometres to the old fort that housed the Mahlabatini police station and charged the culprits. They paid an admission-of-guilt fine. They were lucky – a few years later everything they had would have been confiscated.

Hendrik drove back to Masinda camp laughing and singing. The game guards told and re-told the story to one another, yelling with laughter when they came to the part where the driver stalled the truck. Word spread fast in Zululand, and there was no poaching in that area for a while.

In the years to come Hendrik and I spent time together in Mfolozi, Hluhluwe, and Mkuze game reserves catching white poachers. It was never a pleasant task, particularly as there was little sympathy from either police or magistrates, who considered poaching a trifling offense and irritating for the courts, but I knew from long conversations with Hendrik that the whites, both the locals and those from afar, had no respect for the law-enforcement capabilities of the Natal Parks Board. We had to catch some poachers and, as Colonel Vincent said, show them that we really meant business. We had made our first impression, and the word would quickly spread.

The house at Gome

3

Ndumu Game Reserve

In 1954 I was stationed at Ndumu game reserve on the Mozambique border. Ndumu at that time had over a thousand amaTonga people living within the boundaries of the twenty-five-thousand-acre park, but I lived alone with some fine game guards who had been tried and tested by my predecessor, Tom Elphick, a man of independent character who was the first resident Ndumu game ranger. He had established a respect for the work of the Natal Parks Board against local opposition and various National Party politicians who passed through on periodic visits and condemned the reserve. In their eyes it had little or no value because diseased cattle could pass through it from Mozambique.

I worked hard at first to learn about the reserve, and within three months I knew where to find the populations of hippo and crocodile, and the best places for birds. Ecologically, I felt that I understood how the pans were filled by the Usutu and Pongolo rivers, and how the amaTonga inhabitants had on the one hand killed the game but on the other hand had played an important ecological role.

Since joining the Natal Parks Board in 1952 I had tried to look at the reserves in a scientific way, learning the trees, birds, animals, and insects, and at the same time concerning myself with physical protection and game-guard patrols. Unknown to my conscious mind, there was a part of me that queried what I was learning. Slowly the questioning became conscious, and I woke up in Ndumu one morning in late May, a time when the reserve was at its most beautiful, with calm, cool days, hippo grunting in the pans and the rivers, and fish eagles soaring and calling with that unrestrained cry that once heard is forever a poignant reminder of wild Africa. On this morning I cried out in response to the fish eagle's cry, "You beauty, you bloody beauty you." I knew of no other way to express my praise to this black-and-white eagle, the king and guardian of the river skies. But with all this loveliness and excitement around me and my understanding of the general ecology, there was a sense of loss. I could not explain the feeling to myself or to anyone else. There was a missing element. I learned later in life when these moments occurred that something new was about to break through.

Carl Jung once remarked that you do not find the book, it finds you. At Ndumu it came in the shape of a book by Laurens van der Post. I had gone to the local store to fetch supplies and my mail and there was a parcel for me. I opened it at once and saw the book *Venture to the Interior*, by Laurens van der Post. I flipped over a few pages and read a paragraph. Instantly I knew that the book was about an Africa I had glimpsed at various times in my life. This was a story of a man I had then never heard of, though eleven years later he would become a close friend.

I ate my supper earlier than usual, looking out over the dark line of fig trees along the Pongolo River to the pans at the place the amaTongas called Baga-baga and the dry sand forest of the Sihangwane where the remaining herd of elephants in Zululand lived a precarious existence. After supper I lit the paraffin pressure lamp and began reading. Three pages later I was engrossed in another world. The words spoke to an unknown part of me. I heard the last cries of the fish eagle and the sound of the hippo leaving the lakes and the river to graze in the early evening; then, only the book held my attention.

The story revealed what I felt to be missing in the understanding of my work and could not articulate: Africa had soul, and my own soul was linked to it. In the wild places that I had worked in and tried to protect, the ancient soul of Africa still lived, and parts of people could connect with it once we dropped our veneer and our arrogance. Ndumu took on a completely new appearance. I looked at the wildlife with different eyes and heard the music of the bush with other ears. It was as though an opening had been hacked into my consciousness and there was overwhelming joy at this discovery. From that evening on I trod the earth differently, yet such was my excitement that I missed the crucial quotation from Sir Thomas Browne: "We carry within us the wonders we seek without us; there is all Africa and her prodigies in us." If I did read it, the words were meaningless. Later they would have deep meaning, when I consciously began seeking the inner path.

The aimless wandering after the Second World War that I had returned from at nineteen years of age began to make sense. So did my fishing for a living on the north coast of Natal, my canoe explorations, and my participation in the canoe marathons. All this and the last two years with the variety of my experiences in the game reserves, along with the unpleasant human encounters, now fused. I realized I was slowly focusing on a journey of inner exploration, but I had no true map. I was constantly torn between the contemplative and the active, with the latter being paramount because my daily work demanded it, but in the hinterland of my mind there lurked this powerful force that had to be fed on other bread.

In my quiet moments, philosophically surveying the world from the mountain ridges of Hluhluwe and Mfolozi game reserves, and on still days boating on the lonely far northern waters of Lake St. Lucia, I was slowly awakened to the knowledge that a path of inner exploration had opened. It was not a step-by-step process, but there were moments of brilliant illumination. The outward demands of my job and the determination to serve my calling unstintingly took up my time.

In June 1954 Ken Tinley, a tall, fair-haired seventeen-year-old boy, was sent to join me at Ndumu. His enthusiasm for ornithology had quickly persuaded Colonel Vincent, our director, that he was good game-ranger material. I fetched Ken from Mkuze station, and as we drove over the Lebombo mountains to Ndumu game reserve I was impressed with his keenness for natural history. Within a week we were no longer senior and learner ranger – we had become brothers. In an old plywood boat a little bigger than a canoe, we explored the Usutu and Pongolo rivers and the different lakes that were linked to the rivers. Ndumu had the primeval atmosphere of old Africa, and to be on the slow-flowing Pongolo River gliding close to the hippo and the crocodile was to journey into a timeless world.

Every day was filled with a new sense of meaning. We were unaware of it, but we were also being taught the values of an indigenous culture. Daily we worked with the game guards or the labourers. Their quiet humour and acceptance of life blunted our Western mind-set and subconsciously led us on new paths. These were wilderness people who had existed in a tough environment of malaria, searing heat, and extreme material poverty, but spiritually they had a richness we could not imagine. They were being moved from the game reserve, and their situation would come back to haunt us. They had been part of the landscape, and although it was true that they had killed most of the antelope, it was their slash-and-burn practices that later enabled the game to increase dramatically when the last person left.

Throughout history men and women have been entranced by wild Africa. It has great depth of soul, and people are gripped by its strange, brooding spirit. The ancient Egyptians, Greeks, Arabs, and Romans took expeditions into its heartland. The Arabs said, Once you have tasted of the waters of Africa, you need to return to have your fill thereat. The Romans said: Out of Africa always something new. Part of their empire extended into North Africa, and they were affected by the rhythms of this ancient continent. They captured many wild animals – lion, rhino, and elephant – and took them across the Mediterranean to the great Colosseum. They used cannabis to calm the animals.

The old wild Africa influenced many of the great men and women of our time. Theodore Roosevelt, president of the United States, hunted frequently in Uganda, and he remembered it always. He writes in his book *African Game Trails*:

> "I speak of Africa and golden joys"; the joy of wandering through lonely lands; the joy of hunting the mighty and terrible lords of the wilderness …
>
> In these greatest of the world's great hunting grounds there are mountain peaks whose snows are dazzling under the equatorial sun; … lakes like seas; skies that burn above deserts … mighty rivers rushing out of the heart of the continent … forests of gorgeous beauty, where death broods in the dark and silent depths …
>
> These things can be told. But there are no words that can tell the hidden spirit of the wilderness, that can reveal its mystery, its melancholy and its charm … the large tropic moons, and the splendor of the new stars …
>
> Where the wanderer sees the awful glory of sunrise and sunset in the wide spaces of the earth, unworn of man, and changed only by the slow change of the ages through time everlasting.

F.C. Selous was Roosevelt's guide, and he had once hunted at Ndumu. He had a great influence on Theodore Roosevelt's life. They spent weeks together in the African wilderness hunting rare species for the Smithsonian Institution. One can imagine the long conversations they had around the fire at night, with lions roaring, hyena whooping, elephants trumpeting, jackals screaming. In the morning, when the thermals swirled, they would have listened to the fish eagle, its long call piercing the stillness and echoing over the lakes, forests, and swamps.

Theodore Roosevelt was the rock upon which the conservation movement was built in the United States, and it was due to him that America became the leader in environmental protection, the establishment of national parks, and wildlife management. You need only glance at the index of Bill S1176, the 1957 Senate hearings about the National Wilderness Preservation Act, to see the profound influence Roosevelt had on conservation in the United States. He foresaw the conservation problems that were to face America.

Roosevelt was the driving force in the American Bison Society. It is estimated that there were 60 million bison on the plains when Lewis and Clark crossed the North American continent in the early 1800s. Roosevelt had difficulty in finding eight hundred bison at the turn of this century. I can imagine that in his mind's eye he saw once again the vast herds of African buffalo and antelope, and the memory drove him on to save the remaining bison.

In 1908 Roosevelt brought all the state governors in the United States to a conservation conference, and it was from this conference that the National Park Service became established in 1916. There is hardly a country today that does not have a national park, and the African experience of Theodore Roosevelt was the motivating force. He and Selous kept up a correspondence until Selous was killed by a sniper's bullet in Tanganyika in the First World War.

Roosevelt said: "Aggressive fighting for the right is the noblest sport the world affords." Many conservationists have been inspired by these words.

Why is it that so many people have been caught in the spiritual web of Africa? Is it not because it was here that mankind took its first steps and emerged from the dark forests to walk upright into the savannah? In a BBC interview with John Freeman, C.G. Jung said: "We do not come into the world *tabula rasa*." Three million years of evolution in Africa is imprinted upon the human psyche, and perhaps this leads to a deep yearning to return to see the red earth, to hear the cry of the fish eagle, the roar of the lion, and the scream of the elephant.

Jung was another man whose life was changed by the African experience. In the autumn of 1925 he visited Kenya and Uganda. He came to learn, before it was too late, something about the archetypal nature of mankind.

He wakes, travelling in a train, at sunrise, and on a steep red cliff he sees and describes in *Memories, Dreams, Reflections*: "A slim, brownish-black figure ... motionless, leaning on a long spear ..." It gave him an intense sense of *déjà vu*, and he wrote: "I could not guess what string within myself was plucked at the sight of that solitary dark hunter. I knew only that his world had been mine for countless millennia."

Jung had reconnected with his own interior Africa, and he always referred to Africa as "God's country." For the rest of his life Jung emphasized how important the African experience had been to him and his work. Jungian psychology has influenced Western thought, and Jung's twenty-two books and the hundreds of analysts who have followed up on his work prove it. He, with Freud, made modern humans aware of the importance of the dream.

Winston Churchill's life was influenced by his time in South Africa in the Anglo-Boer War, sleeping on the veld under the southern blaze of stars. Hunting in Uganda, the Battle of Omdurman, and his desert days touched his psychic depths.

Laurens van der Post tells a story, too, in his book *Venture to the Interior* of his incarceration in a Japanese prisoner-of-war camp in Java, when his men were in extremely poor spirits after being made to watch the Japanese bayonet a prisoner. Van der Post writes:

> Africa came to my rescue. I talked to them about the animals of Africa for two and a half hours, about the bush, the plains, the great free mountain tops and immense skies, about a life that was a continuous trek. A journey without walls or streets to hem it in. The sense of doom, the transmuted memory of the killing receded.

He told them stories of baboons, lions, elephants, and rhino, and soon they were laughing. "I realized then how deep, how life giving and strengthening, was this vision of Africa," he said.

My time at Ndumu game reserve had been the opening of the door to the soul of Africa and to the understanding of its impact on others – Greeks, Romans, Arabs, Theodore Roosevelt. *Venture to the Interior* had been a vital key. The journey inward was progressing, and somehow I knew that life would produce the next book or document that would lead me deeper into myself, but problems in the outer world had to be dealt with.

Political storms over the fate of the game reserves in Zululand were growing more serious by the day. The land hunger of the white farmers and the government trying to appease them as well as fulfil promises to black people were leading to a climax. All the game reserves except Hluhluwe were threatened by deproclamation. At the stroke of a ministerial pen and without debate they could be eliminated. Those of us who worked in them lived in a world of uncertainty. Apart from Hluhluwe game reserve, no game reserve was completely fenced. It was only on Ndumu game reserve that a start had been made. Boundary adjustments were another major problem.

Through necessity I learned to play the political game. There was no hope of having any influence on national politics, but I knew that we could play a part and have an effect in the politics of wildlife conservation, later to become environmental politics. Politicians of both main parties at that time were frequent visitors to the game reserves, and I learned the art of lobbying. My connections from my canoeing days with the English-speaking press were invaluable. Radio was controlled by the Nationalist government, but we found friends who helped at least to publicize our game reserves. There were two journalists on the Afrikaans press who appreciated the honesty of our cause and what it meant for the future of South Africa. Their help at critical moments was of incalculable value.

A game ranger was at the bottom of the social scale, and the Natal Parks Board was disliked intensely. To walk into a bar was to invite a fight. Ranchers adjoining the Mkuze game reserve were poaching on the Crown lands, and the local magistrate was himself a culprit.

New rangers were being appointed in Zululand, and they were resented by the old staff. I had to try to keep the peace yet ensure that we moved with the times. There were days on end when I felt physically ill with the strain. So much for the romantic notion of the game ranger. What we were engaged in was a battle for the earth, and we in wildlife conservation were fighting part of the rearguard action. I said this to Colonel Vincent, our director, and he said, "Yes, Player, but it will be a bloody good rearguard action." A former staff college officer in Lebanon, he had long ago appraised the situation.

4

Mfolozi Game Reserve

In 1955 Ken Tinley and I were transferred to Mfolozi game reserve. I tried hard to persuade Magqubu to join the new game-guard force I was recruiting, but he declined, saying that next year he would be ready. He needed time to repair his huts and sort out family problems, but he was always willing to help on specific matters. His knowledge of the game reserve and its historical background made him a valuable source of information. We were joined by a new ranger, Jim Feely, who had just been recruited by Colonel Vincent. Jim, a brilliant ornithologist, was a voracious reader and outstanding naturalist. He, too, was seeking the path. We thought we had discovered the way when we began to read Paul Brunton's book *The Secret Path*.

Brunton answered many questions and opened us to new ideas that emphasized the mystery of life. I remember lying in the shade of a marula tree near the Madhlozi guard camp reading *The Spiritual Crisis of Man* from cover to cover when I had returned from a long foot patrol over the Mtunzini hills to a pool on the Ngamazaneni and Nkonjane hill. I grew increasingly excited at the insights Paul Brunton offered and the magnitude of the crisis he was writing about, yet when I snapped the book closed, looked to the surrounding hills, felt the sun burning, heard *Cisticola chiniana*, the gabor goshawk, and the *cheerio-cheerio* call of the *Tchagra australis*, I knew there was still an important dimension missing. For me wild country had become a place where I was finding out more about myself than ever before, and Jim Feely with his wide reading of game management provided the blinding illumination that connected instantaneously with my psyche. At the back of a book on wildlife management by a man named Trippensee was a list of the fundamental principles of the wilderness concept.

In an instant every wild experience I had ever had came together with the intensity of the equivalent of an atomic flash. The word "wilderness" now described what I had experienced, and images poured into my mind. One was the canoe marathon I had pioneered between Pietermaritzburg and Durban in 1950. The summer storms in the gorges were terrifying, with lightning striking the ironstone cliffs and thunder so loud that it made my sternum rattle. Here was a moment of oneness with the landscape, a drifting into a transcendental state that lasted during the intense thunder reverberating in the gorge.

There were more images, of the years working on Lake St. Lucia: patrols on the lake in an old, leaking clinker-built boat. I grew to love the vast expanse of water and the infinite variety of life that abounded in it and along the shores. It was a moving experience to wake up in the morning and see bright flashes all around from leaping silver mullet caught by the sun. Pelican on the way to feed came gliding low over the green dune-forest hills, and flamingo in all their pink glory fed on crustacea in the shallows. The chorus of birdsong, from gulls, terns, herons, crakes, gallinules, warblers, longclaws, barbets, and robins echoed all over the still morning waters, but above all this sound there was the pounding of the Indian Ocean crashing on the rocks near Cape Vidal, a reminder that it was the source of all life. I would sit in the boat, entranced with the music of Africa.

I remembered the blinding midday heat when the whole world seemed to stand still and hold its breath, moonlit nights when the amaTonga people drummed on the eastern shore, the murmur of the surf accompanying and creating a music.

Trippensee had pulled all this together for me. What I had been having were what we today call wilderness experiences. I had had no terminology, no word to express, to explain how I had been affected by these contacts with the wild. Now here was the word. I was filled with an excitement, a deep thrilling, and a surge of enormous energy. This was not only the word, it was the path.

My life entered a new phase. There was meaning now, and everything that had gone before was the foundation for the work that lay ahead. I realized that the game reserves not only were vital for the conservation of wildlife, but they could be sustenance for the human spirit and lead to a better understanding between people. They could be the core of a renewal of mankind. They were the new sacred places of our world. My imagination knew no bounds. I was filled with an evangelical fervour. I saw the importance of setting aside wilderness areas within the parks, because it was obvious to me even then that there were people within our own organization as well as outside that would insist upon increasing development inside the reserves. I knew, too, that walking and canoeing in wild country would for some people become a spiritual journey that would lead them to a greater affinity with the parks.

The first task was to have a wilderness area set aside in Mfolozi game reserve. Jim Feely and I decided that everything south of the tourist road we planned from Mambeni gate across the Black Mfolozi River causeway up past Mpila to the Mtunzini hills and back past Mbuzane would be the wilderness area. At that time the fate of the corridor of land between Mfolozi and Hluhluwe was still in the balance, but we were determined to get it and the southern Crown lands. We wanted this to be part of the wilderness area.

The need for greater public support for our work was imperative, and one morning I had the idea of wilderness trails. I reasoned that if we could give people the opportunity of walking on the landscape we had been privileged to explore and to love, surely they would love it too and want it to be retained in a wild state. The more I thought about it, the greater grew the excitement. We agreed that all our friends who had visited the reserve and had spent only a short period walking down the banks of the White Mfolozi had been moved when they watched the white rhino and the few other animals that were slowly growing in number after the *nagana* tsetse-fly holocaust. This had to be the way we must go. I knew this was the path to follow if we hoped to keep the reserves. There was also the question of our Zulu neighbours. They had to be convinced about the value of the reserves not only in the practical provision of meat from game, but in the historical importance to them as well. The Mfolozi valley was the heartland of the Zulu people.

Our intense discussions about wilderness continued while we were stationed at Gome outpost in 1955. We lived in the wood-and-iron shack built by Hendrik van Schoor in the midst of the most spectacular landscape. We had only to walk half a kilometre to the nearest hill to be among the white rhino. Other game was slowly beginning to increase, and the mountain reedbuck whistled at our approach. We had learned the difference between their whistle and that of the common reedbuck. This place was enveloped in the old African soul, and there was no better environment to be in to talk about wilderness.

The gap between our evening conversations in the wildness of Gome outpost and the practical reality of implementation of wilderness was going to be difficult to bridge. But because of our isolation from the rest of the world we could talk sensibly – at length and in depth and detail – without interruption or distraction, unless it was a passing rhino, a new bird sound, or an insect my companions did not know. To save this country had become an urgent mission. In the position of senior man I was expected by Ken and Jim to persuade those above us.

I had already experienced bureaucratic snags in my quest to have walking treks in the game reserve. One senior board member had rounded on me. Did I not know that it was illegal to get out of your car in any game reserve or national park in the whole of Africa? This was true, but I knew that he had his eye on Nqabaneni, a prominent and historically important hill overlooking the White Mfolozi River, as a site for a hutted camp. There were old roads made during the tsetse-fly campaign that we were beginning to close off because they made access to Nqabaneni easy. The camp would have a wonderful view, but it would be visible for miles around. The soul of this part of the reserve would be destroyed. I kept firmly in my mind the fundamental principles of the wilderness concept, particularly that "scenery and solitude are intrinsically separate things, that the motorist is entitled to his full share of scenery, but that a motorway and a solitude together constitute a contradiction." The board members' hostility to the idea had not gone unnoticed by some of the senior staff, who were decidedly unhelpful and in some cases deliberately obstructive. There were senior officers who were not in favor of wilderness areas. To them it meant locking up land. To me, Jim Feely, Nick Steele, Ken Tinley and others among us it meant saving the reserve from concrete and roads and unlocking human minds to the beauty and importance of this special landscape. Fortunately, our will prevailed at this time.

I had discovered in my career that any new idea was viewed with suspicion and had if possible to be cunningly introduced, but it was comforting to remember Dean Swift's remark. He said, "You can always measure the worth of an idea by the number of dunces who gather against it."

To some of my seniors the whole wilderness idea was nonsense. Despite working with wildlife and in the reserves, the wilderness aspect had made no inner connection in them. This made my companions angry, but anger did not help to convince people. Fortunately, Colonel Vincent, who had had his own personal encounters with the wilderness of Africa on his ornithological expeditions with the great Admiral Lynes, clearly understood and appreciated what we were talking about. So it was a matter of being persistent and doing the groundwork thoroughly.

The most important document I ever received was from the United States. It was Senate Bill S1176 of 1957, the Senate hearings on wilderness. It was the best secret weapon in our armoury. It contained every argument for and against wilderness. I still have it in my library today, its pages worn, marked, and tattered from much use. The Americans were in the middle of their great battle to have a wilderness act accepted, and through Howard Zahniser of the Wilderness Society I had access to years of accumulated literature. No one knew that their arguments were going to be used with such telling effect in saving a small piece of wilderness in Zululand, South Africa.

Having a wilderness area set aside was only one of the problems in running the game reserve. Since its initial proclamation in 1895, the future of Mfolozi game reserve had always been insecure. Too many people eyed it for other uses. Jim Feely, Ken Tinley, and I were constantly at odds with cattle ranchers. We watched in hopeless rage the cattle being taken into the bush-cleared zone below the Mtunzini hills in Mfolozi game reserve. This was the area cleared during 1947 in an effort to prevent the tsetse fly from moving into the tribal areas. Early one morning Jim Feely and I sat on Lubisana hill and watched a cattle rancher deliberately lighting grass fires. We ran down, yelling and shouting at him. I will not forget the look on his face at the sight of the two dervishes rushing at him. Later we encouraged the cattle into the corridor where they were bitten by infected ticks, and nearly a hundred died. This was the end of the cattle invasion for a few years.

The bush-cleared area was always a great attraction for the cattle ranchers, but it was prime white rhino habitat. The grazing was abundant and, with water available in the rivers in winter and in the pans in summer, they increased in number.

I had no illusions about what we were up against. The Nationalists had been in power for ten years, and regarded the game reserves of Natal and Zululand as things to be bartered. There was no true feeling for them in government circles. With the exception of some English- and Afrikaans-speaking officials – and they had to be very careful about their jobs – we received nothing but cold hostility. Only Douglas Mitchell, leader of the United Party in Natal and vice-chairman of the Natal Parks Board, and some of the braver members of the United Party in the provincial council, stood in the way of deproclamation. In the forefront of the staff Jack Vincent encouraged us to stand firm. His courage never wavered, no matter how the odds were stacked against us or how limited our resources.

The magistrates regarded poaching as a trivial offence and fined poachers the measly sum of ten shillings, though our game guards had spent days watching or tracking them and then were beaten up while making arrests. The magistrates also treated us with contempt and behind our backs and sometimes within our hearing referred to us as Die Varkeraad (The Pigs' Board), or the Fun and Games Board.

Mfolozi was bordered by five magisterial districts, and in some cases it was a day's journey over badly corrugated roads to the relevant court. Cases would be deliberately delayed and game guards caustically criticized by the magistrates or humiliated by the public prosecutor. On one famous occasion it was so bad that Hugh Dent, who at the time was ranger in charge of Mfolozi, lost his temper when a game guard was being unfairly criticized by the magistrate and the interpreter was misinterpreting the guard's evidence.

Hugh, a fluent Zulu linguist, marched up to the bench, grabbed the magistrate by the throat and began dragging him over the bench. Police and court officials rushed forward to stop him before he beat up the magistrate. There was hell to pay. I remember the shock and fear I felt when Hugh phoned on the party line to tell me what had happened. I was afraid for him. He could be charged with assault, and there was the wrath of the chief conservator and head office to face. Dragging the magistrate over his magisterial bench by the throat was a most serious offence, but somehow the affair was smoothed over.

Hugh was such a decent soul; he was liked by everyone. His father had been chief inspector of black schools until Dr. Verwoerd's secretary for black education made his life a misery and destroyed a magnificent educational system. His grandfather had been a missionary at Nongoma and was deeply respected and loved by the Zulus. For this and other reasons, no charges were pressed.

There was an element of fanaticism among some of us in our protective love for the game reserves, but I knew that without it we would not have been able to withstand the pressures. The opinion of the local English-speaking farmers was just beginning to turn in our favour. Friendship with the ex-servicemen sugarcane farmers was helping to sway them toward a more tolerant attitude about our work. I lobbied at every opportunity, concentrating on the Women's Institute, Rotary groups, the Monzi Farmers' Association, the Zululand Public Bodies Association, and anyone else who would listen. My passion for these small remnants of wild country was limitless. My life had been dedicated to their survival, and in my own personal way I intended using every trick in the book.

In the time I had spent at Mfolozi it was obvious to me that if we were not successful in having parts of the adjoining Crown land added to the Mfolozi game reserve, it had no future. Across the White Mfolozi River was a vital piece of land, Mdindini. It was Crown land in the shape of a chicken's head that stuck like a knife into the heart of Mfolozi game reserve. Under the 1897 proclamation of the seventy-two thousand acres of Mfolozi game reserve, the boundaries were from the junction of the White and the Black Mfolozi rivers at Siyembeni up the middle of the two rivers to the Mandhlakazi footpath, which crossed from river to river below the Mtunzini hills. The path had long disappeared and only men like Magqubu Ntombela knew where it had been. Fencing in the middle of the river was impossible, so if the adjoining land fell into other hands it would only be a matter of time before administration became hopeless. In the dry season and in the summer, too, game crossed freely from one side to the other. If we did not get the land it was a foregone conclusion that it would be occupied by displaced people or by cattle ranchers, who were already on the southern boundary of the buffer zone. The Nationalist government policy of removing "black spots" and black people on farms was leading to a massive influx to any vacant land. The buffer zones fell into this category, and the Native Affairs Department, as it was then called, saw the Crown lands as places to put surplus people.

Overpopulation in the Msinga–Tugela Ferry reserves and internecine feuds going back into the past drove people to safer havens. In 1956, Msinga tribesmen had already begun colonizing the country west of the Mtunzini hills. Sometimes they simply displaced longstanding and traditional owners in the adjoining tribal reserves by killing them. A heavy pressure was building up rapidly, and if we failed to get the extra land, life for the Mfolozi game reserve, its animals and curators alike, would become untenable. In the context of the overall availability of land our requirements were very small, but they were vital for the survival of Mfolozi game reserve. The land on the south and in the west was the most critical. We also needed to acquire the corridor, the unallocated Crown land, between Mfolozi and Hluhluwe game reserve. This was approximately forty thousand acres, but encroachment was already considerable. The obvious and most logical step for best use of the land was to join the two game reserves together, but I was aware of the pain of the original inhabitants being removed.

The blame for the indecision and the human misery of displaced black people lay with the Nationalist government. They had total control of the central legislature, the civil service, the police, and the army, yet they were so preoccupied with putting racial laws on the statute books that they ruled with disastrous inefficiency in so far as looking after the land was concerned. There was no national conservation plan, decisions were made on an *ad hoc* basis, and wild lands were the lowest of any priority they might have had in mind. I always found this puzzling, because deep down the Afrikaner is a person of the land.

To be critical of everyone in the Nationalist government would be unfair. There were some incidents involving political leaders that turned the tide at a crucial moment. The Mkuze game reserve had been under threat since it was first proclaimed in 1912 and even before, when it was known as "the magistrate's reserve in mufti." Every year of its existence saw new dangers and the possibility of instant deproclamation. Each conservator wondered when the end would come. Poor Singie Denyer, the officer in charge, lived in constant fear. I was desperately concerned when the Jozini dam was proposed, then built. Land inside the reserve was surveyed and pegs marked out irrigation farm plots. Yet I knew that only when it was actually deproclaimed and occupied would we have lost.

It was, however, eventually saved because John Vorster, the prime minister after Dr. Verwoerd, visited the reserve and was deeply impressed after sitting at a waterhole and watching herds of game come down to drink. He said, "This place is too important to be turned into farms. It must stay a game reserve."

We took heart and renewed the battle for the corridor. Thirty years later it too was proclaimed, but what a story lay between.

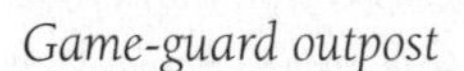

Game-guard outpost

5
The Lion Moves South

In 1957 I was stationed at Charters Creek on the western shores of Lake St. Lucia, and I had recently married my wife Ann. At the end of the year I was instructed by Colonel Vincent that I was to go to Mfolozi game reserve in May. Hugh Dent, the ranger in charge and an old friend of mine, had resigned from the Natal Parks Board and was taking up an appointment to lecture in art at the Durban Technical College. He had trained in London as a portrait painter and wanted a break from game ranging and the bureaucratic dictates of head office, but the bush was in his blood and I knew he would be back.

I had mixed feelings about leaving Lake St. Lucia. Some of the most miserable as well as some of the happiest days of my life had been spent caring for this vast expanse of water, the animals and birds and the surrounding dunes, but I had no hesitation about returning to Mfolozi. I had been stationed there many times and loved the reserve deeply. Apart from Ndumu, it was one of the last wild game reserves in Zululand. However, in the six years I had been in the Natal Parks Board, great changes had taken place on the borders of Mfolozi.

I remember standing on Mpila hill in 1952, 1953, 1955, and even in 1956, looking west and seeing no sign of human habitation. In 1955 Hugh Dent, Jim Feely, and I had walked from the Madhlozi game-guard camp that I had established on the western edge of the game reserve, to Nkonjane hill, the farthest point of the western buffer zone and the end of the white rhino range. We saw a few isolated *imizi* (homesteads) in the area. In May 1958, only three years later, this had changed dramatically. A mass of people, mainly displaced from the Msinga district, had come over the western hills and were threatening to begin building homesteads inside the Mfolozi game reserve.

The day before returning to Mfolozi game reserve I had taken Ann to Nongoma, where she gave birth to our first child, a son we named Kenneth James, after my friend Ken Tinley and James Player, the first Player to arrive in Natal, in 1850. The journey had been nerve-wracking. The Land-Rover bounced over the corrugated and dusty road. Ann's waters had broken and contractions were coming in quick succession. She was calm and without complaint. Outwardly I tried to show confidence, but inwardly I was in a wild panic. We had to stop for petrol, and when she suggested I should perhaps have clean newspapers and an unused razor blade handy, my heart began to pound. The journey seemed interminable, and the road up the steep hills grew worse and the ruts deeper. The eventual sight of the Catholic mission church at the foot of the hills was for me a view of paradise. Handing Ann over to the Catholic nuns was a relief beyond description. Half an hour later our son was born.

I returned that evening to Charters Creek on Lake St. Lucia, packed our furniture, and left the next morning for Mfolozi game reserve. There was a concrete causeway over the Black Mfolozi, and as my vehicle splashed through the clean water I remembered one of the first times I had seen Magqubu. He was with a gang of labourers filling in potholes. He saw me, and with exaggerated leaping up and down he pushed a wheelbarrow full of stones. It was an insight into the way he always acted by example, never asking anyone to do something that he himself was not prepared to do, and do better. The labourers with him laughed delightedly as only Zulus can.

In 1956 he took over as head game guard of Mfolozi under Hugh Dent. All Magqubu's life, from the time he was twelve years old, he had been associated with the reserve. He had served the first game conservator, Vaughan Kirby, and his two successors, Roden Symons and Captain Potter. Magqubu's mentors had been Mali and Mankenke Mdhletshe, two of the most famous and courageous game guards in Zululand. From them he had learned wild animal lore, and from his father and uncle he learned the history of the Zulu people.

I was taking our furniture into the Mfolozi house when a game guard came up the path. He greeted me, and we talked about reserve matters. Then I clearly remember him saying, "There is a story that a lion has crossed the Usutu River." I muttered something polite and carried on getting the house ready for Ann and our son.

Later in the morning Magqubu Ntombela arrived with a great flourish, his extraverted personality preceding his physical presence. He gave me a salute fit for a field marshal, then we shook hands with some emotion.

After our greeting, he gave me a situation report on the game-guard force, how the good ones were faring, where the lazy ones were stationed, how many more guards we needed, as well as new firearms, and how old .303s should either be rebarrelled or replaced. Magqubu's statements were to the point, and once he had made up his mind nothing could shift him. He was adamant that two game guards who were drinking and bringing women into their outposts should be fired. So it went on for another two hours. The game reserve was our whole life, and for us everything revolved around it.

Magqubu spoke at length about the squatters who were coming in busloads to the Biyela, Mtetwa, and other tribal areas adjoining the reserve. "They are now well into the five mile," he said, referring to the buffer zones surrounding the game reserves.

When he finished I casually mentioned what I had heard earlier from the game guard about the lion.

"Yes," Magqubu said. "There is a story that a big lion has crossed the Usutu."

He knew no more than that a game guard at Ndumu had told a game guard at Mkuze, who told one at False Bay, who passed the information on to Nathaniel Nkwanyane, the tall, aquiline-featured man who was Norman Deane's *induna* (head man) at Hluhluwe. He in turn had passed the word to someone at Mfolozi.

"There were lions here before," Magqubu said matter-of-factly.

"Do you think they will come again?" I ventured, sure that the answer would be no, because of the development in Zululand.

"This is their country," Magqubu said. "There is lots of food for them to eat here. Why should they not come back? I can remember seeing them just over there." He pointed to the lower part of Mpila hill not far from where we were standing.

"How many were there on Mpila?" I asked.

"There were three," he said. "One big male and two females. They used to hunt all over the reserve, but Mpila was a favourite place because in the summer when it is hot they could lie in the shade and feel the cool winds."

"What happened to them?" I asked.

"They left," Magqubu said, "because people were always trying to shoot them."

Most of the morning had passed before he took his leave and walked away down toward the game-guard quarters where he had a hut about four hundred metres from the barracks. He lived alone and cooked his own food. I watched his strange gait, a rolling sailor-like walk, but there were few men who could keep up with him. Uphill and downhill he would go at the same pace and without water too, even on the hottest summer days.

Nick Steele, who had recently been transferred to Mfolozi from the Hluhluwe game reserve, came down to the house and we talked about the problems the game reserve was facing. Uppermost in our minds was the squatter invasion. We knew that, ecologically, the boundaries of Mfolozi reserve were inadequate to ensure the survival of the white rhino that were our special concern.

We talked very briefly about the lion rumour because it was all so speculative, and in any case it was over a hundred miles away.

Weeks later there were more rumours of this great lion that was coming down from northern Zululand. Masuku Mzwabantu, the tall Zulu *induna* of Nick Steele's game guards, came to the house to pay his respects to our child.

"He should be called Ingonyama [lion] because he came at the same time as the lion," Masuku said. I laughed and said the child was so small it would be better to call him Uchakide, for the slender-tailed mongoose. I was joking, but Masuku took me seriously, and Kenneth became known from then on as Uchakide.

There was much work to be done in the game reserve, and one of the first tasks was to employ suitable Zulu labourers and game guards. Nick Steele, Magqubu Ntombela, and I worked from the workshop attached to the garage outside our thatched house overlooking the White Mfolozi River. Some time was to elapse before money would be forthcoming to build an office, so the workshop had to do in the meantime. This had been my fate wherever I had been stationed, and had it not been for Ann's competence, far too much time would have been spent on administrative paperwork. To begin with she was paid nothing, then later she received the equivalent of five rands a month. This did not bother her. She was not in it for the money.

When the word went out that work was available, many men came from the tribal areas surrounding the game reserve. They arrived, most of them barefooted, some in Western dress but most still wearing the *beshu*, the Zulu kilt, around the waist, and a khaki shirt. They had wonderful faces: handsome, strong men, the sons or grandsons of the Zulu warriors who went out to fight the British at the great battles of Isandlwana, Kambula, and Rorke's Drift. The men we interviewed had lost none of the warlike nature of their forefathers, and they wanted to join the game-guard force because they would wear a uniform and be taught how to shoot with a rifle. They smiled and tried to cajole us into taking them all, but we were restricted to a few and so selected the strongest and the bravest. When a candidate that Nick Steele and I approved of stepped forward, we would look at Magqubu standing at the edge of the makeshift desk, his face stern and his arm proudly displaying the sergeant's stripes.

"Where is your *muzi*?" Magqubu asked. The man would reply, and then Magqubu asked, "Who is your father?" He seldom needed to ask much more because he had such an intimate knowledge of the surrounding families, and if there was a flaw he gave a barely perceptible shake of his head. The man had failed the test.

When the game-guard vacancies had been filled, we looked for men to serve in the labour gang, which would repair roads and work on camp construction or bush clearing. They filed forward, looking apprehensively at Magqubu, because they knew that we were dependent on his opinion. I was always impressed by the difference between Magqubu the disciplinarian and Magqubu the storyteller.

When the right men had been selected, a paysheet was made up, their *dompas*, or identity book, number was recorded, and a quick check was made to see if they had paid their tax. Potential game guards were marched off to the barracks, and the labourers were placed in the care of the *induna*. We had working with us some of the finest human material imaginable. Man management is never easy, but no one I had ever worked with submitted to discipline so quickly. The old Zulu order survived not because of, but in spite of the efforts of many governments and the machinations of Sir Garnet Wolseley after the Anglo-Zulu War, when he split Zululand up into thirteen small kingdoms. The white man and the Zulu were to live with this mistake for a long time. Despite the history there was a feeling of mutual respect, but I found it hard to understand how the Zulus could still love the British after what they had done.

A rest camp of square huts on the top of Mpila hill was still under construction, and John Kinloch, a former sugar farmer from the sugarcane country on the north coast of Natal, had been appointed to manage the camp. There were only five whites in the game reserve, but we lived at that time without fear of anyone, surrounded as we were by Zulu game guards and labourers. Ann was the only woman except when, once a week, Magqubu's chief wife, Tabete, would visit him, bringing special items of food. We were isolated yet considered ourselves fortunate to be living in this landscape of koppies and acacia savannah intersected by two great rivers.

The land was alive, and there were moments in the night as well as odd hours during the day when one was aware of the *genius loci*, the spirit of place. It was a land that had been inhabited by human beings for a long time. Early Stone Age artefacts lay scattered on the sun-facing slopes of hills. Old Iron Age forge sites were everywhere, and Bushman or Khoisan paintings were faintly evident in those overhangs and caves that had not been desecrated by subsequent invaders. No part of the game reserve was untouched by Zulu history, and it was Magqubu, patiently and over many years, who was to be my instructor in the oral history of this exceptionally beautiful and exciting place. Nowhere in my subsequent travels all over the world did I have the same deep sense of attachment to a landscape. It was in this terrain that the most ancient of hominids had hunted, mated and named the multitude of features. I was aware of their presence from the first time I walked on the rhino and game paths. I was later to understand why Magqubu described the animals as brothers. Their presence activated archetypal forces within the psyche, and at times I felt I was moving in another dimension.

What I had experienced as a game ranger over the previous six years had prepared me for the great test of leading men, learning, and taking the Mfolozi game reserve into the tourist era along with the management, capture, and translocation of the very rare and endangered white rhino. I had my hands full, too, with the initiation of wilderness trails and the political fight to secure the boundaries of the game reserve. I saw it as my task to win over to our cause both the white and the surrounding Zulu neighbours. Wilderness trails and the private organization, the Wilderness Leadership School, that I had founded, would play an important part.

At the end of May 1958 there was factual evidence of a lion in Zululand. Cattle had been killed, and lion spoor was seen in the sandy soil of the northeastern sandveld. The amaTonga people were complaining to the native commissioner, and he sent the police to investigate. Their reports made it abundantly clear that it was a lion that was doing the damage.

Everyone assumed that the lion had come into Zululand from Mozambique, but later there were rumours that a lion's tracks had been seen in the lowveld of Swaziland on the western side of the Lebombo mountains. There was not a permanent lion population in Swaziland, so any lion in the country would probably have come from the Kruger National Park, which was not far from the Swazi boundary. North of Maputo in Mozambique there were many areas where lions occurred, and in the past a few had made their way south, then east, to the elephant park near the village of Bela-vista. The park had a big population of elephant that roamed in and out of the reserve at will, depending upon the season and which fruits were ripe. Years of heavy poaching had wiped out most of the smaller game, and only ordinary reedbuck and red bush duiker survived in any numbers. This meant that any lions would have had to turn to killing the cattle of the amaTonga people who lived inside the reserve. Only a few beasts would die before the amaTonga would have been after the lions, hounding them with dogs and shooting at them with old muzzle-loaders. The lions in the Maputo Elephant Park were transitory, using it only as a place of passing refuge.

Nobody knew for certain where the lion had come from, but its first major hazard in entering Zululand was the Usutu River. The river forms part of the boundary between South Africa and Mozambique, where it plunges through the deep gorge in the Lebombo mountains to its junction with the Pongolo River. The Usutu then turns and flows northward, becoming the Maputa River. It finally pours its waters into the bay of Lourenço Marques, or Maputo as it is now. Few people are aware that the river actually carries more water than the Vaal, one of South Africa's best-known rivers.

The lion had already created its own mythology. No one had heard it roar or even had a glimpse of it. There was something ghostlike in its movements, and local tribesmen said it was the avenging spirit of a senior Zulu chief who had been driven north in Shaka's time. He was now coming back in the shape of a lion to claim his land. This was a conscious expression of the unconscious wish for a return of Zulu power. The lion as an animal was revered, and the Zulu word for 'lion' is one of the praise names for the Zulu king. There were other, more frightening stories of its being the reincarnation of a lion that lived in the 1870s. This beast became the most cunning man-killer in the history of the Tonga people. They pleaded with David Leslie, a famous hunter of that period, to hunt and kill the monster. With some difficulty David Leslie and five hundred amaTonga warriors cornered it in thick bush and killed it, but not before the lion, totally unafraid, had defied the whole group and charged, injuring a warrior before it died.

In May the river level drops, but there are still deep channels along its course, and big crocodiles cruise up and down, feeding on cattle, goats, and often people. So wherever the lion crossed there was a chance of its being snatched by a crocodile. There were amaTonga tribesmen, too, all along the banks of the Usutu who would kill the lion to protect their cattle. Vervet and nsamango monkeys and baboons lived in the giant sycamore figs that line the riverbanks. They would have spotted any lion that passed near their territory and created a hullabaloo of chattering or barking until the lion moved off. This would quickly have attracted the attention of amaTonga women collecting water, or *abafana* (young boys) herding cattle, and they would have reported at once to the nearest homestead. By the time it had reached the Usutu River and traversed the thickly populated areas of either Swaziland or Mozambique, this migrant lion would have learned that it was safer to travel at night; in the daytime it lay hidden in patches of bush, resting and sleeping.

In the early part of June the lion left the border regions and trekked south. Its movements could be traced by the dead cattle it left. Some of the cattle owners put poison in the carcasses, hoping that the lion would return, but months of human persecution had made it extraordinarily clever, and it never returned to a beast that it had killed. It continued south across the dry areas of Maputaland between the grasslands near the sea and the dry bushveld country on the west. A tribesman reported losing two goats, but by the time he had gathered his neighbours and his dogs the lion was miles away, padding silently south toward a goal that it had fixed in its feline brain.

In the grasslands west of the high forested dunes lining the sands of the dark blue Indian Ocean there were many pans and one big lake, Sibaya, named because its shape resembles a Zulu cattle kraal. This habitat was marked by lala palms, the raw material for the local amaTongas' *bisulu*, a potent but high protein drink. West again of the palms was dry, almost arid thornveld where the pans were seasonal until the Pongolo River was reached. The lion needed water, so it would have gone toward the pans country to slake its thirst, then moved west again. It miraculously escaped the attention of the amaTongas, who daily gathered around their respective lala palm trees, filling big Portuguese wine jars with jam tins of the precious juice, greatly thirst-quenching in the hot weather. The amaTonga have always been recognized for their superlative tracking skills, and in the sand-veld following a spoor was not too difficult. Yet the lion continued to elude any pursuers. It crossed and recrossed the Tongaland plains without molesting a human being. This saved it from too much attention.

From the Mozambique border to the Mkuze River, which is the northern border of the Mkuze game reserve, is a good forty miles as the crow flies. In the way the lion walked, it probably covered about three times this distance, but it had survived, and stories of its cunning were magnified.

The man in charge of the Mkuze game reserve in 1958 was "Singie" Denyer, always known by this nickname. He came originally from the East Griqualand district bordering Natal, spoke Zulu fluently, and had given many years of devoted service to the Mkuze game reserve. He came to Zululand to work in a store in the Hluhluwe district, then he joined the government veterinary department and worked in Mfolozi game reserve during the 1930s and 1940s *nagana* campaign.

I remember him telling me one evening that Deneys Reitz, who was minister of lands under General Jan Smuts, had visited Mfolozi and said, "When I had Ndumu game reserve proclaimed, I did my duty to God and the hippo."

Singie knew the land, its people, and the wildlife. He loved to tell stories, some of them outrageous: one was about a python with its head in one hole and its tail in another, and the distance between the two holes was thirty feet! He would tell a story with deadly seriousness, but those of us who knew him looked into his eyes, and when there was a twinkle, we knew he was joking. He developed a reputation of being a yarner, inclined to pull a long bow, but it never bothered him, and he would go on to tell even wilder stories.

In the 1940s Singie was transferred by the department of veterinary services from Mfolozi game reserve to Mkuze. The reserve and its abundance of game became his life, and he and his wife Dawn worked to ensure its survival. They faced what at times were almost insuperable difficulties.

Mkuze was proclaimed in 1912, and it was looked after by the magistrate who had his offices at the village of Ubombo on the top of the mountain. The reserve was under constant threat of deproclamation, with successive governments vowing to hand it over to cattle farmers or to find some other use for it. When the Jozini dam was built, the game reserve was earmarked for agricultural land, and farms were pegged out to be irrigated. The Natal Parks Board was told it would have to give up the Mkuze game reserve in exchange for the corridor between Mfolozi and Hluhluwe game reserves. Those of us in the field were determined to keep both areas, and we worked hard looking after the influential political people that Douglas Mitchell, the vice-chairman of the board, brought from Cape Town during parliamentary recess. There were other people we personally invited to join our cause. It meant that we spent many hours lobbying.

The arguments against retaining the reserve were always specious: for instance, the reserve doesn't pay, or it's too dry, or it's a disease danger, or it's overstocked, or no visitors will ever go there because it is too hot. Singie spent his life refuting these arguments and doing his best to lobby anyone he thought would be an ally for his game reserve. If a passing dignitary happened to comment favourably on any aspect of the game reserve, Singie made sure the whole world knew, and he had no hesitation in embroidering the statement. We were good friends and had spent many hours in the bush chasing poachers or catching impala at night, which were distributed to farmers keen to re-establish game on their depleted ranch lands. Singie publicized this to the full, and by the time he finished talking, Mkuze game reserve was responsible for stocking every ranch in South Africa. The impala from "his" game reserve were unique. They were stronger, bigger, faster than any other impala in Africa.

On one occasion we chased some white poachers and discovered to our consternation that one of the killers was a well-known magistrate. We pressed on and did our best to catch the man, but he was too clever and he hid the evidence. Singie turned even this to the advantage of Mkuze game reserve. "Can you imagine," he would say to anyone who would listen, "one of the most important magistrates in South Africa was prepared to stake his whole career, his life almost, on a chance to go poaching in my game reserve. What other proof do you need to know that my game reserve and my animals have no equal? Can you imagine a magistrate of that rank, of that eminence, risking everything to pinch one of my impala? He knew that the finest game-guard force in Africa guarded the place, he knew that our spies were everywhere and we had wind of his coming weeks before he arrived." (This was true.) "I even knew what car and rifle he was going to use," he said. (This was untrue.) "Let me tell you, if anyone is in any doubt at all about why Mkuze game reserve needs to be saved for posterity, what further proof do you need than this particular case?"

Singie spoke with the earnestness of a revivalist preacher talking to a Southern Baptist gathering. People may have smiled, but no one doubted his sincerity.

Some years previously, in 1956, Singie had telephoned me. He claimed that a lion, the biggest in Africa, had come into his reserve. "Now no one will ever be able to deproclaim this place because this is the only reserve in the whole of Zululand that will have lions. Mfolozi may have its white rhino, but we have the lions," he said, using the plural. "You must come at once and verify it," he urged me excitedly.

It was a long, bumpy, dusty, and tiring drive, and it was some time before I got to Mkuze. Singie at once took me in his truck to the spoor he had carefully covered with branches. The wind had been blowing and the tracks were now not too clear, but there was no doubting the pug marks of *Felix leo*. The lion seemed to be heading north, and Singie had to admit sadly that no one had actually seen it.

"It is true that the lion was passing through. It came to Mkuze for a brief respite to eat impala, the famous Mkuze impala, and now it has gone," Singie said.

The excitement died down and life returned to normal. Singie was bitterly disappointed and very angry when a local farmer said he didn't know the difference between a hyena's spoor and a lion's, but Singie was right. There was no doubt that it had been a lion. This lost opportunity to give his reserve another boost was a great blow to Singie.

In May 1958 the Mkuze River held little water. Scattered pools on the edges of overhanging banks became gathering places for many species of wildlife. A short walk along the riverbed and near the pools would reveal a diary of the night's events. Impala, nyala, kudu, wildebeest, zebra, steenbok, baboons, monkeys, jackals, and the occasional leopard: a record of their presence was there for any keen observer to see.

Part of a game guard's duty was to patrol the riverbed, because any enemies of the reserve had to cross it to get inside. Poachers with dogs were constantly on the lookout for an unwary animal. A quick dash into the reserve, and the dogs would be yowling and snapping at the flanks of an antelope or warthog that had turned to face the adversaries. One lunge and a thrust with a broad-bladed assegai, a gurgle and rattle in the throat, and the animal was dead. Blood seeped into the sand and hungry dogs licked and nuzzled the kill while the poachers, using razor-sharp cane knives, hacked branches and made carrying sticks. With its legs tied, the animal would be hoisted up and within a few minutes the men could re-cross the Mkuze to the comparative safety of the tribal reserve.

Game guards passing along the river were able to read every detail of this quick raid, and the area would be mentally recorded, because people have a habit of returning to the scene of a crime. This type of poaching had a certain glamour. There was always the danger of being caught and the possibility of a fight with the game guards. Young bloods in the tribal reserve looked upon this experience as a form of initiation. It was a way too of cocking a snook at the government, and, besides, the stolen meat tasted good. There was time to grill it over the fire, drink marula or lala palm beer, and tell tall stories of battles with the game guards and narrow escapes from black rhino.

The game guards looked forward to catching the poachers, for it was for them also a kind of sport. There was the pleasure of taking the prisoners to the main camp and then to the police upon the mountain at Ubombo. They could look in at the trading stores, talk to the girls, and buy a bottle of illicit liquor. Then at the court case there would be even more time to spend at the stores and talking to the girls. If it meant staying over a night, they would be able to indulge in a good drinking session and perhaps a little dancing too. The fact that the magistrate always seemed to be on the side of the poachers was puzzling, but it was all part of the game.

The snare men, who were a different breed of poacher, took greater care in crossing the river. Wire stolen from fence lines or old railway cables or post office telephone lines made excellent nooses. These men would pick their crossing place with care and go to great lengths to hide the evidence of their passing. Enough snares to cover nearly a mile of game paths converging on the isolated pools would be laid. It required extraordinary skill to disguise the snares, the crossing place, and any sign of their own presence.

Rangers and game guards hated this kind of poaching because it meant a long and tedious wait at the snares. Sometimes this required days of just sitting and watching. There could be no smoking or even washing because the noses of the poachers were extraordinarily keen, and they could pick up the scent of a man at a hundred paces or more, depending on which way the wind was blowing. There were times when the snare-laying men were frightened off by accident. A game guard might be passing through the area and give his position away by smoking a cigarette or talking or whistling. The poachers would fade into the bush and then, suspecting a trap, would never return to their wire nooses. Weeks later the unusual activity of jackals or hyenas or perhaps a gathering of vultures would attract the rangers or game guards to an area. What they found was not a pleasant sight: rotting carcasses covered in a white cream of seething maggots, a head, its bulging eyes staring into space, filled with an unbearable agony, a death from lack of food and, more importantly, water in an arid area, and the slow closing of the windpipe as the animal struggled to free itself and, in its frantic twisting and turning, the noose slowly tightened. Sometimes a passing hyena or jackal would hasten death by biting chunks of meat from the still-living body. Animals in snares died horrible deaths.

Poetic justice once caught up with a snare poacher who heard approaching game guards. He panicked and tripped, falling into his own snare. In his haste to get away the noose tightened on his throat and he experienced what an antelope went through. His strangled cries guided the guards to him and he was released before he choked to death.

The only way that the work of these poachers could be curbed was first to check the human spoor of people who were entering and leaving the game reserve illegally. Poachers would take incredibly elaborate measures to hide the evidence of their coming and going – walking backwards on tiptoe, running and jumping from one point to another, dragging branches or laying leaves – anything to distract attention from their presence. Their expertise prevented them from having to spend a long time in a prison cell. These poachers were animal-like in their cunning and slipped like shadows in and out of the bush, going barefooted and dressed in the flimsiest of skins, a small *beshu* at the most. Snares were carried over their shoulders, and in the right hand was the *celemba*, a sharp cane knife, its handle covered with an animal skin stretched tightly over the original wood. This stopped sweating hands from slipping. Poaching was a way of life, and some made a good living from it, selling the meat to fellow tribesmen, and the skins, pounded to a soft chamois, found a ready market.

The game guards, some of them ex-poachers themselves, or certainly with relatives who indulged in the illegal game, were constantly on the lookout. Any patrol along the riverbed and its banks was conducted in a most practical and intuitive fashion. They looked for any tiny and insignificant sign of someone having crossed. Daily they had to report in detail everything they had seen to Majuda, Singie Denyer's Zulu name. With his knowledge of the language and the people, Singie would question and re-question the game guards. Singie was then too old to walk on extended patrols, and this made him even more keen to know the smallest detail of events in the reserve. The game guards were his eyes and ears, and their accumulated reports allowed him to know everything that was going on in the reserve. He knew too what was happening in the surrounding tribal areas. Game guards going home on leave attended beer drinks, listened to the gossip, talked to their wives and children, and heard more gossip. Anything of interest would be passed on to Majuda. Anything they may have missed or forgotten to pass on would have been picked up by the house cook, an old and loyal retainer of Singie and his wife. Singie was extremely well informed about everything that was going on in the Maputaland lowveld. In his own way he was as much part of the country as the riverine sycamore figs and the umbrella-shaped *Acacia nilotica* trees.

The news of the lion crossing the Usutu River and its southward trek had made no stir beyond the amaTonga tribesmen in the Pelindaba sand country and the Makatini flats. It had certainly not been reported by any Natal or national newspaper, but Singie Denyer had heard of its presence, and as it trekked on silently southward he listened carefully to the bush telegraph provided by his game guards and the workers in his reserve.

One can imagine the excitement of the patrolling game guards, making a normal but detailed check along the Mkuze River looking for any faint sign of their enemies the poachers, to see a strange spoor. "Ibubesi – the lion!" they would have exclaimed and, filled with the importance of the news, hurried off to tell Majuda. But not before they had absorbed all the evidence: a hair lying on the sand, the size of the spoor, the steepness of the bank it descended, other animals that may have scattered away from its presence, its faeces and what was in the dung – goat, cattle, antelope, or dog. When they had all the information they would have taken the shortest path to headquarters and Majuda. They knew how jubilant he would be.

Singie, listening, would nod his head encouragingly. "Yebo, yebo!" (Yes, yes), he would say, as a game guard, vying with one of his mates, remembered another tiny detail. The size of the spoor grew in the telling, but it was obvious that it was a big lion.

The lion stayed in the Mkuze game reserve for a few days, and some of the remains of its kills were found by the guards. Singie could now hardly contain himself, and he had the largest spoor covered with forty-four-gallon drums cut in half. He couldn't wait to tell everyone, and as luck would have it, Douglas Mitchell, the vice-chairman of the Natal Parks Board, happened

to visit the game reserve. Singie lost no time in telling him about the lion, its size, colour, and everything else about it.

"Have you seen it?" Mr. Mitchell asked suspiciously.

"No," Singie said.

Mr. Mitchell might have looked sceptical, wondering if it was another one of Denyer's yarns.

Singie drove him out toward the old airstrip that had been used by aircraft in the *nagana* campaign days. It was sandveld, and the lion spoor had left a deep impression in the soft red sand. Singie moved the half-drums away, and with a flourish pointed out the spoor. Douglas Mitchell examined them carefully, and after a short silence he said to Singie, "Yes, Denyer, there is no doubt that is a good-sized lion."

Singie told him all he had learned from the game guards. Douglas Mitchell, himself a Zulu linguist who had a rapport with the black people, understood and appreciated how Singie had collected all his information. Nevertheless, because this was not the first lion to reach the Mkuze reserve, it was now a matter of waiting and seeing if it would turn round and head back north toward Mozambique, as another lion two years previously had done.

6
May Patrol

After a few weeks at Mpila I left with Magqubu on a familiarization patrol. My last long walks had been in 1955 and 1956.

May is the month when the cyrtanthus blooms, a small red flower that grows on the rocky hillsides of Mfolozi. Its appearance brings notice of a change in seasons. The sun does not scorch the skin anymore, the land becomes quiet, and sound is carried a long way. It is a time of *imithi iyahlanguka*: the trees begin to shed their leaves.

We left at first light and walked from the main camp of Mpila past the Momfu cliffs, then down through the bush to the Mpafa River. While we walked along the paths I could see Magqubu was scanning everything around us. The spoor on the ground told him exactly which animals were ahead and how long it was since they had left their imprint. A piece of dung, bark off a tree, a broken twig, or a scrape on a rock were enough clues to tell him a whole story. This he knew by observation and experience, but he had other more powerful and subtle senses that gave him an even greater awareness of what was happening. He had learned to fuse his observation and intuition enabling him to know when we had passed an animal even though he had not seen it.

The path led through a dense reed bed, making it impossible to see more than a few feet ahead. Magqubu stopped in the middle of the reeds and said we had passed a white rhino bull on our right. I did not question it, but doubted how he could know. We climbed the bank on the other side, and Magqubu looked back and pointed. There was the white rhino bull standing on the edge of the reeds. How did Magqubu know? It was as though the animal had entered into his consciousness. Over the years I was to experience this same phenomenon many times. I always walked behind, watching him closely. He would have his head turned to the left or right, but he always knew what was on the opposite side. His knowledge of animal habitat built up over a lifetime of work enabled him to anticipate what species of animal would be in a particular clump of bush. At the same time his intuitive radar-like power went beyond experience and knowledge – it was

supernatural. He understood the moods and rhythms of the land. Magqubu stopped again to listen to the monkeys chattering excitedly in the Mantiana kloofs, an insistent sharp sound, and he said the way they were calling meant they had seen either a snake or a leopard. He had hardly spoken when we heard the long sawing cough of a leopard quickly followed by the angry guttural noises of the monkeys and the alarm barks of a sentinel baboon.

I had already worked in Mkuze game reserve with outstanding game guards such as Sighodlo Mbazine, who once tracked a man on horseback over stony ground where I could not see even a scratch; Samuel Mtetwa, who was my first guide into the mysteries of Lake St. Lucia and the high surrounding dunes. In Ndumu game reserve on the Mozambique border there was Catuane Tembe, a short, thickset, immensely strong man who had grown up on the Pongolo and Usutu rivers and in the swamps and sandveld. He was another game guard who knew the animals and the land, and there were others, too, at Mkuze game reserve. But even the combined skills of these men could not match Magqubu's. It was not fair to try to compare, because each was an expert in his own way, but Magqubu had been given or had developed extrasensory perception.

We reached the deep pool below a rocky ledge in the Mpafa stream. It held water even in the driest of times and provided ideal habitat for large pythons that lay in wait for the game to come and drink. We approached quietly and saw the brightly colored snakes lying on the hot black rocks, absorbing the autumn sun. They slithered off when they saw us.

Magqubu began to make a fire. He gathered a handful of grass, fluffed it up, added some small dry sticks, made a movement to check the wind direction, struck one match, and the fire was burning. He was aware of my looking, so he made fire-making into a ritual, humming to himself as he put one stick upon the other with slow deliberate movements. The filling of the billycan, cutting the supports to hang it over the fire, was a public show, but many times he would do this anyway to entertain himself. He unpacked the billycan from his old rucksack and I got out the tea and sugar. He filled the billy, then used his penknife to cut sticks to hang it over the fire. These were still the days without tea bags, and one waited until the water was boiling, then tipped a handful of dark tea leaves into the billy, took it from the fire, and tapped it to get the leaves to settle on the bottom. The Mpafa stream in the dry season of May was salty, not enough to stop the water from being potable, but the taste was unmistakable. Later in the season, when the animals were more dependent upon it, the water level dropped, became saltier, and had the additional flavor of animal urine. It would have to be very bad water not to assuage an Mfolozi thirst.

The smell of woodsmoke drifted through the air, its strong scent overpowering the faint smell of the pythons and the surrounding bush. There are subtle scents of shrubs, bushes, trees, and flowers that hang in the still air of May mornings, and one learns to identify them as though they were birdsong. We had walked through many different types of vegetation over the years, and I remembered them most from the scent of crushed leaves and the feel of the bark. I resisted learning the Latin names because it depersonalized the trees, putting them apart from me. With Magqubu it was a different kind of learning. Walking behind him I was absorbing knowledge through a process of osmosis, example, and imitation.

We lay resting in the shade of a schotia tree, the fire dying down and the strong scent of the *umThombothi* beginning to fade. Sunbirds and orioles fluttered in the branches above us. It was quiet, yet the world was full of sound: the trickle of water from the second pool on the Mpafa stream, hadeda ibises calling upstream, and a chanting goshawk. I had begun to doze in the warmth of the sun and became dimly aware of the ground hornbill whose booming call came from the direction of Nqabaneni krantz overlooking the White Mfolozi River. My one ear was on the ground, and I could hear the reverberations of the call. Magqubu with his boundless energy was awake, alert, and aware of the sound. It is an abiding memory. No matter where we were he was on guard. If any danger threatened, his posture would change, and he would be ready for whatever might happen.

The deep booming calls of the ground hornbills reverberated, lulling me to sleep. Dimly I heard Magqubu move and begin to talk quietly to himself. I opened my eyes. He was nodding his head and walking with long strides like a stodgy English colonial official, and saying "Umuthi muni, umuthi muni?" (What tree is this, what tree is this?) He saw I was awake and he spoke louder. He became the ground hornbill, and anyone who had ever heard or seen the bird would at once have known it from the sounds and the movements Magqubu was making.

"You know the *insingisi*, but do you know what it says? You will have seen that they usually walk in pairs," he said, "but sometimes there are six and perhaps more, but there is always a leader and he walks ahead and he is asking his family as he is calling, 'Are you eating, are you eating, are you eating well?' And then they reply and they say, 'We are eating, we are eating well,' and then he will say again, 'Are you eating, are you eating, are you eating well?' and they will reply once more, 'We are eating, we are eating, we are eating very well.' Then when he comes near the *msinsi* [erythrina tree], he will say, 'Umuthi muni, umuthi muni?' 'What tree is this, what tree is this, what tree is this?' And then the family will reply, 'Msinsi, msinsi, msinsi, this is the msinsi tree.' And so they will carry on. So you see you have to watch carefully and listen to what they are saying and when you do that, then you really start to learn about the birds."

The ground hornbills were coming closer, and Magqubu began his *insingisi* dance and song again. "Umuthi muni?" His head moved exactly like a ground hornbill's, and when I turned my back it was hard to tell the difference between his voice and the sound of the birds. They melded into one continuous song. When the birds were really close he whispered softly and indicated I should follow him. We climbed the slight ridge, and in an open glade there were six huge ground hornbills walking ponderously like old men, their heads moving up and down, and their red, white, and black feathers contrasting with the grey bush. Magqubu watched the birds intently. It was obvious that no part of their behaviour escaped his observant eyes. He nodded his head in time to the birds' movements and sang their song quietly to himself. Something disturbed them and they ran a few feet, then took off, flying with slow and heavy wing beats, white flashing distinctively on their wings. Soon they were out of sight, and I heard the songs of other birds again.

Watching Magqubu and the ground hornbills had captured my entire attention. I had been oblivious of other sounds and what had been going on around me. This was Magqubu's way. His personality was so strong and his acting so impressive that you were naturally attracted to him and saw or heard little else until his performance was over.

He tipped the dark tea into my mug, his hands unaffected by the heat from the billycan. I remarked upon it, and he laughed and said that as a child, when the fire went out at his *muzi*, he would run to a neighboring family, pick up a glowing coal, and run back to his huts, throwing the coal from hand to hand. I said "Hau!", the Zulu expression for amazement. He picked up a red coal and ran around to demonstrate how he used to do it when he was a child. He passed me and I smelled burning skin and exclaimed that it must be painful. He smiled, and as though to prove a point, crushed the coal out in the palm of his hand. Magqubu then told me how fire was made when he was a child.

"To make a fire for us in the early days was very hard," he said. "We had first of all to find a piece of hardwood like the *umBondwe* [combretum], and then we would cut and shape this so that it looked like a pencil. Then we would find a piece of softwood like the fig or the *umPhahla*, and then we would clasp the dry fig or the *umPhahla* between our feet and then start to roll the pencil-shaped hardwood. Sometimes you would get tired, and when this happened you handed it over immediately to another person and they would hold the softwood between their feet and so it would go on until there would be a glow. We would then put tarchonanthus twigs on top and blow and blow and blow, and at last the fire would start. Once we got it burning we put on *uGagane* (Dichrostachys). Then we would get the *umBondwe*, and get that burning until we had a full fire. We used to use the smokeless wood because it gave a much better light in the hut; also smokeless wood did not ruin the special clothing of the women, who had gone to a lot of trouble to make their clothing.

"To make fire was not easy. That is why we kept it alight, and the *umBondwe* was helpful. When we had used the fire or cooked over it, we would take the ash and put it over the red coals, and in this way the coals would be kept alive, so that when we wanted to get the fire going again we would come along and take the ash off and then throw some tarchonanthus or some grass on, and in that way the fire would be lit.

"But there were times when the fire went out, and that meant we then had to look around the hills, and where we saw smoke we knew that the neighbor had a fire. We would go to the *muzi* and ask for one of the coals, and throwing it from hand to hand we would run to our own muzi, put it in the fireplace, and in that way get our own fire going again.

"Today it is easy. You take a match and you light the fire, and there is paraffin for lighting and you have electric light which comes from the machine up on the hill [the generator], but I remember how hard it was to make fire and to keep the fire going, so when I strike a match I remember all this and I respect that time and I respect the match."

I drank the tea and Magqubu spoke more about the ground hornbill, saying that the Zulus respected this bird and no one would kill it because it brought the rain. There were, however, times when during a prolonged drought a ground hornbill would be killed and thrown into a river in a ritual to bring rain.

Magqubu had no peer as a storyteller, and he could go on for hours, never leaving the central theme of his story but continuing to embellish and repeat. When he was fully in his stride there was no stopping him, but he was never boring because he brought so much variety to the story with his singing and imitations.

It was on this day while we rested beneath the schotia tree on the Mpafa River that he first told me the story of the *mpafa* (*Zizyphus mucronata*) tree. I was tired after our walk and even more fatigued at the thought of the distance we still had to travel. The Mfulumkulu plain and Ngqoloti hill lay between us and the caves where we were going to spend the night. I made a move as though to say he could tell me about it later, but he ignored me and in his clear and beautiful Zulu began talking about the *mpafa*. It was not long before he was on his feet, demonstrating every detail of his words, whistling the bird calls if I did not recognize the Zulu names, and repeating the same phrase over and over with infinite patience if he saw there was something I did not understand. I watched and listened to him, hypnotized by the unfolding story of this tree of which I would now forever be conscious. My poor knowledge of Zulu was no impediment on this warm May afternoon, and my anxiety to reach the Mhlopeni caves was forgotten. This was a masterpiece of theatre, storytelling, and a lesson in ecology that embraced all aspects of the natural world and the human interaction with it, physically and spiritually.

"The *mpafa* tree is the tree of the people, the animals, and of the birds and insects," Magqubu said.

His voice had a sonorous rhythm and I listened, heard, and was caught up by it, yet was still aware of the blue sky above and vultures gliding in the thermals. The fire had gone out, but the combination of acacia and *umThombothi* woodsmoke hung in the air, and there was the smell of soot on the billycan and tea leaves that had spilled on the ground.

A vervet monkey chattered upstream. Magqubu hesitated for a moment, imitated the monkey, and recaptured my full attention.

"The original name was always *mpafa*," he said, "But it was changed to *mlahlankosi* [bury the chief]. It has another name too for those who respect it. It is called *mlandabantu* [fetch the people].

"When a chief or a king died he was buried sitting up and then the grave was laced with the *mpafa* branches. Each branch was intertwined with the other, so closely that no human hand could get through. This would keep away the people who wanted a part of the body for *muti* [medicine] or to *loya* [cast a spell upon] someone. The grave would also have an *mpafa boma* [enclosure] built around it, so thick that neither people nor the hyena nor jackal would be able to penetrate."

Magqubu then made the long mournful whooping call and the giggling laugh of the hyena when they are frustrated by not being able to get to meat. He sniffed the air, his shoulders hunched and his legs bent like a hyena and he loped like this strange beast of the night, head turning and looking back.

"Buqo, buqo," Magqubu whooped. He explained that *buqo* meant the smell of decaying flesh, and this is why the hyena made the sound. It was crying out for meat.

He called out the animal's praise name: "The ugly one who carries a young beast on his shoulders. The eater of all rotten things and anything left over by others. The one who has no hair."

He dwelt on the character of the hyena, how it stole his goats, came into the *muzi* at night and took the young calves or the fat sheep. He danced around, imitating the sound of the hyena whooping, a calf lowing, and a sheep bleating as it was dragged from the kraal. He picked up my stick, brandished it in a defensive way, beating off a hyena attack. He called upon the *amadhlozi*, the spirit ancestors, for help, interspersing the human shouting with the deep-throated whoops, giggles, and screams of the hyena. Women yelled and children cried, and the cacophony of sound grew in intensity as the drama increased.

"You who carry the baboon on your back and circle the *imizi* at night, we are not afraid of you because your dry dung, when it is burnt and mixed with water, stops the diarrhoea in our children," Magqubu cried out.

When he talked and cried like the hyena, we were there in the night, with that weird, mournful sound echoing amongst the krantzes, lingering in the groves of sycamore fig trees, and then we were entering the *muzi* to steal the beasts. There was nothing about the hyena he did not know – its walk, its cry, the bone-crushing power of its jaws, and its cunning stealing of the domestic stock.

"Yebo, mpisi [Yes, hyena], I know you well. You who share the hole with the warthog," he cried out.

He stopped for a moment, laughed, and we were both back in the bed of the Mpafa stream. Then he explained how in the late afternoon warthog made their way to burrows that had been dug by the *sambane* (antbear), where they waited for the occupant hyena to emerge. In the early morning, when the hyena came back from hunting or feeding on the carcasses of dead animals, the warthog would emerge to begin foraging for grass and roots.

"It is the hyena who is the most intelligent, but the *mpafa* thorn can stop this clever animal from getting to the graves of the chiefs," Magqubu said. "Look at the thorns."

He grabbed a branch, broke a twig, and showed me the thorns, hooked on the one side and straight on the other, the leaf dull on one side and glinting on the reverse side. This is why the Voortrekkers called it the *blinkblaar wag-'n-bietjie*, the shining leaf wait-a-little tree. When those thorns hooked into your skin, you were forced to "wait a bit."

Magqubu described in detail the construction of the impenetrably dense *mpafa* thorn enclosure. A gate was built from the poles of the gardenia tree, and for a year a man guarded the grave. At night he carefully brushed the sand – Magqubu made all the movements of cutting small branches and smoothing the sand – then in the morning he would inspect the entrance to make sure no one had been near during the night. He walked slowly from side to side, showing how the man carefully examined the ground.

Magqubu rested after his exertions, and I saw a faint line of perspiration on his upper lip. Had he entered the world of acting, he would have been a star. He could say more with the lifting of an eyebrow, the movement of an arm, or a change in the tone of his voice than many actors I saw on stage and screen. Whatever he was talking about or describing he became part of, but when I pulled out my camera he became stiff, standing fixedly to attention.

Magqubu held the twig of *mpafa* in his hand. "Mlandabantu," he murmured. "When my father died at King Edward Hospital in Durban, his body was brought back here to the *muzi* at Macibini [The Place of Small Pans or Lakes]. We buried him and planted the thorns around the grave."

He had shown me at his home the small mound surrounded by the white flowering yucca plants, a species from California and the dry west of America. It flourished in Zululand and helped to protect *imizi* and the cattle, goat, and sheep enclosures, but nearby was the *mpafa* too, its symbolic value deeply rooted in Zulu culture.

"I have shown you the grave, but the body came back without the spirit," Magqubu said. "I had to go to Durban to fetch his spirit so I took a small piece of the mpafa tree with me. I went to the hospital, asked which bed my father had died in, and then I laid the branch on the blankets and called out to the spirit, 'Woza, Baba [Come, Father], I am here to take you home.' " Magqubu spoke slowly and with nostalgia, expressing his love for his father. It was a veneration that touched me because I had heard my father speak of my grandfather in the same way.

"When the *mpafa* had lain on the place where my father died, his spirit entered the *mpafa* and I began the journey home. But there were two of us, my father's spirit and myself. I caught a bus and paid the conductor for two tickets, one for my father, the other for myself. I had to catch a taxi from the bus stop to the station. The *mpafa* lay on the seat next to me and I spoke to the spirit of my father, pointing out the buildings, the Indian mynah birds, and the flags flying at the government building. It was good to talk with the spirit of my father, and I thanked him for all he had done for me when I was growing up on the hills of Ongeni." Magqubu pointed over the Mantiana hills that lay behind us. "You went to Ongeni when you first came here," he said.

He meant in 1955, when I had been sent to take over the patrolling of the game reserve from old Willie Foster, called by the Zulus Mashiya after his bushy eyebrows. Magqubu's memory was uncanny.

"You put a game guard camp near my home, but you called the place Madolofia" (prickly pear).

I remembered Magqubu stopping me at Masinda, which was the headquarters of the reserve in 1955, and telling me that Madolofia was not the right name. He had explained in his usual direct but polite way that the hills were his birthplace and they were called Ongeni. He gave me a history lesson about the early conservators and said that when he had been employed as a young boy by Mali Mdhletshe, the *induna* in 1914, Vaughan Kirby had brought in prickly pear plants and instructed the guards to plant them all over the game reserve because there was a bad drought and the wild animals needed food.

"My father planted the *madolofia* around the huts, but the place is Ongeni," he repeated.

The sun was now dipping in the west, and I was anxious to move on because I did not like the idea of walking through the dense bush below Nqolothi, or climbing that steep hill in the dark. I said something, but Magqubu brushed my concerns aside.

"I know the paths better than the rhino do," he said with mild irritation.

It was not a statement made in bravado: it showed his knowledge of the country and it superseded the need for unnecessary caution. He was naturally brave too, unafraid of facing death in any shape or form. His belief in

Shembe the Zulu prophet and the Christian sect that he led had, if that were possible, reinforced the instinctive Zulu bravery he inherited from his long line of ancestors.

Magqubu insisted on finishing his story.

"We are talking about the *mpafa* – *mlandabantu* – and when I went to Thekweni [Durban] to fetch the spirit of my father. The taxi took us to Durban station," he said, voicing the noise of people pouring onto the railway platforms.

"I bought two tickets at the *stimela* [steam train], one for my father, one for myself. The train left for Mtubatuba in the night and I bought food for the journey. When I ate, I spoke to my father and said that I was eating for him too. I put the *mpafa* branch on the next bunk. The other Zulus in the compartment respected my father's spirit and did not lie on the bunk. During the train journey while I was awake I spoke to my father and told him about the country we were traveling through. There is the Mgeni River, the first one we cross on the way to Zululand, then Mdhloti, Thongati, the Mhlali. In the reeds I could hear the frogs and the *titihoye* [crowned plover] calling, but the noise of the wheels and the puffing of the engine, they drowned out all other sounds."

Magqubu made a noise like the clicking of railway coach wheels and the long whistle of the steam engine. I had travelled that route many times in my early days as a game ranger and could visualize the exact places Magqubu was talking about. His description of the country showed his memory for every tiny detail, the coal sparks flying through the air from the chimney of the engine and the cane fires burning on the hillsides. He described the long bridge over the Thukela River and how the carriage lights were reflected on the water below, the scent of the burning coal in the engine, and the cane smoke.

"The train stops at Empangeni in the early morning so that people can buy food. I bought bread for my father and for myself. At Mtubatuba I caught the bus and once more got two tickets for the last part of the journey home. There were people in the bus who recognized me, but when they saw the *mpafa* branch, they did not speak because they knew that I had a relative with me."

Magqubu paused, looked at me, and asked if he should make the fire for tea again. He understood my fear and was mildly teasing me. I fell for his trick.

"Ca – no. Please finish the story," I said, convinced that we would be walking to Mhlopeni in the dark.

"I took the *mpafa* branch," Magqubu said, lifting his hand and standing on tiptoe. "I pushed it into the eaves of my father's hut, which was made with the same *umuNga* [*Acacia karoo*] poles we had brought from Ongeni when the government removed us in 1945. They said that when the *nagana* was over we would go back, but it was not allowed."

Magqubu was to return to this tragedy in his life throughout our long association. He never forgot the people who had moved him and his family from the ancestral lands they had occupied for generations. Telling the *mpafa* story brought the memories back because all the spirits from the graves around the abandoned huts had to be fetched with *mpafa* branches and taken to the new settlement on the hill overlooking the Macibini pans. Magqubu was silent for a short while, and I could guess that he was thinking of his youth in the Ongeni hills. I remembered those hills well from my first stint at Mfolozi and even earlier, on a misty day in 1953 when Hendrik van Schoor and I caught a local Hlabisa man poaching. It was a place of great beauty and serenity, different from the dry heat of the land between the White and the Black Mfolozi rivers. Mist covered the hills in summer, and the common reedbuck whistled shrilly from themeda and hyparrhenia grasslands. I had seen enough of that country to be gripped by its spirit. I appreciated Magqubu's feelings and understood his constant reference to that land on which he once had lived. It was part of his soul.

"My father, yes my father, he beat me when I was a grown man with two wives. When I put some of the *mpafa* branch in the eaves, I remembered everything about him, and I said, 'Father you are now home with us and we want you to keep the peace in this *muzi* of the Ntombelas.' This is how I brought my father's spirit back from Thekweni. I then slaughtered a beast and everyone in the *muzi* feasted that evening, the men together, then the women, then the children."

Magqubu had finished the story of fetching his father's spirit with the *mpafa* branch, but there was more to come.

The afternoon shadows were lengthening as we sat overlooking the second pool in the Mpafa River. One of the pythons had poked its head out from a cleft in the rocks, then quickly withdrawn when it saw us. The birds were still active in the schotia tree. A scarlet-throated sunbird, the red vivid against the black feathers on its tiny body, fluttered next to a red schotia flower, the two reds together for a brief instant. The air was still and I could hear the beating of its tiny wings. Blue waxbills, mousebirds, and finches drank from a puddle of water downstream, and the white-browed scrub robin sang from a euclea bush. Baboons barked from the cliffs on the southern side of the Mantiana hills. Magqubu told me that the hills were named from the little grass birds (cisticola) that rose as you walked through the grass and gave their *ti, ti, ti yana* calls. Deep kloofs ran up the sides of the hills, and when we walked past in the early morning we had disturbed a small herd of buffalo that hid there and I heard a soft bellow. Magqubu had cocked his head, listened, then said it was a buffalo cow calling its calf. The animals were beginning to recover from the continuous slaughter during the tsetse-fly campaigns.

Magqubu had spent his life living and working in the game reserves of Zululand, particularly in Mfolozi. I looked at him now – sitting upright, his back against a branch on this beautiful May afternoon. I was struck by his high cheekbones and wondered if this was not the clue to his genius for wild-land understanding. Somewhere in his ancestry there was Bushman blood. It could have accounted for so much of Magqubu's character, his extraordinarily long-distance eyesight, his knowledge of plants and trees, and his sheer physical endurance and sense of humour.

The little people had certainly inhabited this land. They were here with the Nguni people, Magqubu's great-ancestors. Trading and intercultural exchanges took place. The Bushmen taught their black neighbours about the plants and the trees, their medicinal values and the poisons that were used to prepare their little arrows. Magqubu had on the walk to the second Mpafa pool that morning shown me a plant that he said would kill a person within minutes if mixed with food. The light-yellow-skinned Bushman girls no doubt attracted the strong Nguni men and would have been brought into the *imizi* as concubines. Magqubu, I was sure, had a Bushman ancestor.

Little now remained of the Bushman occupation of this landscape. There was a painting of an eland in an overhang on Nqabaneni hill, more paintings on a rock face in the Hluhluwe game reserve, and another in the Ciyana hills, but everywhere we walked there were stone artefacts, axes, digging tools, and stones for scraping skins. Their spirits were here, too, tangibly present.

Magqubu tapped his knee with the *mpafa* twig, a clear sign that he wanted to continue the story of this important tree. He completed the story of the human association by telling me that if a person died in the *muzi*, he or she would be buried nearby, and those who carried out the burial would take herbs and be cleansed. In the morning the family who carried the dead body would go out, chop a branch from an *mpafa* tree, and bring it back to the *muzi*. They would spit on the branch and speak aloud to the cattle, sheep, and goats, telling them that there had been a death in the *muzi*. The branch was chopped into two pieces and one was thrown into the cattle enclosure and the other into the goat pen.

At the time of the big battles at Isandlwana, Kambula, and Inyezane in the

Anglo-Zulu War of 1879, the bodies of many men lay on the veld and were eaten by the animals and the vultures. Magqubu hopped with his arms outstretched like a vulture, making its cackling guttural sounds. He circled, stopped, then pecked like these gaunt birds.

"The bones were mixed together," he said. "No one knew which body they came from. The relatives of the men who died walked from their homes carrying a piece of the tree, and when they came to the battlefield they held up the *mpafa* and called out the name of their father, brother, son, uncle, cousin, or the man from their area, and they would say, 'We have come to fetch you, to take you home to your *muzi* on the hills of Hlabisa, or Hluhluwe, Nongoma, Mahlabatini, Lebombo.' The people would then turn and walk back, and all the time speak to the spirit in the *mpafa*. When they drank at the streams or ate at homes on the way, they would do so twice, as I did for my father. At home the *mpafa* twig would be put into the eaves of the huts, a beast killed, and the dead person would then join all the other *amadhlozi* in the *muzi*."

Magqubu's description was so vivid that I visualized the long line of relatives, singing and chanting, carrying the *mpafa* as they made their way along the footpaths to the battlefields where the warriors had fallen.

Magqubu said, "You must know that this is not only a tree of the people but of animals too. The branches carry the spirits of people, but all the wild animals, and cattle and goats too, eat from this tree. It is food for the spirit and the body. You must *hlonipa* the *mpafa*."

The monotonous call of the red-fronted tinker barbet began from the depths of the green leaves and scarlet flowers of the schotia tree. *Tink, tink, tink*, going on and on. In October when the heat is almost unbearable, the repetitive *tinking* sounds are enough to drive one mad. In Zimbabwe, where I once lived, the persistent brain-numbing song is said to drive people to suicide. On this balmy May afternoon its song mingled with that of the other birds, but I was aware of its constant higher pitch.

Magqubu stood up and sang, softly at first, then louder. He began dancing, and from the rhythm I knew it was a dance about the tinker barbet. His sense of timing was perfect, and while he sang, the tinker barbet's call seemed to get louder, drowning out the other birds. Magqubu stamped his feet in time to the bird's *tink, tink, tink*, and he sang, "My hammer, my hammer, my hammer is too heavy."

His feet thudded against the hard ground and his voice rose and fell in time with the bird's call. Here was a dance in honour of the little bird, elevating it and preventing its nerve-racking quality. Magqubu's song repeated, "My hammer, my hammer, my hammer is too heavy," his feet thumping and shaking the earth; the combination of the bird's call and Magqubu singing rose above the other sounds and echoed upstream into the surrounding bush. Man, bird, and land were at one. Magqubu ignored me and concentrated on entering into the spirit of the birdsong. I found myself hypnotized by his movements, the repetitive *tinking*, the words, the warmth of the afternoon sun, and the smell of the bush. It wafted over the stream bed, the lingering scent from the ashes of the fire, mixed with dry white rhino dung, crushed leaves, mud, water, rocks, and the tang of my own sweat and Magqubu's sweat on our khaki shirts.

I was aware, too, of the dust in the air and traces of scent from animals that had been drinking at the pool before we arrived. I could not, as Magqubu could, distinguish between the different animal scents except those of white rhino and buffalo and the sweetish smell of wildebeest. These animals were now pouring into the corridor of land between Mfolozi and Hluhluwe game reserves because Hluhluwe had been saved from the *nagana* slaughter campaign. We had begun hunting them for rations in the headwaters of the Nyalazi River, and I had learned to identify their smells. There were other animal scents I knew, like the pungent odour of the leopard when it had been lying up in the reeds or under a fallen sycamore fig tree, but my knowledge was limited compared to Magqubu's, who, as we moved through the bush, could name the individual species that had walked past. On the morning's walk he had stopped in a patch of dense bush, held up his hand, and sniffed the air.

"Kudu," he pronounced.

"How do you know?" I whispered.

"I know its scent," he said quietly.

He had hardly spoken when there was a deep, gruff bark ahead of us and the sound of a big animal taking off. Magqubu took me forward, studying the earth until he found the clear and unmistakable imprint of a large kudu.

In my semi-hypnotic state I counted the *tinkings* of the barbet, which had now reached eighty, then the bird stopped. Magqubu sang for a minute or more, caught up in his song, then he hesitated and shouted out the Zulu name of the bird.

He was quiet for a moment, and I saw him glance into the sky. I knew he was checking the time in much the same way that we would look at a watch, but time for him meant how many daylight hours were left to do whatever he wished. He sat down on a rock in the waning rays of the sun, picked up something from the ground, and turned it round in his fingers. As all good storytellers know, this is a way to excite curiosity and capture attention. With Magqubu this came naturally. His extraverted personality compelled you to watch him no matter what he was doing. I looked at the object he had picked up.

"This," he said, "comes from the *mpafa*. It is its fruit. Everything eats it, even *msimba* [wild cat]. No animal or bird passes this tree."

My mind had drifted but I was brought back to the present when Magqubu said emphatically, "All animals eat the berries of the *mpafa*. White rhino, black rhino, genet cat, aardwolf, guinea fowl, francolin, doves, zebra, wildebeest, impala, nyala, kudu, grey duiker, bushbuck, steenbok, wild pig, nsamango monkey, but it is not only the berry that is eaten.

"Woza, look here," Magqubu said, beckoning me to an *mpafa* tree. He described how small antelope like the grey duiker and the steenbok eat the leaves on the lower branches. Slightly higher, the impala ate the leaves; nyala antelope browsed at the next level, but like the impala they too fed on the tender branch shoots. Next came the kudu. Magqubu put his hands up behind his head to show how the great kudu bull with its lyre-shaped horns came slowly to the tree, nibbled on leaves, and when the branch was bare put its head into the tree, twisted its huge neck, and broke the higher branches. Some fell to the eating height of the small grey duiker and the steenbok. He brushed dry grass aside, examined the earth, and pointed to the faint V imprint of a duiker's hoof.

"The kudu works here for the other animals, the duiker and the steenbok. But the warthog and the *ngulube* [wild pig], they cannot reach up high, so they feed on the fallen leaves."

He pointed to a big branch which the kudu had broken and which now lay stripped bare on the ground.

"The eland, it eats the branches and the leaves and again some fall onto the earth to help the other animals," he said. "Right at the top of the tree the giraffe eats the leaves, branches, and the thorns."

He made a sweeping movement with his head, opening his mouth and showing how the giraffe with its long neck could reach any part of the tree, slide its big lips or curl its tongue, and strip leaves, thorns, and the softer parts of the branch. "*Indulamithi*," Magqubu said. This is the Zulu word for the giraffe, "he who is taller than the trees."

Magqubu stalked forward, holding his torso upright, one hand behind his back brushing away flies like a tail, and he cantered a few yards, a perfect example of the horselike motion of this wonderful, strange beast of nature. The Voortrekkers called the giraffe a *kameelperd* (camel horse). They relied upon the Bible as their guide to all things, and this strange animal resembled the horse they knew and the camel in the Bible. Hunters would gallop up to it, being careful to avoid the long legs because one kick was death, then shoot the animal, and in most instances they took only the tail because it made an excellent fly switch. The rest was food for the jackal, the hyena, the vultures, and the maggots, leaving only the sun-dried skin on the veld.

In great detail he told a story that I later came to realize was the essence of ecology.

"This is food," he said, "for the monkeys and the baboons, but it is also seed. From this berry another *mpafa* tree can grow. The *iGwala-gwala* [purple-crested lourie, its onomatopoeic Zulu name arising from the sound it makes when it is disturbed and flies away], guinea fowl, *toppies*, orioles, all come to the *mpafa* – *mlandabantu* – the *mlahlankosi* tree, and they eat."

When mentioning each bird and animal he gave its call or showed its flight. With the baboons he made the movements of their climbing up the branches, grunting, barking, screaming at one another, the old dog baboon pinching the younger ones who tried to leap out of his way, the females in oestrus seductively sliding past the male. The defecating and urinating, the careful movements to reach the ripe brown berries at the end of a branch, ignoring the vicious hooked and straight thorns, and stuffing the fruit into the mouth and dropping some when the pouches were too full. The lifting of the eyebrows, the yells of aggression with teeth bared. And all the time Magqubu was saying what the baboons were talking about. His repertoire was phenomenal, even to the little squeaks of the babies riding on the mothers' backs or hanging under their stomachs. A movement, a gesture, and he had unmistakably captured the character of the animal.

Magqubu called me and led the way along a game path away from the water. He looked intently at the ground. "Nango!" (There), he said, and pointed at a partially digested *mpafa* berry that had rolled into a tiny crack on the path. "This is the seed of a new tree," he said, and repeated the long cycle of the defecating process of baboons and monkeys.

Farther up the path he pointed to a dry conical baboon turd, poked at it gently with a stick, and out of it came more *mpafa* berries, all ready to be washed into the cracks of the earth with the first rains. We followed the path until it disappeared into overhanging grass. He pushed the grass aside, got down on his hands and knees, and showed me the tiny shoot of an *mpafa* tree in the earth.

"It is not only the monkeys and the baboons that plant the *mpafa* trees," he said. "When they are eating the berries and drop some of them on the ground because they have been fighting, or are frightened, there are many other animals that will eat." He described the movements and sounds of warthog and bushbuck hearing the baboons and monkeys in the *mpafa* tree and knowing that berries would be falling. The warthogs grunt and make a clicking sound, and Magqubu acted out their quick movements, then their sudden stopping if there was anything suspicious, standing dead still and staring ahead. He was able to transform himself into any animal in an uninhibited, unselfconscious, and uncondescending way. He knew the animals since childhood and loved them as part of his world. He had hunted, legally and illegally, killed, and eaten the flesh with relish, cured the skins and dried the bones. The animals had their place and man had his, but they shared the world together; they were much more than *nyama* (meat), they were spirit too. The circle of life around the *mpafa* tree showed the interdependence of all living creatures, and he had observed and recorded every minute detail of this life. While I carried my notebook and pen, looking and writing down and in so doing detaching myself, he absorbed it all because this was his world and every living thing was a neighbor. During his amusing but extremely informative description of the behavior of the baboons in the *mpafa* tree, he related other little incidents, insights into the relationship he had with the baboons.

"They are our brothers," he laughed. "Look at their hands. They have fingers just like us. They eat like us and enjoy the fruits we do, the sycamore fig, they know the *nconco*, the sweet fruit. When the *umNcaka* [red ivory] berries are ripe they know and are watching. They try to get there first, and in the days when the kings and the *indunas* ruled this land, men were sent to guard the sweet berries until enough had been collected for royalty and headmen. Then other people were permitted to eat, but we always left some for the baboons. In times of great drought we all suffered because of the lack of water and food, and we would take *mbila* [maize] from our granaries, which as you know are under the ground in the cattle kraal."

"Yes, we took those mielies and spread them out on the ground beyond the fields so that our brothers could eat too. When there was lots of food and they wanted to steal our mielies or *mabela* [sorghum] from the lands, we chased them away. But in the droughts it was different, we gave them food. They can talk too, just like you and me." He saw the surprise on my face and laughed.

"We hear them talking, and listen, but they don't talk when white people are near," he said with mock seriousness.

"Why?" I asked expectantly.

"Because they would be caught, made to work, and have to pay poll tax," and he giggled.

In the long years that lay ahead working on the capture and translocation of the white and the black rhino, patrolling Mfolozi game reserve, and fighting poachers, or during the fires that swept in during the hot dry season, on the wilderness trails we initiated and led for the Natal Parks Board, and during fourteen years of working at the Wilderness Leadership School, Magqubu was to tell and retell the story of the *mpafa* tree. It was never boring. There was always something new, a different slant or elaboration. The *mpafa* tree was the symbol that held the world of human, animal, bird, insect, and the red earth of Africa together in a symbiotically physical and spiritual relationship.

I am sure that Magqubu told or tried to tell other people for whom he worked in the reserves the *mpafa* story, but I suspect their response was either scientific curiosity or a passing interest. Magqubu saw something in me that responded at another level to this incredible story, which could be summed up in one Zulu word: *hlonipa*. My initial response to the story was to become caught up in Magqubu's tremendous enthusiasm. He put everything of his own character into the story, acting it all out and enjoying his own show, yet no matter what he said or did there was never a loss of dignity, even in his eighty-ninth year, when his features had softened and he was much more relaxed. He was able to let go more, but he still retained his dignity in every situation.

In the month of April, when the leaves of the *mpafa* first turn yellow, the tree stands out in the green, grey, and brown landscape like the colourful standard of an army in the Middle Ages. I could never look upon the landscape and the yellowing trees without thinking of Magqubu and his stories of the abundance of life that surrounds it.

7

Shadows of the Afternoon

It was late in the day by the time Magqubu had finished the story of the *mpafa* tree. He shouldered his old army haversack, called out "Asihambe" (Let us go), and we climbed out of the depression of the Mpafa stream and followed the bank until we reached a well-worn rhino path heading in a southwesterly direction. Magqubu walked ahead, moving at a fast pace, his short squat body powered by his extraordinarily strong legs. Unlike many Zulus, his calf muscles did not have much definition, but his thighs had the traditional shape of Zulu royalty. Had he wanted to he could have outdistanced me easily, but he listened to my breathing and stayed three to five paces ahead.

The path followed the contour through euclea scrub, dipping in old dongas and heading now toward the White Mfolozi River. We crested a rise, and I could see Nqolothi hill and the long afternoon shadows creeping down its slopes. I did not have to concentrate on any dangers with Magqubu ahead of me, neither now nor in the thousands of other kilometres I was to walk behind him. There were many administrative concerns, personality conflicts, and other worries on my mind. I was sorting through them as we walked, but gradually and almost imperceptibly the atmosphere of the land enveloped me.

It was a landscape that had been occupied by humans for hundreds of thousands of years: early hominids, Bushmen, and Nguni clans. Men had fought here with great savagery against one another. Dingiswayo, the Mtetwa king, was killed by the Ndwandwe people, and Shaka, the founder of the Zulu nation, had in turn chased the Ndwandwe people out and fought their chief, Zwide. I was partially aware of some of this history because in 1955 I had seen the broken maize-grinding stones littering the Mfulumkulu plain. The guards had told me it was Shaka and his warriors who were responsible, thus making sure the Ndwandwe would not return. The land had a mood that in this fading May afternoon transported me into a realm of the mind and body much deeper than I had ever experienced. The chanting goshawk called from a dense patch of bush, trumpeter horn-

bills flapped overhead with their characteristic one-two-three flight. A bush-buck barked in the distance, and a grey duiker bounded across in front of us, diving and weaving through the bush. Words could not describe the poetry of this ancient land. What I was connected to was the spirit of place, all life past and present intermingling at different levels and forming an intangible bond with the hard earth beneath my feet.

For a distance I floated rather than walked, then there would be a break in the terrain, or the sharp shriek of a monkey that had spotted us. This brought me back from my mind wanderings to the beaten rhino path and Magqubu walking at his steady pace. I became conscious of my body, the branches of trees touching me, sweat trickling down my forehead and dripping over my eyes or running down between my shoulder blades. I could feel the firmness of the compacted rhino-trodden earth through my vel-skoene. My socks rubbed against my heels and the burning start of a blister jabbed at me. Magqubu's head bobbed up and down above the top of his haversack and I could hear his breathing, regular and without strain.

Then everything seemed to fade away, and it was only my mind moving high and above the path. For an indeterminate length of time I was like a bateleur eagle soaring above and gliding with wings hardly moving. I did not fight anything in myself, but I drifted into different states of mind, then into my body. It was a form of self-hypnosis in which one part of my mind was absolutely still, and part of the landscape unmoving and unchanged. The other part was very much aware, my senses so sharply acute that eyes, nose, and ears missed nothing: a blue waxbill feather being pulled by tiny black ants across the path; dry, caked mud clinging to a tree where a rhino had rubbed off the mud from a wallow; a dead tick caught in the mud, the outer shell glinting in sunlight for a split second before my eye passed, focusing in short flashes on other things. A boulder dark at the base and white on the edge where warthogs and wild pigs had rubbed. A depression in the churned earth where they had braced themselves.

The sun dipped behind Nqolothi hill, and we walked in the shadows. I heard the sharp-pitched whistle of the mountain reedbuck that lived on the flat tops of Nqolothi, their calls noticeably shriller than the common reedbuck. We reached the thick Ndlovusiyashikana bush at the base of Nqolothi hill.

Magqubu's pace slowed and his body movements changed. He exuded an air of caution. Every metre we walked deeper into the gloom of the bush heightened his awareness of possible danger. There were big pans here, some still holding a little water where trees had protected them from the sun. Others were dark mud, the consistency of thick porridge, and rhino and warthog had been wallowing. There were signs of them everywhere – dung, dropped mud, tracks, and scraping marks against trees. I was now no longer floating. My senses had become aware of Magqubu's vigilance expressed through his body actions. We were slowly enveloped by the bush and had to bend low to pass under overhanging thorn branches. The nocturnal rhythm was beginning, with white-browed scrub robins singing and *toppies* calling in concert as they do when they see a snake. It was a persistent kind of chatter but without the urgency of a warning. The guttural cries of crested francolin in front and behind startled some *hadeda ibises*, who flapped and screamed out their piercing calls. This warned rhino ahead of us, and they snorted loudly. Magqubu stopped, cocked his head slightly, and listened. The rhino snorted again and Magqubu relaxed, turned, smiled, and said, "Mkombe" (white rhino).

He had hardly spoken when there was a deep bellow followed by a growling sound like the beginning of a lion's roar. Then the bush erupted and the din was frightening. The sound of breaking branches and loud scrapings as rhino rubbed against one another penetrated the still evening. The enclosed surroundings accentuated the noise, and I could feel my heart thumping against my chest. The ancient human response of flight-or-fight and the surge of adrenalin to assist either course flashed into my mind.

I watched Magqubu. He stood facing the sound, his head moving slightly, following the movement of the animals. He held up his hand, showing five fingers. How did he know there were five rhino when we could not see through the bush? Again it was an intuitive knowledge and the combination of all his senses. There was a sharp cry, like a cat mewing. Magqubu bent down, peering through the bush, then he indicated with his hand that the noise came from a calf. He held his hand up again, showing four fingers and the fifth bent over: four adults and one calf.

He jerked his head and we walked quietly away, taking another rhino path that led to the southern slopes of Nqolothi hill. We skirted round a big pan where there were many signs of rhino. Magqubu sniffed the air. I did the same and could smell rhino. I said, "Mkombe." He smiled and pointed to a path, then showed me five sets of tracks, one of which was of a calf. He patiently drew out each track, showing me the differences, but they were so slight that by the time he moved from one to the other I had forgotten the previous one.

We were now totally in shadow, and I knew it would be dark within an hour. I whispered that we should move, but I needed to know how he could identify the exact number of five rhino that we had heard. I asked him quietly, and he said he knew by the sound. He moved his body around, making the rasping noise of rhino rubbing against rhino, then against trees, and the calf's catlike sound and the suckling noise as it drank from its mother. My hearing is acute and has always been my most important sense, but this was phenomenal audible observation. He was able to differentiate between the tones, his mind taking in and eliminating unnecessary information and coming up with answers upon which our lives could have depended. I do not see colour until the word is mentioned or I consciously think about it. It is like saying to myself, Look at the landscape, what colours do you see? Then they start to materialize. Sometimes they are so vivid that they force their way into my consciousness. It was only after I had stopped smoking that my sense of smell improved to allow me to be aware of subtle differences in scent. I had to concentrate, whereas Magqubu took everything in, filtering out what was not important, but retaining it for further identification if needed. I can never recall a moment when he was not focused on his immediate surroundings.

The light in the sky was changing when we began the steep climb up Nqolothi hill. I was sweating and breathing heavily when we reached halfway. I called for a rest. Magqubu laughed and stopped. "Sinda" (heavy), he said. It was a polite way of acknowledging my fatigue.

I turned and looked east while he pointed with bent forefinger and named the individual hills and the ranges lit up by the fading rays of the afternoon sun. A long line of dark-green sycamore fig trees marked the course of the White Mfolozi River. Patches of damp sand glinted where warthog and wild pig had been digging for water near the reeds. The cliffs of Nqabaneni glowed a soft orange, and the themeda grass stretching from the Mantiana hills to Little Mpila and the Greater Mpila was a numinous red, emphasizing the origin of its Afrikaans and English names: *rooigras* and red oats grass.

He pointed out other hills – Siyembeni, the junction of the Black and the White Mfolozi rivers and the scene of one of the greatest hunts in the history of the Zulu people. Shaka Zulu had a line of pits dug between the two rivers, then the game was chased into them by warriors. The carnage must have been immense because every local Zulu knew the story. Magqubu began to sing softly as he pointed at the junction. He sang the praise names of Shaka Zulu, how he had taken refuge with King Dingiswayo of the Mtetwa people, fought Zwide, and been a friend to the whites who had landed in ships at Port Natal. It was a spontaneous association with people and the land, a praise to Shaka's amalgamation of the Nguni clans. For Magqubu, Shaka's spirit was still here, moving across the brooding landscape.

Magqubu began to chant and dance. I stopped him and said we should move on because it would be dark by the time we got to the top of Nqolothi hill. For Magqubu this was an order that he obeyed without question, but I was to learn over many years that he would return to the story. It was a mark of respect for whomever he was praising and a subtle reminder to me that the *amadhlozi* were not to be treated lightly. It was a power Magqubu had, but at that time I had no inkling of it. I was still caught up with the arrogance of a white time-scale and lack of sensitivity for any other culture when it impinged on what I was doing or wanted to do.

We climbed up the last slope of Nqolothi, reached the tabletop, and heard the mountain reedbuck whistle all around us. "Nxwala," Magqubu said, giving them their Zulu name. We looked back east again and I asked Magqubu the name of one hill that was now prominently etched against the eastern skyline. "Dengezeni," he said, and began again to explain the origin of the name, how Shaka led the Mtetwa warriors against the Ndwandwe people. Shaka's men smashed all the clay pots and the grinding stones along the ridge of hills. Shaka ordered them to leave nothing alive.

I urged Magqubu on down the western slope of Nqolothi toward the caves below Mhlopeni hills where we were going to spend the night. I did not know that before the year was out I would have an experience at Dengezeni that would smash through my own container of arrogant superiority. If the psyche can be likened to a clay container, a vessel of beliefs, customs, and attitudes, part of mine was going to be broken and recast.

It was dark when we followed the steep path down to where the Mhlologazane (A Place of Little Suspicion) stream enters the White Mfolozi River, but the hills in the west were now lit up. Magqubu wanted to tell me the origin of their names, but I impatiently urged him on. I was tired and very thirsty and hungry. I suspect that Magqubu may have chuckled inwardly at the sharpness of my tone, but he showed no sign. He did stop and say that in the thickening scrub at the foot of the hill lived one of the few black rhino in Mfolozi at that time. As always he was right, and he had the last word, too.

We skirted the bush and walked over the flat rocks to the cave. I dropped my haversack and sat down, leaning wearily against rocks in the cave, still warm from the afternoon sun. Magqubu did not rest. He at once began gathering driftwood that still littered the banks from the big flood of 1957. He found a suitable cleft in the rocks, took a handful of dry reeds, and when the fire caught he blew and added small sticks. The flames blazed, their reflections dancing on the walls of the cave. A hyena whooped across the river from the direction of the Madhlozi camp and Magqubu pronounced, "Mpisi," as though I had never heard one before. For him it was an acknowledgment of the present moment. I stretched out, enjoying the variety of scents of the woodsmoke, the reeds burning, acacia, and a hardwood I guessed to be a combretum. I called out and asked Magqubu, "Umuthi muni?" "UmBondwe," he replied as he went off into the night to find another log. *UmBondwe* is the combretum hardwood, and the coals stay hot for a long time.

Honour demanded that I do something. Magqubu was fifty-eight, I was thirty-one. I was already calling him "the old man." I got up grunting, and I heard him ask, "Uyapi?" (Where are you going?)

"To get water," I said.

He disagreed and said he would do it as soon as he had enough heavy wood for the night, telling me I should rest because it had been a long day on my knee having to climb Nqolothi, which was named for its steepness.

"You have to bend over as you walk up," said Magqubu.

I ignored his concern and made my way over the rocks to the river and scooped the billycan full. By the time I got back, Magqubu had gathered more logs and cut suitable sticks to hang the billy on. He was indefatigable.

The main chores over before preparing food, he now went a few yards into the darkness, and I could hear him praying. His Shembe religion had a powerful grip on him, and he embraced it with obvious joy. It was no hardship to pray after a long walk. When he returned I asked what he had prayed about and he said he had thanked God for bringing us safely through the day. It made me ponder my own religious state. I certainly believed in a god, some superior spirit. Whenever I had trouble I was quick to ask the help of God, yet I could not call myself a Christian. It was a long time since I had even been in a church to worship. The last time was when I attended the wedding of my friend Jim Feely, when he married Molly Kennedy in the little village of Kwambonambi in 1956. I sang the hymns and went through the ritual, but it did not move me. A change would be a long time in coming.

Magqubu filled his small three-legged pot with water. It was the one he told me he had bought for five shillings in 1925. He hung it next to my billy, and it shone in the firelight. He took a cloth bag from his haversack, waited until his pot boiled, then poured in mealie meal. He explained that it was meal that gave the Zulu people their strength, but he criticized the white man for refining it. This meal came from his own granary. It had been ground by his chief wife, Tabete. She visited Magqubu at his hut, which was separate from the game-guard barracks. She was the only person he would allow to cook for him. In his years of working for the early game conservators of Zululand – Vaughan Kirby, Roden Symons, and Captain H.B. Potter – as well as officials of the veterinary department in the *nagana* campaigns – R.H.T.P. Harris, Willie Foster, and Dr. Kluge – Magqubu had made many enemies. He was ruthless in enforcing discipline. Whatever law the white man laid down in the running of the game reserves, Magqubu made sure it was carried out. Labourers laid snares near their camps when they were working in the field. Game guards stole an extra round of ammunition so that they too could poach a buck when no one was around. Magqubu had informers. He would quietly investigate and catch the offenders, who would never forgive him, nor would their relatives. The easiest way to kill him would be to slip poison into his food. It was a traditional Zulu way, and impossible to detect.

One of the worst times for Magqubu was in the 1940s, during the last big *nagana* campaign. All animals within the Mfolozi game reserve, and the surrounding buffer zones, except the white rhino, were killed. Hluhluwe game reserve under Captain H.B. Potter's leadership was spared. The veterinary department insisted that with rare exceptions the meat was not to be taken. Magqubu suffered badly in the enforcement of this instruction. Meat was prized food, and to see it left for the vultures, jackals, and hyenas caused resentment. The wholesale slaughter also went against the Zulu way of living with the animals. Hunting and killing took place, but not on this scale. The senselessness of it affected Magqubu psychically in much the same way the North American Indians were affected by the extermination of the plains bison. When I said to Magqubu that Shaka's great hunt was a massacre, he replied that it was for food and sport with Shaka personally taking part in the hunt. "Nyama," he said firmly.

I told him that early explorers had written about the elephant hunts conducted by Shaka, Dingane, and Mpande, how the kings had sat on top of Nqolothi and directed the hunts.

"Yes," Magqubu said. "It was for the ivory the *abelungu* [white people] wanted. The elephant were not killed for nothing."

I knew he was implying that we had killed for no proper reason. He was right, and the proof lay all around us. In early Nguni times there was game everywhere in what is now KwaZulu-Natal. The white man initiated the slaughter of animals and the transformation of the landscape. Now all that remained were the pocket handkerchief-sized witness areas we call game and nature reserves. We should be deeply ashamed.

Some of the statements of early hunters like Baldwin, Dunn, Drummond, and Cornwallis Harris leave no doubt in one's mind that the killing of game was to satisfy the blood lust that lurks in the hearts of men. The *nagana* campaigns in later and supposedly enlightened years were no different. The purposeless killing of wild animals, birds, and wild people, to say nothing of ourselves in pointless wars, needs much more investigation by the depth psychologists. Yet, paradoxically, the modern hunter has contributed more to wildlife conservation than have many of the people who criticize hunting.

While we were eating his *sqamba* (hard maize-meal porridge) and drinking coffee, Magqubu began to tell me how he had been saved by the Zulu prophet Shembe, but I refused to listen. It did not stop him talking, but I persistently interrupted him, asking him about the old beliefs and the old times. Many years were to pass before I was to listen with rapt attention to his remarkable story of an internal journey of great psychic and religious importance.

After we had eaten, he carefully washed his little pot, tying the leftover *sqamba* in a piece of white maize sack. He never wasted food and was extremely careful of his diet. No butter or fat.

I lay on the hard rock, my head on my haversack and my body covered with an old Second World War military overcoat. It would be a long time before we had the luxury of sleeping bags. Magqubu sat near the fire, singing a hymn quietly to himself. It was a beautiful night, and from the overhang I could see the clear sky with the blaze of southern constellations. The Mtunzini hills were outlined against the last light. Hyena called from the direction of Madhlozi camp, and I heard the faint drumming from the people who were invading the western buffer zone near the Hlungwana River. There was trouble coming, and the next few years of my life were to be spent fighting to get some of the buffer zones incorporated into Mfolozi game reserve.

We were also there to chart a trail for the people we intended bringing on foot next year. I knew that if we could make individuals as passionate about this remnant of wild land as we were, there was a chance of saving it for posterity. Having the concept of a wilderness area accepted had been a bitter administrative struggle.

"Nango ikanka" (There, the jackals), Magqubu shouted. Their cries were ringing out from the bush-cleared zone. They disturbed crowned plovers, who flew up near us. The sound took my thoughts to my youth in the Transvaal, when I remembered hearing them for the first time on a moonlit night in an open field near our home in Lyndhurst. The Afrikaners called the plovers *kiewietjies*.

Magqubu was singing a hymn. He had a good voice and sang with the fervor of a deeply religious man. I thought again about my own religious beliefs. As a child my maternal grandmother had taken me to Sunday school at the local hall. A banner strung across the room read "God is Love." I did not know what it meant. I listened obediently to the Bible stories but was not touched or moved. My grandmother had strong religious faith, and I recall looking at her in amazement when she went through the Christian rituals. They meant nothing to me. It was something that you just did. Lying in the cave on this lovely African night in a land inhabited by wild animals with their own mysterious rhythms made me feel part of the universe. I could identify with the sounds of the night, the scents and the atmosphere. There was a tone and a rhythm that was beating in time with my soul. Some part of me had always been here, and everything that was happening around me evoked this sense of connectedness. There was a peace here, not in the general sense of the word, but in an alive way. One part of me remained quiet and calm while the other thrilled to all the wild sounds, each one arousing a different response. I wondered and worried if this made me an animist. Fear of Christian hell and damnation constantly lurked within me, threatening to erupt and put down anything opposed to it.

Walking through the Zululand landscape this day and hearing Magqubu talk about the life surrounding the *mpafa* tree, the audible contact with the rhino, feeling the spirits of the people – kings, indunas, warriors of Zulu and Nguni, and going further back to the Bushmen – this had gripped me. Here was a drumbeat of the earth that permeated my entire psychic being. This was for me a religious experience. What I took to be Christianity was imposed upon this, a growth that the ancient part of me rejected. It was a paradox I was incapable of properly understanding, but a healing through a dream would come twenty years later.

The work that I had been involved in over the past three years had been painful. I had come up against some extremely unpleasant people. In many ways it had been a shattering experience. Some of the worst aspects of human behaviour emerged when people went fishing, or when farmers' crops were threatened by wild animals.

The memory of some of the incidents made me sit up in anger, and I must have said something, because Magqubu rolled over and asked me what was wrong. There was no way of explaining my emotions and range of thoughts since we had eaten his *sqamba* around the fire. More than half a lifetime had passed. I tried to explain in my limited Zulu how important this particular patrol was for the future of the Mfolozi game reserve. I told him how next year we would be bringing people out here on foot, walking from the Mpila rest camp. He nodded as though this was to be expected. He had an ability to accept things, even though at the time they seemed outrageous.

Magqubu threw a handful of dry reeds onto the fire and it flared up, lighting his strong face and the holes in his ear lobes. He filled his three-legged pot with water from the billycan and put it on the fire. I passed him my tin of condensed milk and the packet of tea. He made the tea and sucked the hot liquid from an old enamel mug, and stared into the fire.

By the light of a torch I wrote up my journal. I had kept a journal since 1946. It was invaluable in capturing the moment, the nuances of conversations, descriptions of country, animals encountered, sounds and feelings. I also used it to vent my frustrations. In 1954, when I was alone in Ndumu game reserve, I kept a detailed daily diary and had continued with this when I was transferred to Mfolozi. When I read it later I was bitterly ashamed of my prejudices.

Strange how one written line of a time long ago could trigger off a whole host of detailed memories. Magqubu could talk nonstop, all of it fascinating information. I would have to keep halting him so I could take notes, but there were moments when the stories were so interesting and Magqubu was in full flood so that I got caught up in the story, became totally involved, and wrote nothing. My limited knowledge of Zulu made no difference. Magqubu would repeat and continue to repeat the same story, telling it from innumerable angles, like turning a diamond around in the light to make the colors flash and fade. His expressions and elaborate acting made certain the essential part of the story was not missed. In the future I was able to tape-record his stories and descriptions of earlier times. When I checked against diary notes it was incredible to see how, after twenty-five years, his memory was so clear.

I was keen to know more about the earlier conservators who had worked in the reserves. Magqubu had served them all, and in typical Zulu fashion had seen through the personas. I decided to wait until the following morning because I knew that once he got going there would be no sleep for me. I finished my tea, said "Lala kahle" (Sleep well), pulled my overcoat up, and with the night sounds echoing against the Mhlopeni cliffs I went to sleep.

8

Stories in Dance and Mime

I woke later to see Magqubu still sitting and looking into the fire. He heard me wake and asked if I had heard the rhinos fighting. I said no. He explained that two rhino bulls had been fighting in the direction of Madhlozi guard camp. A few minutes later I heard a scream and a roar that sounded like a lion. The noise started again: deep bellows, growls, and high-pitched screams.

"Listen," Magqubu said, cocking his head.

I heard the distinct clicking of horns, then dull thuds. Magqubu was on his feet, and in slow motion showed me how the rhino were fighting, first head to head, then horns locking, pushing and straining. He made all the sounds, down to the variable pitch in the roaring and screaming, followed by the bodies battering each other, acting out the battle of these two primordial giants. The sounds floated across the open veld, and Magqubu danced what they were doing, how they approached each other, lips curled, bodies straining. It was a strange scene in the firelight, Magqubu showing in dance how the animals were fighting. His body swayed like a marionette, but instead of strings it was the sounds of the animals in the night that made him move.

I was tired after the long day; added to this were the mental worries of the responsibility of taking over the game reserve, and with it the white rhino. Whether I liked it or not, fate had placed for a term the future of this gravely endangered ancient animal in my care. I knew from my previous time in the reserve that if we did not include sections of the adjoining buffer zones it would be practically impossible to administer the reserve and ensure the survival of these rare animals.

I thought about Magqubu while he danced the rhino fight and realized it was his religion, innate Zulu discipline, and natural cheerfulness that had enabled him to survive what must have been incredibly confusing years. Years of protecting the reserves and all the angst that went with combating black poachers, not only the physical dangers and surviving violent attacks, but the moral strength required to resist pressures from the relatives of the men who had been apprehended, then the confrontations with the white hunters, and latterly the *nagana* tsetse-fly campaigns. Earlier in the day at the *mpafa* tree he had alluded to the trials he had been through, but I was later to hear the details.

I fell asleep again after hearing a leopard coughing at the bend of the river. Magqubu answered it, and that was all I remembered until the early morning sun flashed into my eyes. I rolled over on the hard rock and saw Magqubu was up, had the fire going, and was cooking *puthu* (porridge) in his pot. The billycan was boiling.

The soft light spread over the bend in the White Mfolozi River, the sand shining in a golden glow that extended out into the bush-cleared zone. The tall themeda grass, dripping wet with dew, sparkled in the growing light. Bird calls rang from the grasslands and the acacia-clad Nqolothi hill. The morning African symphony had begun. Guinea fowl squeaked like rusty hinges, and crested francolin replied from the bush. Cisticola flitted in the grass, disturbing the dew-covered stalks, and larks and pipits sang as though taking their cue from each other. I sat listening, absorbed by the beauty of the birdsong and the light that grew stronger, now flooding the landscape. I turned and looked at the cave wall, where a mocking chat had landed on a small ledge. Its black, red, and white feathers blended with the shadows on the ledge, and only when it flapped its wings in quick succession did its form become visible. It whistled its own little song, then a *Cisticola erythrops* called from the nearby reeds, and instantaneously the chat imitated it.

I heard the snort of a rhino a moment before Magqubu said, in his matter-of-fact way, "Nango mkombe" (There is a rhino).

Coming over the ridge in front of us, a cow with two calves walked toward the river. Red-billed oxpeckers moved along the backs, around the ears, and under the bellies of the rhino, managing to keep their balance. They pecked quickly, stopped, and pecked again. One must have seen us, for there was a soft *churr*, *churr*, and the big cow in front hesitated for a moment until the birds churred again. She stopped and turned slowly, facing in all directions, and the calves came up to her, turned, and faced outward. They formed a star formation, a perfect defence posture. The oxpeckers took off, churring loudly, but returned when no danger threatened and began running up and down the rhinos' backs, feeding again. I watched them through my binoculars, fascinated at the interaction between the rhino and the birds. It was nature's example of the early warning system.

I was reminded of the time I was stationed at Ndumu and Lake St. Lucia game reserves. In the summer when the crocodiles laid their eggs on the sandy banks, the *dikkop* (stone curlews, *Burhinus vermiculatus*) laid theirs not far from the crocodile nests. If you walked too near, the *dikkops* would take off with their piping call, and the crocodiles rushed into the water. At Ndumu, Ken Tinley and I observed the little common sandpipers taking leeches off a crocodile's neck and the side of its mouth.

The rhino walked down the path through the themeda grass. Forktailed drongos had now appeared, and they fed off the dense mass of flies on the flanks of the rhino. The birds landed on the ground, taking off and swooping upward to catch a fly.

The rhino followed a deep rutted path to the river, pushing through reeds and disturbing *Cisticola erythrops*, the little brown birds that flew to the drooping tops of reeds and called. A greenshank flew downstream, its three-toned whistle echoing against the krantz, a lovely sound reminding me of boating on Lake St. Lucia in wooden clinker boats down the eastern shores on May mornings, and of the long canoe journey in 1956 with Ken Tinley down the Pongolo River from Otobotini to the Ndumu game reserve. We were at one with that river for many days, with birds, hippo, and crocodile creating a primordial setting. The greenshank was on the sandbanks, and its call was a continuous musical backdrop to our journey.

The rhino were drinking now. The calves jostled the mother and tentatively made their way into the water, breathing heavily, then taking long, satisfying draughts. I could clearly hear the appreciative smacking of their lips. The three animals drank long and deep, then stood with water dripping from their mouths, the sun reflecting on the droplets as they rolled off and fell into the river. Its thirst satisfied, the younger calf playfully butted its elder sister, who trotted a few steps, then whirled to face the baby. This disturbed the oxpeckers again, and they flew off, churring. The cow looked up anxiously for a moment, then dropped her head, and it drooped just above the level of the river. She stood there while the calves played and the drongos flew in quick bursts, catching the flies disturbed by all the movement.

Magqubu glanced up from stirring his little three-legged pot. When the porridge was well cooked he shook the wooden spoon vigorously, and some of the meal dropped on the ground. "That is for the *amadhlozi* of the Ntombelas and the Players," he said with a quiet laugh. Then he took a handful, squeezed it into a hard little ball, and ate it with relish. He knew how to cook it. I enjoyed eating it because its taste was different from refined porridge. A good plateful was very filling and could keep you going all day. The old Zulus had worked out a perfect diet for the climate.

While we drank tea, Magqubu spoke of Shaka and said how he had come hunting in this area. Magqubu's great-grandfather had been one of the senior men in Shaka's *impis*, and in the oral tradition he had passed on many stories to the young Magqubu when the family sat around the fire in the huts. If he was anywhere near as gripping a storyteller as Magqubu, those evenings must have been exciting. One could imagine the children in their traditional *beshus* watching every move and listening to the intonations of their *babamkulu* (grandfather).

"Shaka used to have men killed, any misdemeanor could be a sentence of death," Magqubu said. "Then the bodies would be laid out over there," and he pointed to the flat ground above the river. He imitated the specks of vultures appearing in the sky, circling and circling, coming lower and casting their shadows on the ground.

"The king's birds. When we eat, the birds must eat too. These were the words of Shaka," Magqubu said, in the voice of his grandfather.

The *hlonipa*, or alternative, name for the vulture is *moya*, from the sound of the wind whistling through the primaries as the great bird circles and comes swooping down to earth. Magqubu pursed his lips and made the vibrating sound of the vulture's wings. He stood up, and with his arms outstretched showed how the birds soared, then folded their wings back and came in to land. The sounds he made were perfect, and you needed little imagination to see the whole scene.

"Shaka loved the *amanqe* [vultures] and the *ingqungqulu* [bateleur]," Magqubu said. "When Shaka ate, the vultures must eat. That was Shaka's law."

It sounded terribly cruel and, in the eyes of modern people, inhuman, yet the discipline it instilled was absolute. Killing people publicly for breaking a Zulu law meant there were few transgressions. Magqubu explained that if a young girl became pregnant before marriage, her whole family and that of the boyfriend too would be taken to a deep pool at the nearest river. Heavy stones were tied around their necks, and they would be thrown into the pool. Witchcraft was punished by pushing a long, sharp pointed stake up the anus when the individual had been tied hand and foot. Magqubu acted out the whole procedure with a frightening description of the individual writhing and moaning on the ground, pleading between gasps of ghastly pain to be released. It is not surprising that as Shaka rose to power and formed his *impis*, making them discard the long-handled assegai for the *iqwa*, the short stabbing spear, the word Zulu struck terror into the hearts of other tribes.

"Shaka knew the white men were coming, and he made his warriors go into the sea and fight the waves. But when the white men did come he treated them well. He wanted their friendship. He gave them land at Thekwini and killed elephant for the ivory they wanted." Magqubu pointed to

Nqolothi hill. "That's where Shaka would sit while thousands of warriors rounded up the elephant and drove them like a herd of cattle below the mountain. Then other regiments would rush in among the elephants and hamstring the animals. Shaka himself would do that too."

Magqubu sang Shaka's praise names and followed with those of Henry Francis Fynn, one of the early white pioneers who won the confidence of Shaka.

"It was in the Ndlovusiyashikana, the thick bush we walked through yesterday before climbing Nqolothi hill, that's where the elephant were killed for their tusks. The name of the place is Where the Elephant Fight. It means fighting for a long time. Perhaps it was because of the hunting that the elephants milled around, fighting for a long time amongst themselves, not sure where to run. The elephants would be tired and go to the stream Indhlovukuma to drink, and then they would just stand to rest."

The sun grew hotter, and we went down to the river, stripped, and bathed. Mountain reedbuck saw us and whistled. Magqubu pointed them out on the lower slopes of Mhlopeni. We watched their rollicking rocking-horse run. Then he stared with the fixed penetrating look of a pointer dog that can see game birds hiding in the grass, out of sight to the normal human eye.

"Nango," he said, pointing in the Zulu fashion.

I searched the krantzes and could see nothing. I ran to my old army backpack and took out my binoculars and carefully looked where he was pointing. He laughed at my irritation. Then I saw it: a klipspringer standing on a jutting edge. Neither ear flicked. It stared at us, and no shouting or waving made it move, but I heard it give a suspicious sneeze-like snort. The camouflage was perfect. The animal was hidden by its dull grey colouring and a slight shadow over its hindquarters, all blending into the background colours of the rocks. Magqubu's eyesight had recognized the shape and instantly known it was a klipspringer. He never needed binoculars.

On one occasion during Hugh Dent's time, Magqubu was patrolling with other guards near Iqaqalempisi (Ridge of the Hyenas). They saw a line of poachers coming out of the game reserve, heading south. Magqubu studied them as they walked along the bank of the White Mfolozi, then they crossed the river in single file. Magqubu spoke to the other guards, describing exactly what firearms and animals the poachers were carrying. The guards, led by Magqubu, ran to head the poachers off and after a long chase caught two men. They were taken to the police station, and after questioning they gave the names of the other men.

When the court case took place, Magqubu in his evidence told the court what he had seen the poachers carrying. The magistrate interrupted and asked how far Magqubu had been from them. Magqubu described the distance, and the interpreter told the magistrate, "About a mile." The magistrate said it was impossible that a man could see such detail in that distance. The prosecutor suggested to the magistrate that they go outside and test Magqubu's vision. Needless to say, Magqubu quickly demonstrated the power of his eyesight and the poachers were convicted.

It was not only Magqubu's vision but his long experience in observing animals as well as killing them and seeing them killed. He knew which species they were from the way the animals were lying as they were carried. The firearms, too, he knew from the shape, whether they were .303 or .22 rifles, shotguns, or homemade weapons. Poachers bored a bigger hole in airguns and converted them to take a .22 cartridge. I witnessed Magqubu's visual powers time and again when we walked in the bush, but he had other senses which even he did not understand or could describe.

The klipspringer stood dead still, staring at us. A troop of baboons crossed the river, quickly passed through the deep places, then gambolled on the white sand. The old dog baboon sat on a big rock watching the troop and looking for danger. Youngsters chased one another, screaming and tumbling, then played king of the castle on a small mound. Magqubu followed their antics and told a story in a language that was a mixture of Zulu and baboon barking, youngsters crying and females shouting. He splashed around in the water, barking, laughing, and crying like young baboons. It was live theatre, a one-act play where Magqubu was taking all the parts and providing the sound effects. His voice rang out among the red krantzes and echoed downriver. The old dog baboon became agitated, making deep-throated warning barks and looking in our direction. I glanced up at the klipspringer. It stood immobile, but the shadows had changed and the sun was shining on it. A lovely little animal, poised to take off if danger threatened.

The baboon troop moved off. They were aware we were harmless. They slowly climbed the cliffs near the klipspringer, and as they drew closer I saw the klipspringer move, and in a flash it had bounded off on its high raised hooves, speeding along the krantz, running over the top, and disappearing.

"Bahambile" (It has gone), Magqubu said. "Hamba kahle, gqoqo" (Go well, klipspringer).

The baboons started performing again, and Magqubu took up the refrain. Shouting back at them, laughing and gesticulating, he continued his baboon-language story about what happened when they came to the sycamore fig trees near the big rivers. The old baboon complains that the

younger ones are stealing the *nconco* – the sweet fruit. The babies protest that it is not true. "It is the red fruit, the red fruit," says the dog baboon. "You are taking all the ripe figs," the old baboon barks, and Magqubu showed how it rushed along the branches to grab the youngsters, who manage for a moment to stay out of reach. "No, no, father, we are only taking the green figs," they chatter back, showing their fangs in fear. They know the terrible power of the hands and nails of the old baboon. But he reaches out, grabs one, and pinches it. The youngster yells out, "No, father, I'm innocent, please father." Other baboons join in the racket, pleading for the youngster to be released.

Magqubu's actions were so real that they captured the baboon behaviour to the last gesture. The baboons sitting on top of the krantz looked down on us, and I wondered what they thought as they watched us hominids in the river. Magqubu saw me looking, and he adopted the pose of the old baboon and translated a conversation that was taking place in the baboon group.

"Hey Joe, weh Joe, who's that down there? They are white and black. One is Madolo, that's his knee. You can see by the way he walks." Magqubu limped around, pointing at my leg. His action was so accurate I had to laugh. One of the baboons barked, and instantly Magqubu was into the story again. "Joe, Joe, are they coming here? Is there a gun? Who is the other? Oh, that's Ntombela. Ntombela, which Ntombela? There are many Ntombelas. Magqubu Ntombela. Qumbu Magqubu Ntombela. Oh, that one from Ongeni? Yes, from Ongeni. What are they doing down there? Catching fish. Fish? The Zulus don't eat fish. No, it's Madolo. He eats fish. Why is

Magqubu there? He leads Madolo. Magqubu who? Ntombela."

Magqubu jumped up and down and stalked through the water with the slow deliberate movements of the baboons. I looked up at the krantzes and the troop was leaving, almost as though they had had enough of the show. Magqubu shouted out, "Hambani kahle, bafowethu" (Go well, my brothers). One female with a youngster on her back turned for a moment, stared at us as though to say, "What on earth are you up to?", then she moved off, following the troop.

Magqubu, now serious, explained about the sycamore fig tree. He said the tree bears three different types of fruit in one season and that the trees can differ. Some of the fruit is infested with insects and even the baboons are reluctant to eat it.

"We call the tree *siza abantu* because in dry periods, when food is short, the women and children go to the river to collect the fruit," he said.

He described how the figs were laid out in the sun to dry, then crushed in the grinding stone and mixed with *amasi*, the sour milk that is part of the staple diet of the Zulu people. The figs gave it a slightly sweet taste. This mixture was added to the *puthu*. Spoons and ladles and bowls were fashioned from the soft wood, and the dry sticks were used to make a fire flare up. Broken bones were set in fig-tree splints.

Like the *mpafa* tree, the fig was heavily used by animals. On one of the first mornings at our new home on the southern slope of Mpila, I was sitting with Magqubu discussing staff matters when he pointed out animals down below on the White Mfolozi. I looked through my binoculars and saw monkeys and baboons moving from tree to tree. The branches were shaking violently as the simians jumped, fed on figs, then moved on. Down below, two bushbuck does and a magnificent ram walked slowly under the trees, followed by a troop of five nyala, the male black, yellow above the hooves, and all the females a soft fawn. They could have been a different species, they were so unlike the males. A short distance away warthog snuffled along, feeding on what the antelope had left. Later in the day I saw white rhino, a kudu bull with big horns, and two waterbuck feeding, a grey duiker following. Bees, wasps, butterflies, and other insects flitted in the trees and on rotting fruit that lay on the ground. Black-collared barbets, bulbuls, crowned hornbills, orioles, and other birds brought another great circle of life to these trees. There had been devastation in 1957, when a flood swept down in May and washed away many of the big groves. A worse flood was to follow in 1963 and the worst of all in 1984, when almost every tree was washed away from the banks.

Magqubu and I got out of the river, having lain in it for an hour, letting the soft dun-colored water flow over us. In all the years spent at Mfolozi the rivers were a godsend. It was possible to drink from both rivers up until the late 1960s, then contamination by human faeces upstream made it impossible, unless you drank it almost daily and became immune. Magqubu had a stomach like cast iron, and there was no water that he could not drink. I suspect that having to drink from the Nyalazi River, with its high saline content, near his home at Macibini had hardened his intestines. The Mfolozi rivers would taste like nectar in comparison.

We lay on the warm red rocks and soon we were dry. A *thekwane* (hamerkop) came flying downriver, and I saw Magqubu edge sideways. I asked what was wrong, and he said the *thekwane* could bring bad luck and even death if it flew over you. Being superstitious, I stood up ready to jump away from the bird's flight. The *thekwane* saw me, swerved in mid-air, and took off in another direction. Magqubu giggled and asked if I was afraid. "Yebo," I said emphatically. He seemed surprised, and I tried to tell him about walking under ladders.

At that moment a flock of crowned hornbills flew over, making their long, bleating, childlike cries and reminding me of when I had seen and heard them for the first time as a boy in Chase Valley outside Pietermaritzburg. My cousin and I were walking through an indigenous forest in the late afternoon when we heard the weird cries. We crept up and saw this incredible bird with a huge double beak. It hopped among the high branches feeding on ripening red berries. I saw the birds again in 1952 on the pioneering canoe expedition down the Mkomaas River. We camped in a gorge, and early the next morning there was a cacophony of sound. It was like a children's nursery gone mad. I grew to love the bird and was always fascinated by its movements.

Magqubu stood up and flapped his arms, giving the hornbill's cry, and he launched into a lengthy story describing how it flew with a flap, flap, flap motion, then shut its wings and glided, calling down the scale. He sang out the praise names.

"Weh umholwane [You, the trumpeter hornbill]. All other birds drink water, they've all got time to drink water; why don't you drink water? They've all got time to drink water; why don't you drink water? All you can do is fly straight in a beeline, *kwe, kwe, kwe.*" He called and flapped his arms in quick succession, then made the gliding motion.

"You go right over the water and over the mountains. While other birds are loafing, you are on your way. Where are you going? You are umkhonto [the spear]. Aha, there is the male. You are going to find a tree to make a nest."

Magqubu moved his head from side to side, like the trumpeter hornbill looking at a tree.

"Yes, this is a good one, the bird says," and Magqubu made the noise of it chipping away at rotting wood. "*Kok, kok, kok, kok*. Now your wife will come and she will go into the nest. You will go to the river to collect mud and you will cover the nest until only her beak can come out, so you can feed her grasshoppers until she has hatched her eggs. When the chickens hatch you will have to feed them, too. You will open the nest and all will come out together, but they will be weak and only able to hop a short distance. The fig tree, *siza abantu*, will help you. You will be able to hide the chicks until they are big enough to fly from one tree to another."

Magqubu sang out the natural history of the birds, using the alternative names, *jubakala* and *umkhonto*. He laughed and said that young Zulu men on their way to court the girls would be delighted if the trumpeter hornbill flew across in front of them along the path. This would be a good omen for the courting. The girls were going to say yes.

"It is the same with the *uchakide*. When they run across the path in front of you, you will be lucky in love."

Magqubu's knowledge of natural lore seemed limitless, and almost everything had its praise name. I made pages of notes in my field notebooks, but it was impossible to keep up with his stream of stories, praise names, observations, and subtle actions that revealed some hidden aspect of the landscape.

We walked back to the overhang, and Magqubu went to the fire, got on his knees, and within minutes had blown the embers into a flame, and he piled *umNqawe*, the *Acacia nilotica*, onto the fire. It caught quickly and burned with a bright red glow, with a good heat and a lovely scent. Magqubu took the billy to fetch more water, and on his way to the river he sang about the *umNqawe* and how the seed has a strong fresh smell and it shines when you rub it. He called out to the impala and said how much they loved this seed, the kudu, nyala, and the goats too. He made the contented munching sounds of an animal eating. I heard the chink of the billy and the gurgle as it filled in the river. Sound carried in this amphitheatre of krantz and river.

I lay back and mused how different and exciting and uplifting it was to have walked with Magqubu. He knew he was acting, but it was a teaching process, and he knew that I wanted to learn from him on a different level from the other white men he had worked with. I had felt the spiritual quality of the land and wanted to know more about it. My ecological scientific education was in progress, thanks to my friends Jim Feely, Roddy Ward, and Ken Tinley, but with Magqubu another form of education was evolving.

What made him tick? He was planted firmly in the world of the old Zulu order, which had its impetus from the fierce discipline imposed by Shaka. He had been brought up with respect for parents and his elders. Even as a man he had been given a beating by his father because the older man thought Magqubu was being too harsh with one of the grandchildren. Magqubu was able to accept life in the true philosophical sense. When I met him he had gone through the pain of losing children to enteritis, one wife to another illness, and relatives all around him. Death was ever present at his homestead. Drought wiped out his mielie and *mabela* and decimated his cattle, and preying hyena fed constantly on his small herd of goats. There had been times when they came right into the *muzi*, went straight for the goat pen and had to be fought off with knobkierie and assegai. Sometimes it was Tabete, his chief wife, and the children who had to fend off the hyena because Magqubu was away working in the game reserves. The grain pit in the middle of the cattle enclosure was the mainstay of the *muzi*, a tradition that was never broken because it meant life or death to the people. Many of his children had been a disappointment to him, but Ikonamangele had proved to be a faithful son, and we took him into the game-guard force.

I watched Magqubu attaching the billycan to the sticks above the fire and carefully placing the *umNqawe* log so it gave off maximum heat. No movement was wasted, and his body was as supple as that of a man in his twenties. His skin shone and his face was firm and strong. It was easy for me to fall into a hero-worshipping role, but I knew that although this was true to a degree, there were two aspects of the situation playing a part. One was the practical: following a man who knew and understood the bush better than anyone else I had ever worked with. The other was his openness and complete lack of fear in talking about his culture, and his real willingness to pass it on to me. We had already established a rapport at an unconscious level, and I knew that it was going to grow. There were practical considerations on his side. I had already improved his wages and had gone out of my way to help him and his family. He did not take this lightly, and what he was doing for me was an acknowledgement to the *amadhlozi* because he saw I wrote down the things that he said, a form of repayment, too. The interplay between us had many aspects, but above all it was practical on both sides.

The rest of the day we explored the Mhlologazana cliffs and looked out into the Biyela country to the south. Mountain reedbuck and klipspringers were common, and white rhino in herds of ten to fifteen grazed in the bush-cleared zone. Magqubu spoke of a pan north of the Madhlozi guard camp where the rhino wallowed at midday. I said I would like to watch them.

"It is too late now," he said. "We will sleep here, then walk there tomorrow, watch the rhino, then walk back to Mpila."

The noises of the night were rhino fighting and a passing hyena whose call echoed loudly against the red cave walls, flickering in the firelight. Drums thudded on the far side of Mtunzini hills, reminding me that people and homesteads were advancing on the game reserve.

I was awakened by the flutterings of the mocking chat, then its imitative calls. It was a bird I always associated with the western area of the reserve, because in 1955 my game ranger companions Jim Feely, Ken Tinley, and I used to overnight in a cave on the Hlungwana River. It had its resident mocking chat, which we greeted as an old friend. We called the place Mocking Chat Cave and used to leave messages for each other there in old soup packets.

Our patrols extended to Nkonjane (Swallow) hill. We had little in the way of possessions, and the pay was barely enough to feed and clothe us, but we were happy and fulfilled in the work. One particular memory remains of clear pools of water in the tributary Ngamazaneni that fed into the Hlungwana river. We camped near them and swam on the hot days, washing off the dust, ticks, and grass seed. The relief of clean water and the chance to swim always put new life into us. We frequently camped at the pools, laying out our greatcoats and using ex-army backpacks for pillows. Blankets would have been too heavy to carry. When we lay in our greatcoats, waiting for the sun to dry the dew and warm our stiff limbs, Ken and Jim competed with each other every time a bird called. It helped further the bird identifying I had learned from Ken at Ndumu in 1954, but I never reached their standard. The game guards had great enjoyment from the competitive spirit, and if they knew a bird they were quick to give its Zulu name, then laugh as we all laboriously wrote it down.

Magqubu had stirred the porridge, made the coffee, and packed his haversack. He was always precise and neat, never wasting anything. I ate my breakfast and drank the coffee laced with condensed milk and sugar. Magqubu busied himself checking that the fire was out, and he poured water on to make sure. The smell of damp wood rose from the ashes.

"Asihambe," Magqubu said, shouldering his pack and the rifle.

We walked, following the bush-cleared line. We saw white rhino everywhere. Being inoffensive animals, they immediately moved out of our way. We passed below Lubisana hill, named, according to Magqubu, because of the milk-coloured water that runs down a gully from the hill after rains. There were antbear holes that had evidence of hyena going in and out; and on the top of the hill a troop of baboons watched our progress. On our left looking west was the long line of Mtunzini (Shadows) hill, and farther north Sokwezela hill. Cisticola called from the grasslands.

Magqubu pointed out where the footpath of the Mandhlakazi people ran. It officially marked the old 1897 western boundary of the game reserve. Sibephu Mandhlakazi was one of the generals who distinguished himself in the Anglo-Zulu War of 1879. When the war was over he became embroiled with the royal Usutu faction. This internecine struggle was the direct result of Sir Garnet Wolseley's policy of splitting Zululand into thirteen different small kingdoms. Poor Sibephu was eventually defeated by a combined Boer and Usutu faction army at Tshaneni (Place of Stones) hill overlooking the Mkuzi River. Dinuzulu lost vast areas of Zululand to the Boers in payment for their help.

While we walked, Magqubu spoke about the aftermath of the Zulu War and how Sibephu and his men would trot along the footpath named after the Mandhlakazi clan. He pointed with bent forefinger in Zulu style to a low hill on the southeast slopes of Mtunzini.

"That is Ntaba-amanina [The Hill of Our Mothers]," he said. "Once there was a fight on the plain below and the women ran up the hill with the beer pots. When the men had finished fighting, the women gave them beer."

Magqubu shed his backpack, laid the rifle down, and began to act out how the opposing *impis* fought. He rushed forward beating an imaginary shield and assegai. His voice rose and fell, battle cries rang out, and men groaned with spear thrusts into the belly. He showed badly wounded men crawling, and other men licking the blood off the spears in triumph. It was a remarkable one-man play of a battle scene with all the accompanying sound effects. I watched as he leapt, cavorted, yelled, screamed, moaned, roared, and finally sang a song of victory, imitating a whole *impi* trotting off in close formation; then he became the defeated men running around shouting in a bewildered way. The victorious *impi*, their voices rising and falling, half-ran half-walked in close formation up the hill, shouting to the women to bring the *izinkhamba* (pots) of beer. Magqubu acted a dozen parts in quick succession, his voice changing tone and sounding like a whole army. Then he sat down, clasped an imaginary *khamba* of beer, and drank with deep grunts of appreciation. He looked at me, saw the amazement on my face, and rolled over laughing and slapping the ground. He stood up, dusted the grass from his clothes, saluted, and calmly said, "That's how the men of Sibephu Mandhlakazi and the Mtetwa fought."

He had given me a history lesson. I tried to imagine my history master giving a lesson this way and had to laugh at the thought.

Magqubu shouldered his backpack, called out "Asihambe," and walked and danced for a hundred meters, then settled into a steady pace.

We continued north, skirting the edge of the bush and following well-used rhino paths. We entered Madhlozi game-guard camp, checked to see if the guards were in – they should not have been at this time of day – and drank water from a forty-four-gallon drum. Magqubu showed me the footprints of the guards' boots. They had obviously headed west to the tops of Mtunzini hills.

My mind went back to 1955, when I established the guard camp as the most westerly outpost of the game reserve. It was a very lonely place at that time and game was much scarcer, but poaching gangs swept through and there were fierce clashes with the guards.

We left the camp, first making a mark on the ground to let the guards know we had visited. They would have seen our spoor and wondered who we were. We continued walking north and reached the pans on the edge of the Mbulungu hills. There was a little water and a lot of thick mud. We hid ourselves in a grove of trees, and Magqubu quickly piled a screen of *Rhus natalensis* to shield us from the rhino. We could hear the animals shuffling in the bush. It was nearly midday, and the heat would soon drive them to the water and mud.

I waited tensely for a while. Magqubu was relaxed, but I noticed that his eyes were constantly scanning the surrounding bush. An hour passed, and I drifted off to sleep.

I was awakened by Magqubu, who touched me with a twig. I looked up and saw five big white rhino approaching in single file. The wind was in our favour, but they were dimly aware of our presence. Their ears flicked, swivelled, and turned. The leading animal hesitated on the edge of the pan, but thirst and the need to wallow overcame their resistance and they plunged in, drinking, sucking up the water in long draughts through their square lips. Magqubu moved slightly, smiled, and made a wallowing action. A bull slopped into the mud, lay down, and began wallowing with loud noises. Magqubu pointed to my camera and indicated I could now shoot as much as I liked. Magqubu never lost his concentration, yet he was not tense. This is what made him so deadly a hunter in the terrible days of the tsetse-fly campaign.

The rhino drank the chocolate-brown water and rolled, wallowing in the mud. When they moved I clicked the camera. One big bull stopped in the middle of drinking, raised its head, and listened intently. It had heard the camera and knew the sound was not natural. When I had enough pictures I lay on my stomach, peering through the rough blind to watch the antics of the rhino. They enjoyed wallowing in the thick mud and gave little squeaks of pleasure. A young calf ran up and down the edge until, taking courage, it plunged in and ploughed through the mud, making such a noise that the adult rhinos panicked. Led by a cow, they all came lumbering out, bellowing. They stopped, quieted down, and began rubbing the mud and ticks off against old trees and stumps. I could smell their bodies and the mud and watched the hordes of flies rise in small clouds when the rhino rubbed hard.

One by one the rhino moved off, going silently down the paths until they were enveloped by the bush. I heard the young calf making the mewing sound when it wanted to suckle. Then there was total silence.

The white rhino is a gentle animal, non-aggressive unless pushed to the absolute limit. A mere clapping of the hands is enough to make it turn tail and gallop off in the opposite direction. The black rhino is different, far more curious and likely to charge if given a fright. When they have been disturbed or persecuted, they turn into instant chargers. One famous black rhino cow in Hluhluwe, called Poking Polly, would stand up on her hind legs and try to hook a person out of a tree. Paradoxically, though, when rhino capture began, it took six weeks to tame the timid white rhino and only two days to have the black rhino literally eating out of your hand.

Magqubu shouldered his pack, looked toward the sun, and said we should begin walking – Mpila was a good four hours away. He set off at a brisk pace, and we walked in the basin of the hills heading east.

Magqubu kept up a steady pace, following the game paths that weaved across the acacia-covered grasslands. In the hollows and where deep clay covered dry streambanks we passed through groves of *umThombothi* trees. Porcupine had been busy, and the bark on the lower trunks had been eaten. I wondered what sort of metabolism enabled the porcupine and the black rhino to eat this tree that is so deadly poisonous to human beings. Above us white-backed vultures and a lappet-faced vulture circled in the thermals, and at a lower altitude the handsome red-and-black bateleur eagle flew in a straight line, its wings motionless. Grey duiker leaped up in front of us, running in quick jumps, swerving, then vanishing into the bush. On our left I heard the impala rutting and the sound of the males clashing horns. With the afternoon shadows spreading across the hills the veld grew more alive and we came across nyala, warthog, steenbok, and white rhino making their way to the pans and the river. A honeyguide flew in front of us, calling persistently, trying to attract our attention. It flitted above us, then sat on branches ahead of us, calling all the time. Magqubu whistled and imitated the sound of the honey badger. This excited the bird even more, and it stayed with us for a long time. The song of the white-browed scrub robin reminded me that it was getting late.

We reached the road at a place Magqubu called Maplangweni, named after a little wooden shelter built in the *nagana* tsetse-fly days, where the labourers of the area were paid. The sun had sunk behind the Mtunzini hills and the sky was aflame. I turned to see the Mtunzini hills covered in a red glow. Was this an omen of things to come? The invasion of displaced people into the western buffer zone, the need to adjust the boundary to the top of Mtunzini, and the inclusion of some of the southern buffer zone were urgent problems. A long, frustrating bureaucratic struggle continued. Our small conservation group was very much in the minority, but I knew that our cause was just. The last two days with Magqubu had not only inspired me but also filled me with a passionate zeal to ensure the survival of this unique landscape with its long history of human and animal occupation. The story of its importance to the Zulu people, because it was where Shaka had walked, emphasized the need for its protection. I had been deeply affected by the landscape when I was stationed here in 1955 and during my brief visits in 1952 and 1953, but these two days with Magqubu had added many dimensions to my understanding of it.

A leopard began calling near the Mantiana hills, and a hyena followed. Soon it would be dark. I had no illusions about the importance of our work and the difficulties that lay ahead, but Mfolozi was part of Magqubu's soul. No one knew it better. I realized I would be depending upon him to guide me in the relationships with the other guards and in learning about the land. The last two days had given us additional insight into each other. I intuitively felt that, despite my faults, he had developed a liking for me. He was prepared to be patient, to teach me and to serve the cause of defending this game reserve, no matter what might come. He was able to bring everything together for me.

Nevertheless, there was still a barrier to be overcome: my sense of white superiority. It pervaded our relationship to such depth that only the most dramatic external experience could break and overcome it. My respect for Magqubu was limitless, and yet we were far apart at another level. Destiny had something in store for us both but especially for me, an incident that would change me in a way that nothing except death could do. I was to be led into an abiding friendship with Magqubu and the start of an inner exploration that was to transform my life.

We reached the game-guard barracks in the darkness. Magqubu went off to his hut, and I heard him singing as I walked the last half-mile to our house on top of the hill. The lights were on, and Ann and our firstborn child were waiting for me.

9

Magqubu the Hunter

Every day there was something new happening in the game reserve: poaching incidents, disputes between the guards or their families, and marital problems, VIP visitors, demands for reports, and the ever-growing threat of displaced people taking up land adjacent to the game reserve. I consulted Magqubu daily over some problem or another. His long knowledge of the history of the game reserve and the surrounding people was invaluable. We were living in dangerous times of transition, and we had to be firm or everything would be overwhelmed. People's problems dominated most of our time. The animals that were our responsibility led their lives in a pattern that nature had ordained. We saw them feeding, mating, trekking to water, and lying up in the shade. It was very seldom that any animal gave trouble of its own accord – usually a human had injured or hounded it.

An old buffalo had been wounded in a fight, and it took to charging vehicles. One of our senior men from head office in Pietermaritzburg had innocently stopped to look at the buffalo, then got out to take a photograph. The buffalo charged, and the man was fortunate to escape. Orders came for me to have the animal shot. Budgets were tight at that time, we were short of rifles, and the only heavy calibre weapon was an old 9mm Mauser. I went with Magqubu and another guard, Gqakaza Ntombela, a nephew of Magqubu's, and later Mcetegi joined us.

Gqakaza was a typical Ntombela, afraid of neither man nor beast. Very much a rural tribal man, he had been part of the tsetse-fly campaign, having been recruited by Magqubu. Later he joined the Mfolozi game-guard force and became one of my men. Many years after his retirement I recruited him again to become one of the wilderness guides for the Wilderness Leadership School.

We left soon after sunrise from the Masinda camp and after half an hour found the old bull. I stalked to within sixty yards, crouched down, took careful aim, and fired. Split seconds before firing, the buffalo was aware of our presence and half turned. I heard the thump of the bullet striking, but I knew the shot was not fatal. My heart dropped. Hunting a wounded buffalo is dangerous.

"You have hit it and it bleeds," Magqubu said when he picked up a tiny blade of grass marked by a speck of red blood. For a second it reflected the rays of the morning sun.

Magqubu looked hard at the spoor of the buffalo. His powers of observation were so acute that once he had the details in his mind they were fixed. No mark, scratch, or chip in the hooves would have gone unnoticed. The depth of the imprint from all angles, the space between running and walking, was instantly recorded and memorized. From a tiny child Magqubu had learned this craft, first taught by older herd *abafana* (boys) in following cattle or goats that got lost in the hills, then by his father, uncles, and cousins when hunting game.

It is not easy for a white man to understand this process. Magqubu knew the ways of animals so well that he could think as they did. He showed his capacity for understanding when I took him to the aquarium in Durban, where he was to give a talk. When the evening was over we walked to the shark pool and watched the grey killers gliding past through the clear glass. Magqubu was fascinated, and when he saw a big shark with remora attached to it he instantly saw the symbiotic relationship and remarked, "Amahlanyati we lawandhla" (The oxpeckers of the sea).

The incident came to my mind as we followed the buffalo, and a flock of oxpeckers rose with cries of alarm. Magqubu held up his hand, sniffed the air, and indicated with his head that the wounded buffalo had gone toward thick bush lining the Nyalazi River. The flight of the birds and the faint odour of the animal's scent had given him the clues. He led us toward the left, away from the direction of the spoor, and within five hundred yards we came upon the track again exactly where Magqubu said it would be. My inclination would have been to follow the tracks, but, as Magqubu showed us later, the animal was waiting to ambush us, a typical ploy of the buffalo. Magqubu walked slowly forward, pointing at the spoor by nodding his head. We entered the bush and I heard the whistle of a reedbuck on the hills and the call of the white-browed scrub robin. There was a tenseness in the air, and I held the rifle at the ready.

Magqubu stopped and stared ahead at the opposite bank, his eyes fixed on something I could not see. He turned his head slowly toward me and indicated something ahead with his eyes. Even at midday there was a gloom in the forest. I stared hard where Magqubu had looked but saw nothing. We stood dead still with only our heads and eyes moving. Magqubu nodded his head again, and I tried to follow his line of sight. Then in the dappled shade behind a dark bush I saw the flick of an ear. I lifted my rifle, the buffalo saw the movement, got on its feet, and trotted away. I fired at its vanishing backside, but it was the waste of a shot.

Magqubu asked, "Did you not see it lying down?"

"No, Magqubu," I replied.

"The *nyati* was looking right at us," he said, and laughed, as he often did after being serious.

I felt foolish, but it amazed me how he had seen the animal, which was so well camouflaged. I sensed that he was slightly angry and disappointed because it would have been an easy shot, but he said nothing. In later years, when our relationship became deeper and more open, he did not hesitate to comment forcibly. We followed the buffalo for the rest of the day, Magqubu painstakingly tracking the spoor over grasslands, stony ridges, and encroaching acacia thickets. I was desperately thirsty by the late afternoon, but neither Magqubu nor Gqakaza mentioned water. We were in the lower reaches of the Nyalazi, where water was scarce. My pride forbade me to call for a halt while Magqubu had the hardest work, crossing and crisscrossing the veld and probably walking double the distance. Later in the afternoon the spoor led to a small ooze in the sand. Flies, bees, butterflies, wasps, and other insects buzzed near the damp sand. Trying to be casual, I dug to get clean water. Magqubu watched, then calmly knelt down near me and expertly dug until the water appeared. He stepped politely back and I drank until my stomach was bloated. I looked at him but he shook his head. "I will drink tonight," he said. Gqakaza bent down and scooped two handfuls into his mouth and said it was enough. Magqubu laughed when he heard my stomach gurgling and the water sloshing from side to side when we walked away, and he imitated the sounds.

The sun was setting, and long shadows spread across the land. Herds of blue wildebeest in single file were making their way to the Black Mfolozi. Zebra with nodding heads followed the same paths. The bush was coming alive as the cool breezes began to blow. Layard bulbuls, Natal robins, and turtledoves were calling. This was a time of day when nature rested before bringing on the night. Monkeys chattered and baboons looked for trees to roost in. Magqubu beckoned me and pointed to a mass of spoor. "We will have to come back tomorrow," he said.

I was deeply concerned about my wounding of the buffalo, although Magqubu had assured me that the wound was slight. I felt that if we stopped now we would never see it again, but we could not go on in the dark. I looked anxiously at Magqubu, then at the complex pattern of spoor that the wounded buffalo had walked into.

"How will we find it tomorrow?" I asked.

"We will find it," Magqubu said, and Gqakaza nodded his head in agreement.

I went home to our house on top of Mpila hill very troubled, fearing that the wounded buffalo would never be seen again. I heard the old lion roaring and grunting below Nqabaneni hill, and I hoped he might get the buffalo, but he was too much to the south.

I awoke early the next morning before dawn and fetched Magqubu, then went to the barracks to collect Gqakaza and Mcetegi. We reached the Nyalazi as dawn was breaking. Magqubu climbed out of the Land Rover and gave orders to Gqakaza and Mcetegi. They moved in a wide circle around the mass of spoor we had seen the previous evening. Magqubu walked in a greater circle, and in a few minutes I heard him grunt, "Nango." I walked over and looked. All I could see was a faint smudge on the grass. "This is the animal," Magqubu said, and he began to walk slowly, following a print invisible to me. Gqakaza and Mcetegi joined him and they both grunted affirmatively.

Carefully and painstakingly Magqubu tracked the buffalo, his sharp eyes picking up clues split seconds before the other guards saw the marks on the grass. He led, pointing in Zulu style, with the bent forefinger. He hummed a herd boy's song softly to himself and nodded as he walked. The spoor disappeared into long themeda grass. Magqubu signalled the two other guards to go in a wide circle, and he walked cautiously into the long grass. I followed him, very much aware that the buffalo could be lying in wait. I had the heavy 9mm Mauser, Magqubu carried the military Lee Enfield .303. The sun was beginning to burn, and my thirst started, reminding me of the difference in our water discipline.

We came out of the dense themeda and Magqubu found the spoor again. He waved his arm, and the two guards walked quickly toward us. They hardly glanced at the track, nodded their heads, and said, "Yebo." Magqubu was already looking ahead, and he pointed to a tiny broken piece of grass, proof enough for him that he was following the correct spoor. His skill was far more than just powers of observation. He was in the animal's mind, thinking just as it did. There were moments when he did not look down but kept his eyes a fair distance ahead. I sensed a form of telepathic understanding between himself and the hunted buffalo that I would never be able to achieve.

The sun grew hotter, and I felt the sweat begin to run down my face. Masses of tiny pepper ticks clung to my socks and began moving up my legs. The day before I had walked into a cluster, and my thighs and midriff were full of bites that itched badly. The more one scratched the worse the bites became, and they could turn septic. As soon as the body warmed up, both the ticks and the itching became more active. I followed Magqubu as he walked carefully, following the spoor. I envied him not being bothered by the ticks. He did not lose concentration as I did, having to stop periodically and scratch. The ticks were able to get into almost impossible places: up the anus, on the scrotum, in the urethra, and, worst of all, between the toes. They were so small that it was only when the itch began that you could find and remove them, and sometimes by then they had already dropped off.

The tracks led to a small spring bubbling out of the grass in the Nyalazi River basin. Here I could clearly see the spoor. The unfortunate animal had drunk and then lay down not far from the water. Magqubu said I should drink because he knew that the buffalo would be heading for the Ongeni hills, where Magqubu had been born. "We will find it this afternoon," he said matter-of-factly, then added that the day would be hot and water not easily found. I drank the sweet clear water and sat for a while, resting and listening to the birds. A four-coloured bush shrike called *kokoviet*, *kokoviet* from the riverine bush on the lower Nyalazi, and *Cisticola chiniana* made its *kiss-kiss-churr* song from the top of an *Acacia burkei* tree. A gabor goshawk flew with swift wing beats between the trees, settled among schotia trees, and began its liquid trilling call.

I was for a few moments transported back to my early days at Ndumu game reserve on the Mozambique border. Ken Tinley came to join me there. He was fanatic about birds, and I was soon caught up in his enthusiasm and learned from him. Listening to calls became second nature and helped attune me to the land. I heard its rhythms and felt its power through the birds.

My reverie was broken by Magqubu saying, "Wozani" (Let us go). The guards shouldered their rifles. I followed Magqubu, who pointed out the signs where the buffalo had walked. We passed over a rocky area, and it was the only time I saw Magqubu hesitate. He signalled the guards to do a sweep ahead, then stared at the rocks, his eyes fixed on something. He smiled and pointed to a minute scratch mark. I looked carefully but could see no more than the line on the rock. Magqubu bent down, examined it, and once again showed me how the buffalo had stood, looking back for its pursuers. Magqubu whispered that it knew we were after it and now it wanted to outwit us, ambush and kill us. Who could blame it? Although I was one of the hunters and needed to kill it because I had been instructed to and because I had wounded it, my sympathy lay with the animal. These lands belonged to the animal and primitive man in a form of balance. I, a modern man armed with a deadly rifle, was out of balance. Many years later with

Magqubu's guidance I would become one with the land, but at this moment I was an intruder.

I knew Magqubu respected the spirit of the animal. I had heard him talking to it when we began the hunt, but he was not going to have any compunction about killing it when the moment arrived. Gqakaza and Mcetegi had the same understanding. The buffalo was an important animal in Zulu culture. In the old days the Zulu tactics in war used the horns and chest formation when they attacked an enemy. It had been brilliantly successful at Isandlwana, to the cost of the British. Buffalo meat was prized above all other animals, and the thought of cooking the steaks of this animal and ritually eating some of the intestines was, I am sure, constantly in their minds. At the same time, the respect and even love for the animal were there in an inner dimension that few white people would ever appreciate or properly understand.

Magqubu pointed with bent forefinger. The spoor of the buffalo turned northwest. We began climbing the low-lying hills toward the heights of Ongeni. The country had opened out into ideal reedbuck habitat, and I heard them whistling all around us when the sun dipped. It is a lovely animal that runs with a rocking-horse motion while it gives its piercing whistle.

Magqubu and the other two guards began to look ahead. They knew that in the open grassland they would see the animal if it was lying down. We climbed higher, and the wind grew a little stronger. It was a relief to feel it on my face and blowing around my sweaty shirt. Magqubu was sniffing the air like a hunting-dog and stopped to inhale more deeply. Then I caught a faint smell of bovine dung. Magqubu pointed and said the buffalo was not very far away. Open grassland stretched to the skyline, then there were clumps of bush on the wet southern slopes of the hills. On another ridge a good three miles away, *Acacia karoo* and other invading acacia species grew like a small forest. Magqubu pointed and said this was where the buffalo would now be lying up. Near us was a spring that trickled into a mud wallow, and the grass beneath the acacias was sweet. He consulted the other guards, and they agreed that he was right. The spoor led off in another direction following the side of a hill. Magqubu explained that the buffalo was not like cattle, which walk straight up and down hills. It went the long way, following the land's contours. Magqubu saw a path that turned toward a thicket at the top of the hill. He had played on these hills when he was a child, so he knew the country.

Clouds were gathering in the south over the Umendo hills, and there was distant thunder. The wind dropped, a sure sign that rain was on its way. A quietness spreads across the African veld before rain comes, and there is a palpable air of anticipation. Rain is life here and the earth waits to draw it up, and the animals know instinctively that green grass will follow. We walked with Magqubu leading, and I thought of the relief to the dry country when the rains came, the scent of the red and the black earth of Africa rising like waves of the ocean bearing down on a shore. The senses are assaulted with the strength of the scent. As we tramped toward the buffalo I wondered what it was thinking in its own instinctive way. It knew there was an enemy following it. The way it had changed course so many times clearly indicated that it knew we were on its spoor, and I had no doubt it had telepathically picked up our intention to kill it.

We drew closer to the bush where Magqubu suspected the buffalo to be lying up, and his body language changed. He moved deliberately and with more caution. His .303 Lee Enfield was firmly gripped in his right hand, and he scanned the landscape. Gqakaza and Mcetegi followed Magqubu's example. I was immensely proud of these men and felt honoured to be with them on this afternoon with thunder rattling in the distance and the grass swishing as we walked through it. The thought of one of them being injured worried me, because I knew they would protect me first, whatever happened. This was the Zulu way. I felt confident of looking after myself, but I was very aware that they were protecting me. We had become one group, and colour and race were irrelevant. They were treating me as they would one of their *indunas*. I was their leader and had to be protected, with their lives if necessary. This was to happen many times in my game-ranging years and I never took this loyalty for granted.

Magqubu stopped at the entrance to the thicket and held up his hand. Gqakaza and Mcetegi stood like pointer dogs, frozen in movement. Magqubu slowly stepped forward. I followed, and the two guards were close behind me. I heard the buzzing of a cicada beetle, and down among the sycamore figs lining the Black Mfolozi a bushbuck barked repeatedly. Magqubu moved stealthily through the acacias. Many of the smaller trees had been broken by passing black rhino. Bloodied ticks embedded in blobs of mud attracted the flies. We followed the path, and the bush became thicker. Magqubu dropped to his knees and peered through the tangled trees. A grey duiker jumped up in front of us. Magqubu had his gun levelled in a flash, saw it was a duiker, and we all laughed, breaking the tension. The noise startled the buffalo from its recumbent position. I saw its black form crash through the trees and I took a snap shot as it came into a clearing. The buffalo ran into the open, then turned and faced us. We all fired. It came straight at us, unaffected by the striking bullets. I heard Gqakaza praise its

courage while he fired another shot with the animal only ten paces away. Mcetegi put in a fatal shot, and Magqubu finished the poor animal off. It had been a long and tiring hunt after an animal that never gave up.

Magqubu walked to the buffalo and tied a knot in the hairs of its tail. This was a mark of respect for its courage and an appeal to the soul of the animal not to haunt those who had brought about its death. He examined the body and found a suppurating wound under one back leg. This was what had caused the animal to chase cars. It looked as though a snake had bitten it, and the poison had infected the whole underbelly. He showed me my first shot. The bullet had lodged in the flesh behind the ears and had done no damage at all. With a flick of his clasp knife Magqubu extracted the dark bullet. Gqakaza and Mcetegi opened up the belly with a cane knife and carefully cut off meat near the gall bladder. They ate the pieces with relish.

We sat resting, the guards getting up periodically to cut off a small piece of the meat they considered a delicacy. The brom-blue flies had already found the carcass and settled on the innards and near the anus. Thunder boomed in the distance and there were brilliant flashes of lightning. A cool wind blew, carrying the scent of rain mixed with the trees and the grass. Magqubu had been sitting deep in thought, then he stood up, half turned, and pointed to the hills just to the north.

"That is Ongeni," he said. "That is where I was born, and my father was born, and my grandfather was born. That is where I grew up. That is where many of my ancestors are buried. It was on those hills that I hunted as a child, then as a young boy, then as an adult. It was from my father that I learnt how to use an assegai and a knobkierie, and how to follow the spoor of the animals that we hunted. When I was an *insizwa* [young man], my father taught me how to shoot with the *mnqonqo* [muzzle-loader]."

Magqubu sat, his face cupped in his hands, and he spoke of his early days at Ongeni.

10

Magqubu's Early Days

Maklwana Ntombela was Magqubu's father. He was son of Nkovana, son of Bidankomo, son of Ngogo, who was an *induna* of King Senzangakhona, an early Zulu king. Then he served Shaka and could imitate the way Shaka spoke. He passed this on to Magqubu. Magqubu would spend hours telling me his lineage and that of Zulu kings, his *indunas* and their praise names. Shaka was a hero of Magqubu's, and we were to walk for over thirty years together in Shaka's footsteps across the Zululand hills.

Magqubu said his full name was Qumbu Magqubu, and that he was named at a time when his father and uncle were having a bitter dispute about cattle. Magqubu's father had returned from the battle of Tshaneni with cattle that had been given to him by King Dinuzulu, who had been helped by the Boers. Many years later a girl in the Ntombela family had married, and Magqubu's uncle Sikhunyana claimed that the *lobola* (bride price) cattle were his. Magqubu's father went to fetch the cattle, and his brother wanted to kill him. The dispute was so bad that Maklwana said he would never enter his brother's huts again. There was a case before the local *nkosi* (chief), and the cattle were eventually brought back to Magqubu's father. Magqubu, who said he was in his mother's womb while this violent disagreement was taking place, was born when the cattle were returned. So his father said his name would be uQumbu Magqubu, Bearer of Grudges. His name was eventually shortened by a magistrate's clerk, who irritably said the name was too long to write down.

"When I was a small boy I was at Ongeni," Magqubu said. "I first saw the world there. I grew bigger, and I started to herd the goats, taking them out in the morning with the sheep. I waited for the other herd boys from nearby homesteads and together we would go off to herd. While the animals were feeding we went into the bush to dig *nsema* [a tuber]. One of us would roll the *nsema* along the ground like a ball, then all of us would throw our *nkangi* spears to see who could hit it first. Those who missed we called 'stab the dog,' and those who hit it, 'hlaba khona' [we have stabbed it]. When the *nsema* rolled to the bottom of an incline, it would be fetched and we would go through the whole sport again. We learned to throw a spear with great accuracy.

"When we grew tired of this game, we cut small knobkieries in the forest to throw at birds. The little bird called *iNcede* [a cisticola], which flies then sits on the ground, kept us busy."

One day an *iNcede* flew close to a boy of the Mdhletshe clan, another boy flung his knobkierie, missed the bird, hit the boy on the head, and he dropped like a stone. They rubbed his head and asked him not to tell his father. He was told to say that he fell and hit his head on a stone, otherwise they would all get beaten by the elders for carelessness. Every day the young herders were out on the hills with the goats and the fat-tailed sheep. They played their hunting games and watched the wild animals.

"We tried to catch the *iNtendele* [francolin] by digging a hole in the ground, then on the opposite side we drove sticks into the earth and set traps for the francolin, using termites for bait. These traps were very successful, and we would work five traps at a time. The birds were taken home in the evening and given to the father of the kraal. They roasted the bird, and the catcher would be given the head and the neck. We were not allowed to give the birds to our mothers because it was believed that if we did, we would not be able to think like men." Magqubu smiled. "The fathers were clever with this story. They liked the sweet meat of the francolin and didn't want to share with the women."

Magqubu grew older, and the hunting quarry changed from tubers and birds to antelope. The Ongeni hills and ravines had good populations of duiker, bushbuck, and reedbuck. They would dig a hole on a path and make a trap using a rope and branches. When a buck was caught, one of the herders would run and call a father, who killed the struggling antelope with a spear. Then everyone in the *muzi* could eat. Reedbuck was considered the best meat, followed by bushbuck and duiker.

"Our ropes were our guns and we set traps in the game trails," he said. "Once, while we were setting a trap, a branch flew back and hit a young man in the eye, and it was torn from its socket. There was no water because we were on the hills, so one of the men washed the wound with urine, which removed the blood. The hole in his face was covered with a big leaf and he was taken home. He recovered." The injured boy was not allowed to cry.

Many cattle had died in the rinderpest epidemic, and later their replacements died too, of *nagana* after being bitten by the tsetse fly. When the herd grew again, one of the sports was to get the bulls to fight. On the way to the dip tank the bulls were put in close proximity and then goaded until they attacked one another. Each bull was a champion of a group of herd boys.

The winning bull would kick the beaten one until it bellowed in pain, and then a winner was declared.

Discipline was severe. Magqubu said that all young boys were afraid of disgrace. They were always being beaten. Older boys and men would hold the younger ones down. Hair was twisted, fingernails scratched on the body, and the boys had to keep quiet.

They would then be asked, "Do you hear what we are saying?"

The boys would answer, "Yes."

"Well, what are we saying?" the elders would ask.

"You are saying we should not do this or that, and we should do no wrong."

The saying goes that a young person who defies a knot that was tied by the elders will not succeed in life. This was drummed into every young Zulu with stick, fist, foot, and by being scratched with fingernails.

They set a trap for a leopard one day and checked several times to see if anything had been caught. On the second day they found all the sticks in the trap missing and they looked up to see a leopard hooked in ropes in a nearby tree. Magqubu's father yelled, "Run!", and they ran until they reached home. Other tribesmen joined them and they took their spears and shields and attacked and killed the leopard. They returned in the evening, the carcass of the leopard on their shoulders, singing one of the hunting songs, and the women ululated and danced when the men entered the kraal. The leopard skin was a great prize. The leopard was skinned at the goat kraal and the pelt was pegged out to dry.

"When we brought the goats back in the evening, they refused to enter the kraal. They ran all over the place," Magqubu said.

I could imagine the yelling and the cursing of the elders and the alarm of the young boys when the goats scattered in all directions. The hyena would have grabbed them in the dark, and the boys would be whipped.

"Eventually we kraaled them at Mdhletshe's *muzi*. Later, when the leopard skin had been removed, the goats would still not enter the kraal. We had to catch some of them and tie them up in the kraal, then the others followed, but they went around smelling the whole area and only after we had covered the spot where the skin dried with dung did the goats settle down."

Magqubu grew up with leopards in the bush a few hundred yards from the huts he and his parents lived in.

"There were many leopards at Ongeni and in the surrounding hills," Magqubu said emphatically. "I saw them with my own eyes. They would catch any goat that strayed. Once I saw a leopard dash out from a patch of bush, and in seconds it had killed a goat. The elders put the dogs on its trail, and my uncle was attacked when he tried to stab the leopard. It clawed him in the mouth, splitting his tongue. He was sick for a long time, unable to eat solid food. Liquids had to be poured down his throat. The wound stank and had maggots in it."

Magqubu described in a matter-of-fact way how, after the leopard had been stabbed to death while it was standing over his uncle, the goat was taken back to the huts. It had been mauled but not eaten. "So we ate it," Magqubu laughed.

"But what happened to your uncle?" I asked.

"The women washed his throat with goat's milk and fed him on *amasi* [sour milk], and he recovered," he said.

Magqubu was now in a storytelling mood. Being so near to his original home was bringing back memories. Gqakaza and Mcetegi cleared a small area in the grass, gathered a few stones, and lit a small fire. Green sticks were cut, and soon buffalo meat was sizzling, yet they continued to eat the raw pieces. Magqubu began another story.

"I was a small boy at the time Solomon was the king. We were going to Nongoma and I carried my brother's sleeping mats, blankets, and clothes. We met up with King Solomon at Chief Mtubatuba's *muzi*. He had been entertaining the king to a big feast. A white ox had been killed for the occasion. There were many of us, and we all walked together to Hlabisa where there was a school, and a German priest lived there. That night Chief Hlabisa killed an ox for us and we feasted well.

"We left early the next day and walked beyond the Mona River where it enters the Black Mfolozi in the game reserve. I went into the veld to relieve myself, and while I was away my elder brother said, 'Magqubu is growing too quickly, and who is going to carry for me? We need to weigh him down to stop him growing.' They quickly undid my pack and put heavy stones in it. When I came back and picked up the pack it was terribly heavy. My brother and the other boys groused at me and said, 'Get moving.' I complained about the sudden extra weight. They said I was talking nonsense and they would leave me behind for the hyenas if I didn't stop talking. At that time the custom was to prevent a young boy from growing too quickly, but I did not suspect what my brother was doing.

"I continued carrying the load for a long way to the Mpompolo River, and we crossed it as darkness was approaching. The other boys decided we should camp there before going to Usutu near Nongoma. When my pack was opened to get the cooking pot I realized how I had been fooled and what they had done to me. The older boys wanted me to remain an *udibi* – a carrier of their mats and blankets. These were the customs of earlier times."

Magqubu at 88 years old

Magqubu laughed. It had been part of the process of growing up.

"We had many customs that have gone. I remember them all because I grew up at a time when the king and the chiefs had power.

"My first memory is of a clear day when my mother carried me from the huts along the ridge that leads to the road from Mtubatuba to Hlabisa. At that time it was a wagon track and went close to our *muzi*. She told me that our King Dinuzulu was being taken by the government to Pietermaritzburg because he had helped Bambatha's people in the 1906 rebellion. I saw the soldiers."

Magqubu described in detail the uniforms the men were wearing. He was intrigued by the hats, and nothing had escaped his observant young eyes.

"When Dinuzulu went, Zululand changed. Our customs were no longer considered important and the government and the missionaries tried to teach us different ways. But we kept on living and, in my father's and my uncles' homes, we followed the old traditions.

"In the early morning before the vultures and the bateleur eagles were circling in the winds and the monkeys were sitting on the branches of the *umuNga* getting the warm sun, my father would tell me to make fire in the cattle kraal, the *sibiya*. In the evening all the men and the young boys who wanted to would gather around the fire. Some of the men carried mielie cobs, which they would roast and eat while sitting on their haunches. Even the very old men had strong teeth and could easily tear the maize off the cob. Talk was easy and many matters were discussed: the weather, hunting, crops, and the cattle. The women stayed in the huts and the young boys stayed with their mothers during the morning sessions. The boys were called *mnqolo*, a derogatory term meaning 'they picked the lice off their mothers'. When the older boys spoke in this way and the younger ones retaliated, there was always a good fight.

"The elders talked about the *amadhlozi* and God, whom they revered and loved. There were times when the people wanted to speak with God, the Great Spirit, and on a hot day they would go up a high hill and break the branches of the tree *msele* as they walked. The blackest man was chosen as the spokesman, either to talk to God or to ask for rain if there was a drought. After the *indaba* [gathering] taking place on the highest point of Masinda hill they would return with the branches, and a black beast would be killed and the black man again asked for rain. Light-skinned people were not allowed to be present.

"The dung of the black ox and the branches were taken down to the Black Mfolozi River, the one that carries away the ferryman. At the river the black men were immersed in water and the dung was smeared on their bodies. On the way to the river they would walk slowly, singing the old songs of the time of Shaka, Mpande, and Cetshwayo. If the ceremony had been a request for rain, they returned to the kraal and ate the beast. Shortly afterwards it would rain. My father was part of these gatherings many times. If there was not enough rain, the whole ceremony would be repeated. In times of extreme drought all the men would gather with their spears and their dogs. They sang, then danced with their feet stamping on the hard ground. Nearly all were barefooted. They were then ready to hunt the buffalo," he said.

Magqubu stood up in one agile movement, began singing a song in his clear baritone voice, gripping an imaginary spear, pointing it, and saying, "There go the buffalo – *abanyama*" (the black ones, a term of respect). He paused for a moment and looked at the dead buffalo lying near us. Rigor mortis had set in and a thin veil of smoke drifted over the carcass. I could smell the intestines and the raw meat cooking on the green sticks. Magqubu then spoke on as Gqakaza and Mcetegi, squatting on their haunches, looked at him appreciatively.

"The men would trot down the hill, running in the same way they did to the great battle of Isandlwana, singing as they ran, and the dogs followed, barking, growling, and fighting with one another until the scent of a buffalo was picked up. Encouraged by the whistles and the shouts of the men, the dogs took off after the buffalo, which always ran for the thick bush.

When it knew it could not get away, the bull turned and faced the dogs, hooking and disemboweling any animal that got too close. With the dogs yelping and barking in excitement the men knew the buffalo was at bay, and they surrounded it and speared it to death."

Magqubu left out no detail, and I was there with the buffalo, lowing and roaring as the blades of the assegais thudded into its body, the spear shafts quivering and smashing off against the surrounding trees. Dogs rushed in to grab the hind legs or lunged to grip the buffalo by the nose. Men, sensing the kill getting closer, went for the shoulder, where the heart lay. Blood squirted out onto earth, trees, men, and dogs. A crescendo of frenzy, then a swift thrust of a spear pushed by the powerful muscles of a tall Zulu, and the buffalo rolled over, the death rattle in its throat drowned by the noises of men and dogs. The dung was gathered and, holding branches, the men trooped to the Black Mfolozi, singing in a slow march-shuffling step.

"The dung would be smeared, the washing ceremony performed, then they would go home and it would rain for many days while they ate the meat of the buffalo."

Magqubu sat down near the fire, breathing a little heavier than normal after the exertion of the vivid demonstration. He spoke more about his growing up on the Ongeni hills and how he and his young friends played on the rocks in a king-of-the-castle game. But it was rough, and he showed me his knuckles, permanently scarred from countless fistfights.

In May 1887 Zululand was annexed to Natal, and in June 1892 the new magistracy of Hlabisa was proclaimed. In the early 1900s the game laws were being strictly enforced, and King Dinuzulu had forbidden the hunting of certain species as earlier kings had done, and now these were white men's laws too.

Zulu constables controlled by the magistrates patrolled the country and frequently visited the Ongeni region, where game was plentiful. Magqubu described the police wearing black uniforms with a little round hat held by string under the chin. Once they came to his *muzi* when his parents were out in the fields. The police told him to grin so that they could see his teeth.

They asked, "This meat on your teeth, where did you get it?"

Magqubu replied, "I haven't had any meat."

The police took a piece of dried grass, gave it to him, and told him to pick his teeth. Small pieces of meat clung to the grass.

"What is this?" the police asked, pointing to the specks.

"Goat's meat," Magqubu said.

They demanded to see the skin. Magqubu and the other children searched for the skin, which was not there, until they found a way to escape and ran crying to their parents. The police followed and asked the parents about the meat. Magqubu's father showed them the skin of a recently slaughtered goat. This satisfied them, and they said the children were telling the truth.

Magqubu laughed. "But it was game meat. It is hard to tell the difference. In those days it was not necessary for the police to catch you in the act of hunting." Hair in dogs' faeces, meat on the teeth, skin or bones were considered sufficient evidence for prosecution.

When Magqubu spoke about his youth he constantly compared it with earlier times, when Zululand was still an independent kingdom.

"The Zulu kings conserved wild animals," he said.

Senzangakhona, Shaka, Dingane, Mpande, Cetshwayo and Dinuzulu all looked after the game. So did Solomon, son of Dinuzulu. People were never allowed to kill wantonly, and there were seasons when the animals could be killed. Buffalo, kudu, and waterbuck were specially protected.

"If a man was caught killing game out of season, or killing a protected beast, he was handed over to the king's *indunas*, and if he was unable to pay for his crime in cattle or goats he was dragged in front of the king and flogged. The beating was terribly severe and the prisoner dare not remonstrate because he would be killed immediately. As the hiding progressed the king would ask if he repented. If the answer was not satisfactory the king would say, 'Beat him some more.' Eventually the king would ask, 'Will you do it again?' The culprit would swear he would never do it again, and the king would pronounce: 'Be careful and go and tell all the people that if they kill a wild animal they are not supposed to kill, they will be flogged like you. Do you hear?' 'Yes, *nkosi* – I have heard.' 'All right then, you can go.'"

Magqubu then made his point.

"If the wild animals had been killed indiscriminately, nothing would have survived when the white men came here."

Later he was to talk about the massive systematic killing of game by the department of veterinary services in the tsetse-fly campaign.

"Wild animals," Magqubu said, "were called *mhlozo* [forage food] because they helped people during a famine. People were saved by eating meat, and because the early Zulu people had no guns, it was not easy to chase and kill an animal with only spears."

He explained that if a big animal like a waterbuck was killed, people in the whole region were informed, and they would come and eat until all the meat was finished. Waterbuck were plentiful, and he had many stories about them.

He told me one story of a poaching incident he was involved in.

"I went hunting at the Mfolozi River with a man named Msilawevondwe Ngcobo," he began. "I was still a young boy. Ngcobo shot a waterbuck, and I and some other boys helped him to carry it to his home. The waterbuck was placed in the *inqolobane* – a small storage hut on poles. The old people called it an *umgango*. Ngcobo cut me some ribs and the liver from the animal to take to my father, who was alarmed when I gave it to him. 'Don't bring the meat into my house. Take it away and hide it in the bush. You know that hunting is prohibited,' he said. My father had sensed something because by the time I came back from the bush, the police had arrived and searched everywhere for the meat, even in the pots. They even went into my grandmother's hut. I knew then that my father was right. If I had taken the meat inside, we would have been in great trouble."

The police found nothing, and they left for Ngcobo's, where they found meat already cooked.

"What meat is this?" they asked.

Ngcobo tried to run away but he was caught. Then the boys who had helped carry the buck were caught, and one of them told the police that Magqubu was involved. Magqubu described how the two Zulu constables took Ngcobo to the storage hut where they found the meat.

"Who shot the buck? Was it Ngcobo?" they asked.

Ngcobo admitted guilt and was told he would have to go to the Hlabisa court the next day. He fooled the police by getting rid of the meat, and when he appeared in court the magistrate gave the police a dressing-down, saying they had assaulted the man. Ngcobo was fined three pounds. A policeman was furious and said to Ngcobo, "You Msilawevondwe [tail of a cane rat] are cunning, but I'll get you."

Magqubu and the other boys were given a few lashes on the buttocks by the police, which made them cry, then they were released. Magqubu went home and reported to his father.

His father said, "If I had allowed you in the house with the meat I would be in jail now. You should know that we hide buck meat in the bush and never bring it home. You do not want to listen, so I will add to the punishment from the court."

Magqubu related in detail his father's voice, facial expression, and the stick.

"He took his stick and beat me while I cried and promised never to go hunting with anyone but him. He continued to beat me and warned me never to involve myself in other people's affairs. He would not stop, and my mother began crying. My father threatened her, saying 'Be quiet, or I'll hit you too. This is my child and I don't want him to do just as he pleases.'"

"He beat me and kept on beating me and when I cried my father said, 'Shut up,' and I quickly wiped away the tears, but my heart and my backside, legs, and body were sore from the hiding."

The description of the beating, his mother intervening, and everything that happened in the *muzi* at the time was given with complete sound effects.

When Magqubu had finished he laughed and said, "That is how I grew up, my father only allowing me to visit the families that he approved of."

When Magqubu reached puberty, he and his brothers went to look for work on the sugarcane farms. He worked for six months and only had a hessian sack to sleep on. He earned six pounds a month plus twelve shillings bonus for uninterrupted loyal work. He saved all the money and gave it to his father, explaining that in Zulu custom there is the adage, The dog fends for his master. In appreciation, his father slaughtered a goat and praised Magqubu to the ancestors, and then they had a feast.

Insangu (dagga, or cannabis) was part of Zulu custom. Adults were permitted to smoke it, and to his dying days Magqubu defended its use fiercely. He maintained that his body was not quite right because he had had to give up smoking it because of white men's laws. When he became a man he used to drink too, but in his eyes dagga and drink could not be compared. One was beneficial, the other harmful. White men's laws put a stop to dagga, yet drink was encouraged.

"When I had grown up," Magqubu said, "I used to visit *imizi* with my father and uncles. We walked because there were no buses, and horses were killed by *nagana*. There were many footpaths, some started by the rhino, which then became our footpaths. I can remember the dew on the *insindi* [themeda] grass and the reedbuck whistling as we walked. They stood watching us because they knew we were not going to kill them at that moment. We were like lions who had had their fill, and the antelope knew it. The wildebeest would run in circles and dance in front of us, snorting and kicking up their back legs. Baboons sitting on the tops of the rocks would bark at us if we had dogs, and the vervet monkeys would chatter. We were brothers to all these animals, we respected them and we liked to have them as our neighbours. There were birds everywhere, guinea fowl, francolins, plovers, bateleur and martial eagles. They called out to us and we replied in their own language. Yes, we killed them too, but for us there was always a purpose, and the birds and the animals knew this because once the killing was done, everything quickly returned to the normal pattern.

"I was aware of all this when I was on my way to smoke *insangu*. We called it 'the story'. It gave us courage and respect. When I quarrelled with somebody I used to say, 'Meet me at such and such a place' at a time of day determined by the sun. I would then fill my pipe with dagga and smoke it. This would bring me back to my senses and set my eyes straight. It helped me to see properly. Even today if I use binoculars or spectacles I cannot see as clearly as I do without them. Smoking *insangu* helped the eyes and you never blinked when you looked into another man's eyes."

Magqubu compared these earlier days with modern times, saying that as dagga was no longer smoked bodies were not fit, but it was not only the lack of dagga.

"We are not fit because we have stopped living the Zulu way. We do things that are not good for Zulus. We do not eat the food we ate in my younger days.

"We walked long distances to smoke 'the story'," he continued.

When they reached a *muzi* and were allowed inside and the necessary greetings were completed, they would sit in a circle and begin smoking and play war games with spit. The ritual included sucking the smoke through water with a reed stem.

"The water used to boil," Magqubu laughed, and he made a popping noise. "When we had smoked a little we started coughing, and my friends said that anyone who cannot cough is not a real man. Then we spat our saliva and everyone knew which saliva was his own."

The saliva was propelled through a hollow reed, and Magqubu made the noise of the spit moving and sizzling in the dust. Saliva attacked saliva, and eyes concentrated on the direction. Later there were deep discussions, and Magqubu said that the dagga centralized the thoughts – it did not allow the mind to wander. One did not engage in a serious conversation without first smoking dagga.

Magqubu maintained that in a race between two men, one who had smoked dagga and the other who had drunk beer, the dagga smoker would cover five miles and the drinker only one. He said that drinking did not allow the expansion of the lungs, and the gut was full of beer, which weighed you down.

"If a man who had been drinking ran ahead of me I would soon catch him up and jump over his shoulders," he laughed.

Magqubu's descriptive powers were at their humorous best when he described a competition between two men – the dagga smoker and the drinker – digging a hole.

With heavy breathing and the sound of liquid rolling around in the stomach, Magqubu became the drinker, digging laboriously away, the spade getting heavier and heavier, the man taking longer rests and the sweat pouring off his body. He would brush the big beads of perspiration away from his eyes, at the same time making stomach-rumbling noises like a huge beer barrel being rolled from side to side. He would be overcome with laughter at his own performance and roll on the ground. Then he would begin the performance again, the slow heavy movement of the spade, taking long rests, moving ponderously, and indicating that the hole after this lengthy effort was no more than calf-deep. He'd belch, saying, "Damn it, damn it," and flop on the ground for another rest, and so the drama of the drinking man would continue, each gesture and remark absolutely correct, the result of a lifetime of concentrated observation. Any actor would have been envious of this performance. The look on his face or the movement of a hand added the right touch at the appropriate moment.

Now came the change, and Magqubu turned into the man smoking dagga. First, the taking of the pipe, *igudu*, and stuffing it with dried dagga leaves. He moved carefully, with the most elaborate gestures, and tamped down the cannabis. Then he picked up a burning coal ember, held it nonchalantly between thumb and finger (as he could do in reality), and pushed it gently into the pipe bowl. He waved a hand, brushing away the smoke from his eyes as he puffed deeply and inhaled. After a minute or two he coughed, his eyes rolled, and he laughed in a high-pitched giggle, "Heh heh heh," and did a little dance, going around in a circle stamping his feet rhythmically. One hand held the imaginary pipe and the other kept time with the feet and slapped his thighs. Then he sang about how he was filled with great strength, his mind clear and fixed on digging a hole. He interrupted the dance to speak contemptuously to the drinker, whom he immediately turned into, standing sullenly and listening. Then he again became the dagga man.

"You and your fat belly full of beer, you who sweat with the smallest touch of the sun, how do you think you can compete with me and my *insangu*? Not only can you never beat me in digging a hole, but if you tried to run against me you would be vomiting" (and he imitated the long drawn-out retching that seemed to start at the anus). "Do you hear me, drinker?" he asked in a loud voice, waving the dagga pipe around, then puffing with great enjoyment and coughing dramatically again.

Instantly Magqubu became the drinker, shuffling from foot to foot, looking shamefaced, and holding onto the fat belly that flops over the top of his pants. "I hear you," he says listlessly and sits on the ground, holding his head in his hands.

"Aha, you hear me, then why do you drink and think that you can beat me in hole digging?"

The conversation and the action between the drinker and the dagga smoker grew faster and faster with Magqubu changing the tone of his voice and switching his body with amazing rapidity yet with a deliberateness that left no doubt about who was who.

"I drink because I like it, not because it makes me work. Do you know how good the taste of beer is on a hot day? Have you had the white man's spirits that go to your head almost before reaching your stomach? Ah, to feel it going into your veins and your legs grow weak and you want to lie with your head on a rock and sing to the sun."

"Sing to the sun?" the dagga smoker says scornfully.

"Yes, and when the singing is finished and the drowsiness comes, you drink a little more and soon you can sleep and nothing can wake you."

"Go away, you drunkard. Now watch me and I will show you that *insangu* is the real power. Look, man, look. Here is the pipe, I light it again and I suck the smoke and my body is filled with strength and my head becomes clear. Now I can work like ten men. I can run up hills, fight a leopard, climb a tree, or chase an impala. This smoke is power, this is what our brothers and our fathers used at Isandlwana – we walked and trotted into the bullets. Heh heh. Now watch me carefully, 'beer man'. Look when I pick up the spade, see how quickly the hole is dug."

Magqubu defiantly picked up the nonexistent spade, laid the pipe down with a loving look, and began to dig with frenzied energy. Dust, earth, and rocks fly out in all directions, and in no time the hole is thigh deep.

"Fool, this is what *insangu* can do," and Magqubu fell to the ground laughing at his own magnificent performance.

Magqubu grew serious and spoke at length about his growing up.

"This is how it was when we were growing up, but the white man's government made smoking *insangu* against the law. We do not know what they saw wrong. Dagga helped many people. It made them work.

"In Durban there was a big house where the workers used to stay. This was in 1914 and 1918. The men all smoked *insangu*, and they were diligent people. When the law prohibited it, people stopped working and many became loafers. Then, those who steal to live appeared. If you were standing in a train queue to buy a ticket the criminals picked your pocket. Stopping the smoking of *insangu* created the loafers; their thinking was not straight. When I was young and smoked *insangu*, which I did properly and with respect, I worked hard, and when I was finished I would think to myself what work I should do next. I collected my father's stock – goats, sheep, and cattle – that did not die in *nagana* times. I counted them and took them to the *sibiya*. If my father called me I responded immediately. Even if a man from another *muzi* called me I treated him like my father. I respected old people. This is what it was like in the days when we were allowed to smoke *insangu*. Drink has now killed that old spirit. I once used to drink myself, this is how I know the difference.

"The worst drink was *isishimeyane*. When a man drank this liquor he forgot about his children. He didn't even know his wife. If they quarrelled he would take a bush knife and hack her. When the police came to arrest him and asked, 'What's wrong, why did you kill your wife?', the drinker would say, 'I don't know. I was drunk.' Even the government hated this liquor. A cup of *isiqatha* or *isishimeyane* was enough to make you drunk. This is the liquor that corrupted the world and made the government open beer halls so the people could buy sorghum beer."

Magqubu also spoke about food in the old days.

"When I was a young boy," he said, "we had no salt, no sugar. Honey from the bees was our sweetness. We found hives in the ground or in the hollows of trees. We took green leaves and laid them on a fire to make lots of smoke, then dropped them on the hive. This made the bees drowsy. If we were lucky we didn't get badly stung. Sometimes we moved too slowly and the bees came for us and we would get so badly stung we could not see out of our eyes, and one boy had to lead the other. Our lips, too, and our ears were badly swollen, but it was worth it because the honey was so sweet. It was only the hives in the *umThombothi* trees we couldn't eat. The poison sap affected the honey, and if you ate some, it was like swallowing burning coals. Today people go to the store and buy sugar.

"We never even had combs. If you wanted to comb your beard and brush your hair you would use a stick. We used a thorn to make our hair stand up nicely.

"Neither men nor women cut their hair because they believed it would take away their energy. If they did do so they got a cold. In the old days there were very few colds; people lived healthily. There was no time for coughing and no time for dying.

"The only time the hair was cut was if sores or a rash appeared on your head. Ringworms made sores, and we got rid of them by applying cow dung. This made the pus disappear. Three applications were enough to get rid of the ringworm. The old people were strong. You do not see many now. I can remember people who were so old they crawled around like sheep. My father walked to Mtubatuba and back every day when he was nearly ninety. I will do the same." Magqubu laughed, bending over like an old man holding onto a stick and hobbling forward.

"When all the game at Mfolozi was killed by 1945, the government told the people who lived at Omendu, Ukuku, Mtunzini, and Ongeni that they had to move. Anything that had blood that the tsetse fly could drink had to go too – cattle, goats, sheep, dogs, fowls – they all had to go. We were told that the people could return when the fly had gone."

The entire Ntombela clan and their neighbours were removed by the department of veterinary services and sent to the low-lying country of Macibini, which despite the meaning of the name, small pans or lakes, was a much harsher environment. It was a trail of tears. Re-establishment for the Ntombelas was very difficult. The contrast of cool, well-watered Ongeni hills with thick forests in the kloofs and ravines with the hot and dry Macibini area was forever in their minds. At Macibini the nearest perennial water was the Nyalazi River, which in dry cycles was salty and bitter. The reason for the removal of the people was the tsetse fly. It was spreading out of the game reserve onto nearby white ranching land, and cattle were dying. The Ntombela clan and their neighbours were told that when the tsetse fly was eliminated they would be allowed to return to the Ongeni hills. The promise was not honoured. Magqubu could never forget his birthplace, and I went with him to it many times and watched him walking round talking to the boulders he had played upon and to the spirits of his relatives, who were buried on the hillsides.

Magqubu said, "For us it was a time of great sadness. The young children cried and kept asking why we had to leave the green hills that looked as far as Nongoma. In the summer the mist would come down out of the sky and the reedbuck would whistle in the darkness. Ongeni was our home."

Magqubu repeated the last sentence in deep nostalgic tones.

We walked back in the late afternoon down the old track from Ongeni to Masinda. In the early part of the century John Dunn had come up that way, using zebra to pull his cart. Magqubu began humming an old Zulu hunting song. Gqakaza and Mcetegi took up the refrain, then they danced and sang, praising the buffalo, the *inyonikayiphumuli* (royal cattle) of the veld. The Zulu kings and the ancestors of the three men were brought into the song of praise. All I could see in my mind's eye was the extraordinarily brave animal coming straight at us, ignoring the bullets until it died.

11

The Lion Comes Home

In early June I had a telephone call on the party line from Singie Denyer in Mkuze. Curious housewives and bored farmers would listen to interesting conversations, and any Parks Board call was in that category. Singie told me with relish that "the biggest lion in Africa," probably the same one as two years ago, had returned.

"Have you seen it?" I asked casually, knowing Singie's predilection for yarns – and I wanted to tease him too.

"No," he said. "But I know how big it is, the size of the spoor, the colour of the mane, and what it last ate before coming into the game reserve. I know more about this lion than it does about itself. This lion is much more important than your white rhino," he laughed. He knew I had used the white rhino in every way I could to publicize the Mfolozi game reserve because it suffered from the same threats as Mkuze did.

"You must come up at once and see the spoor. Mr. Mitchell has just been here and confirmed everything," Singie said triumphantly.

The mention of Douglas Mitchell would have made every listener to the conversation take notice. Both Singie and I knew it would not be long before there were wild stories doing the rounds of the Zululand bars and farm coffee circles. Singie was aware that someone would tip off the press, and this was exactly what he wanted. Rangers were not allowed to give press statements. This was a firm rule from head office, but the story of this big cat was now about to become news. A local stringer was tipped off "confidentially" by a telephone listener who embroidered the story by mentioning Douglas Mitchell. It would not be long before it was filed with a newspaper in Durban. Singie repeated everything at least twice to make sure that everyone listening in heard. A series of clicks on the line, the cackling of fowls, barking of dogs, chimes of clocks, squawls from children, and even someone spitting, confirmed it.

"You must come here," Singie pleaded. "Leave that country of yours and come here to a paradise."

I left the next day. Singie greeted me with glee and took me to the forty-four-gallon half-drums that protected the spoor. He moved a drum away and pointed dramatically to the tracks. I stared and walked around for a good three minutes, examining every detail. I dropped onto my hands and knees, examined the spoor microscopically, then sniffed it. I turned up my nose and Singie looked at me in alarm.

"Well, what do you think?" he asked.

I pronounced it to be the biggest hyena footprint I had ever seen. Before Singie could reply I added that to rely on politicians to assist with identification was foolish. Everyone knew they exaggerated.

Singie took a step back in surprise, then realized I was pulling his leg, and said, "Voetsak" (Go away).

We had tea on the veranda of his house and talked at length about the lion, and laughed about the telephone conversation. We knew that within a day or two the news would be in most of the newspapers. This helped to bring attention to Mkuze, and we needed something else to take the public's mind off crocodiles. For over a year the public, through the newspapers, had directed a concentrated attack on the Natal Parks Board over crocodiles. This had been exploited by some Nationalist politicians as an opportunity to have game reserves deproclaimed and the land turned over to farmers. Pineapples had recently been grown near the False Bay nature reserve, so this area was a main target. Through friends in the press I had exposed the political machinations, but it was difficult because there was an instinctive loathing for the unfortunate crocodile. In early June the Hluhluwe delegation of the Federation of Women's Institutes urged its congress to pass a resolution calling for the extermination of all crocodiles in Zululand. Public ignorance of wildlife conservation matters was going to take a long time to overcome.

"*Ja,* the lion of Mkuze, it will help to distract attention from the bloody crocodiles. Hell, everyone goes on about them every time I go into the village in Mkuze. We must get the lion into the news," Singie said.

"Don't worry," I said. "The old busybodies on the party line will have passed on the news by now."

The story would be in the papers within a day or two, but content and presentation were anyone's guess. We did know that it would draw some attention away from the crocodiles. We were heartily sick of the incessant rantings from chambers of commerce, farmers' associations, and women's institutes in Zululand. Hardly a day passed without more garbage being written about the dangers of crocodiles. Faked photographs showing groups of crocodiles on the doorsteps of houses at St. Lucia Estuary had become commonplace. In reality the crocodiles were forty miles away, minding their own business.

The Natal Parks Board partially succumbed to the public outcry and political pressure. I was ordered to employ a man to shoot any crocodile appearing near any of the tourist camps on Lake St. Lucia. I spoke indignantly to Colonel Vincent, the director. He looked at me and said, "You are in charge of the operation." He needed to say no more. A crocodile hunter arrived, and I issued him with a leaking boat, failing torch, and totally unreliable rifle. He complained that I really did not want him to kill any crocodiles. There was no point in replying. I looked at him and the equipment and shrugged my shoulders. He did not stay long and departed for better pastures.

I took my leave of Singie and Dawn Denyer after a splendid tea and made my way back to Mfolozi via Nxwala Estates and the dry drift across the Msunduzi River. I stopped for a while to look at the sea of reeds covering the Nsumu pan, a favorite hunting ground for white poachers and the scene of many tough days for me. On one occasion in 1953 I was shot at repeatedly.

June is a marvellous month in Zululand: balmy weather, clear skies, and little wind. There is a scent of dust, dry leaves, and a smell of game. I stopped at a big kigelia (sausage) tree, its red flowers alive with insects and sunbirds. Never had I seen such a variety of the lovely little glossy sunbirds with their long beaks probing into the flowers. I crossed the drift and looked up at the silent krantz on my right and the large open-mouthed caves. Eighty million years ago this land was under the sea.

I left the valley and made my way south along the road toward Mhlosinga village, named after the groves of fever trees in the swampy places. I stopped again and looked back over the flat-topped acacia trees stretching eastward toward the distant coastal dunes. It was a beautiful afternoon, and so still that I could hear pods falling through the branches of the trees. Over on my left I heard the faint cry of a jackal hunting near the Mkuze game reserve. I wondered about the lion, and I knew that a time of great danger had come in its southward trek. This land was owned by white farmers, most of them Afrikaner cattle ranchers. They were deadly shots, and a wandering lion would get short shrift. I uttered a quiet prayer to the great Creator and asked him to be merciful and let the lion live. The odds were heavily stacked against it, and it was a miracle that it had reached the Mkuze game reserve. Jackals called again in the distance, a reassuring sound and perhaps an omen that the lion would survive. They were, after all, the followers of the lion.

My life was full, but I was concerned about that lone lion trekking south. Would it, like the other lion, return to the north, or would it continue south? I thought about those enormous footprints that Singie Denyer had shown me. This really was a big lion.

I arrived home at Mpila late that evening, and the following morning Nick Steele rode over on his horse, Zoom, from the Gome outpost. I told him what I had seen at Mkuze.

We were both romantics and hoped to have all the former species that once existed in the Zululand game reserves brought back – the cheetah, brown hyena, wild dog, elephant, and eland. We hoped that the leopard population would increase too. Its numbers were low because the *nagana* section of the veterinary department had placed bait cattle to attract biting flies in almost every patch of bush in the Mfolozi game reserve and in Hluhluwe. These were the areas where the leopard liked to hide, and the disturbance drove them away. Snares were also set by *nagana* personnel for any unwary leopard. The skin was extremely valuable, equal to six months' pay, so any chance of catching one was worth the risk.

"I really wish that lion would come here," Nick said. He knew as well as I did that the cultivated land and masses of people could easily prevent it. "But don't forget," he said hopefully, "there is that hippo, Huberta; she walked south from Richards Bay through Zululand, into Natal, right through Durban, and into the Cape."

Nick was right. That wandering hippo was a miraculous wildlife incident. It became so famous that it was revered. Initially, everyone thought it was a male. Only when it was killed by farmers in the Cape did someone realize it was a female. The name was changed from Hubert to Huberta, and Hedley Chilvers wrote a charming book, *Huberta Goes South*, about her wanderings.

"*Ja*, but she was shot," Nick said. "She was a hippo and would gain people's sympathy. You can imagine how little sympathy a big lion will get on a cattle farm, and even less in a city."

Ann appeared at the door and said that tea was ready. Tea took precedence over everything, for a little while anyway. We walked to our house, which had one of the finest views in Zululand.

From one window you looked toward the east and the coastal dunes, from others lay the dry Mtunzini and Ukuku hills, and in the far west, the hills of Mahlabatini. Out of the kitchen window were Momfu cliffs, the White Mfolozi River and the big fist of Mdindini, and behind it the Gome hills. It was a view that I never tired of looking at. In summer there were many anxious moments. The roof was thatched and lay on top of a net of eight-gauge wire. If lightning had struck, the resulting fire would have been out of control in a few minutes. We relied for our safety on a lightning conductor and hoped that the stories the salesman had told us about its efficacy were true.

Nick and I continued our conversation in the house. New huts had appeared east of the Mtunzini hills and there were well-founded rumours of hundreds of people arriving in the Mahlabatini district and making their way to the vacant land. The squatters – unfortunate, displaced people – had become the greatest problem facing the Mfolozi game reserve.

To make matters worse, our western boundary was a line on a map. In the south and the north it was the White Mfolozi River and the Black Mfolozi River, respectively. A river boundary was impossible to fence, and furthermore, the boundary line was in the middle of the river. We were not prepared to give up a square inch of territory and knew that if we did not get at least some of the Crown lands adjoining the reserve, it would eventually be impossible to administer our area. The Mdindini bend, shaped like a harmless chicken head, was in fact a dagger poised at the heart of the Mfolozi reserve. If that land became populated by squatters – and they had already started to move in farther south – we would not be able to control the poaching, and the loss of grazing for the white rhino would become critical. With the intrusion of the six squatter huts on the east side of the Mtunzini hills, we had already lost the high ground. Poaching parties planning a raid into the reserve had all the advantages. Observers posted along the ridges of the Mtunzini hills could see for miles into the game reserve. And one of our most important game-guard camps, Madhlozi, now lay half a mile from the nearest hut and in view from every high point. The squatters occupied them all. The moment game guards moved out on patrol from their camp the poachers would be alerted, and one sharp whistle was enough to warn men laying snares or on their way to hunt with dogs.

I had written many reports on the situation, and so had Hugh Dent when he was in charge. I lobbied everyone who would listen to me, and I invited my old friends from the press to come and see what was happening. Every day brought more bad news, new worries of proliferating huts along the southern and western boundaries, and a steady intrusion of people into the corridor, the strip of Crown land that joined the Hluhluwe and Mfolozi game reserves together. I knew that Colonel Jack Vincent had placed the subject on the agenda of every Parks Board meeting. He forcibly expressed his views on the seriousness of the situation, but apart from a few of the board members, most were unconcerned once they left the boardroom.

Nick Steele and I had by this time begun to treat Mfolozi reserve as though it were our personal property. We were as sensitive to what happened to it as a spider would be to an insect landing on its web. Nick looked to me as the senior man to fight the issue and achieve something. I expected those above me, especially Colonel Vincent because he cared deeply, to do something to relieve the pressure. Colonel Vincent had to rely on the board to take action or to give him instructions and backing. There were politicians on the board. Jim Grantham was a member of the Executive Committee of Natal, one of the most senior positions in provincial government, and Douglas Mitchell was a member of parliament who had a big say in the United Party, the chief opposition party to the government.

However, neither Jim Grantham, who came from a farming constituency, nor Douglas Mitchell, who had good friends in the government, could afford to rock the boat too much. If they had expressed publicly everything they felt about the government's maladministration in Zululand, the repercussions could possibly have soured the government's attitude toward the game reserves even more. These two men were doubtful about my reports. They told Colonel Vincent that I was exaggerating what to them was a minor issue. He defended me and seized the opportunity to invite the two board members to visit the area during a staff inquiry, as they were part of the subcommittee concerned. They accepted, and the Colonel phoned to tell me the news. I was delighted, and looked forward to showing the board members that, far from exaggerating, I was understating the case.

Winter was upon us. Reedbuck whistled, the *isikhele* francolin called from down in the bush along the river banks, and Shelley's francolin sang out its monotonous, *I want some beer, I want some beer*. We heard a white rhino bellowing from the pans in the Magunda bush below Dengezeni. A troop of baboons gamboled on the sands of the river, the older ones barking loudly and the youngsters screaming when they were chastised. A hyena left an antbear hole and gave its first deep *whooop* of the evening. The atmosphere of the reserve changed. A nocturnal rhythm was beginning and would ebb and flow until the first fingers of dawn light.

"This is a wonderful place," Nick sighed, staring out at the grey bush all around us and listening to the sounds. We had become part of it, captured by wild atmosphere, the bravery of the Zulu game guards, and the long history of the reserve.

In recent historical times the Zulu had lived and fought here. They were plagued too by the tsetse fly, the rinderpest, and east coast fever, a virulent cattle disease. Shaka had made his reputation in the hills we could see from the house. Dingiswayo, who became Shaka's patron, had built up the Mtetwa empire in the valleys below us and was killed by Zwide Ndwandwe, who by sorcery had obtained some of Dingiswayo's semen. Shaka chased Zwide Ndwandwe and his people out of the Mfolozi valleys into the country north of the Pongolo. Before this happened there had been a decisive battle at Nqabaneni, the hill overlooking the White Mfolozi River, its name meaning "The Little Fort." It was called The Hill of Refusal, too, because

Zwide fled rather than face Shaka and his men. Then, over the last sixty-three years, there had been an ongoing fight to maintain the area as a game reserve, a continuation and extension of the kind of protection that Shaka and Dingane had given it when elephant ivory and rhino horn were valuable trade items.

When Nick and I parted, it was dark and the night sky was ablaze with stars. "Give it hell tomorrow," he shouted, referring to the visit of the board members, as he walked towards Mpila camp.

The following day I accompanied the director and the two senior board members of the Parks Board on a tour of inspection of the western areas. I did not have to talk much. It was obvious how serious the situation had become. Even from the top of Mpila hill we could see smoke from the fires of the huts right next to the game reserve boundary. There was no need to stress the importance of having the high ground inside the reserve. Douglas Mitchell reminded me of the visit of the prime minister, J.G. Strijdom and the minister of lands, Paul Sauer, and the minister of justice, C.R. Swart, in 1956.

"Do you remember?" he said, "We talked about high ground at that time. We also asked what we were to do when fired upon by armed poachers. The reply was 'Shoot back'. Do you remember that, Player?" Douglas Mitchell asked.

Mr. Mitchell's recollections brought back memories of having to chase white rhino into prominent areas so that the ministerial party could view them. Jim Feely and I met the party at the newly built Mpila rest camp. Mr. Mitchell called me aside, and his blue eyes seemed to pierce me as he said, "I want the P.M. to see white rhino." His voice was stern and uncompromising. "There has been a fire on the Mtunzini hills and many rhino have left the reserve," I said apprehensively. "Well, get them back" was his curt reply.

My heart sank, and I said to my ranger colleague Jim Feely, "Who the hell does he think I am, the bloody Pied Piper?"

We had game guards and rangers running all over the reserve secretly driving rhino toward the roads. At the end of the day we had shown the prime minister eighty white rhino. That evening Mr. Mitchell took me to a view site on Mpila hill. The Southern Cross appeared in the sky, and he said in a kind voice, "Sorry you had to be a rhino herd boy, but we made good friends for the game reserve today."

He was one of the few board members who understood why we wanted wilderness areas in Mfolozi and Lake St. Lucia. It was a concept that fitted into his own philosophy, because he had ridden on horseback all over Pondoland when he ran a trading store there. When he was over seventy years old he got onto a horse and went with us into the game reserve, riding among the rhino to see a disputed boundary for himself. He did not drink or smoke and he had great stamina. He was able to make long political speeches without tiring. There is a story that he was at a political meeting in his constituency and he told his audience that he was a man of peace but that destiny had decreed that he should constantly become involved in discord. "I must say," a voice mused loudly from the back of the hall, "you co-operate rather well with destiny."

Douglas Mitchell's reminder of that earlier visit made me realize how he cared for the game reserves. At the end of every parliamentary session he would bring prominent members of the government to the Zululand game reserves. It was a complete break from their normal lives, and, out of the view of the public, they were able to relax and discuss other issues. Douglas Mitchell lobbied for their support when they were back in parliament.

When Mr. Strijdom left Durban by train for Pretoria, he was asked by a newspaper reporter about his visit to Mfolozi. The prime minister said that he had seen Mfolozi's famed white rhino, which, unlike the black rhino, was an enemy of mankind. (This of course is not true.) The newspaper man, trying to lead Mr. Strijdom on, suggested that there might be some moral to be drawn from the prime minister's description.

"No, there is no moral to be drawn," Mr. Strijdom said. "I'll leave that to the newspapers." And he smiled. The reporter said that this was surely the first time that a "lion" had been in the reserve. Again the prime minister (dubbed by the press the Lion of the North) laughed and replied, "Not really. They tell me there used to be lions there, but that they were exterminated."

Almost exactly a year later a real lion was on its way to Mfolozi, and Zulu power was returning to the land.

Mr. Mitchell, in an old felt hat and a big overcoat, looked at all the huts and agreed that the situation was worse than he had imagined. He was angry about the inefficiency of the government and said he would take the matter up with the minister of lands. Jim Grantham nodded emphatically, saying, "Yes, Douglas, it is a parliamentary matter." Colonel Vincent and I exchanged glances. I am sure he felt as I did: Grantham was grateful to pass the buck. It was a hot political issue in the making.

On our way back to the camp Mr. Mitchell talked about the lion spoor he had seen in Mkuze. "Denyer certainly wasn't pulling a long bow this time," he said, and he described the petrol drums that covered the spoor and the stories the game guards had told Singie Denyer.

That night I was pleased to be able to tell Nick Steele that the visit and inspection had been a success. I believed, too, that between Colonel Vincent and Douglas Mitchell, the government departments responsible for allowing the chaotic situation to develop and continue would be pressured and urged to take action.

It was perhaps fortunate at the time that we did not know three more years would have to pass before the government took action. By that time there were thousands of people in huts all along the edge of the western and southern boundaries. Police and a detachment of the navy had to be called in to remove the displaced people, but not before there had been a massive poaching raid on the reserve. This story has been told in Nick Steele's book *Game Ranger on Horseback* and in my book *The White Rhino Saga*.

We had much sympathy for the squatters. They were victims of overpopulation and internecine fighting in the Msinga valley, but we had to ensure the sanctity of the game reserve and the white rhino. We had a duty to the wild creatures. They too deserved a place in the sun. The only herds of white rhino left in southern Africa were in Mfolozi, and it was a heavy responsibility. There were nights when I could hardly sleep for worrying about the rhino. It would only take one cow infected with anthrax to come into the reserve, and the rhino could have been wiped out. I felt, too, that with the historical value of Mfolozi to the Zulu people and to the nation, we had to fight with every weapon to make sure the game reserve survived. I knew that it was here in the valleys of the Black and the White Mfolozi rivers that a spiritual understanding between man and the land could be renewed. I had already begun to plan the wilderness trails in my mind, but without the land we could do nothing.

After talking to Nick I had a report from a new learner ranger, Noel Mast, who had been on patrol in the Mcetshwanene area on the northern end of the Ukuku range with game guards from the Mbuzane outpost. They were experienced men with many years' service, but they had been shaken by a particularly nasty encounter. Over fifty poachers in one band were hunting warthog and reedbuck when they were surprised by Noel and the guards. Noel courageously tackled the gang, and with the help of the guards captured three poachers. A gang this big was far too much for our small forces and created a potentially serious situation.

Noel described the incident and said that there were men running all over the place, and at one stage he had found himself in the middle of them. I was alarmed because I knew how lucky he had been, and the game guards confirmed my fears.

"We were lucky today that no one was killed," they said. "We were right in among the poachers and one quick thrust with a spear would have meant the end of one of us."

This was a prelude to the trouble we were to have in this area for the next three years. Only a month later Magqubu and his son Ikonamangele Ntombela were attacked by a gang. Ikonamangele was stabbed, and when Magqubu went to his aid and grappled with a man twice his size, Magqubu's rifle went off and the poacher was shot dead. We all knew that it was only the removal of all the unfortunate squatters, and a good fence clearly demarcating the game reserve, that would bring an end to an explosive situation. It would be a long time in coming. Politicians and officials were slow to act.

The government was experimenting with social engineering and thousands of men, women, and children were forcibly removed from farms and other areas. Many of these people were dumped in the Tugela valley, which was already overpopulated and badly eroded. It is little wonder that they trekked toward Mfolozi and the adjoining vacant Crown lands. We were only too happy that they should be given land to settle on. Our requirements were minor in comparison, but without some of the high ground and land away from the rivers that could be fenced, Mfolozi was doomed. Government departments continued to dilly-dally.

The day after the board members left, fires broke out all along the Ukuku ridge and inside the game reserve on Mbulungu hills. We fought the fires well into the night, but large areas were burned out. Every day brought fresh troubles of some kind or another: poaching, fires, vehicle breakdowns, personality conflicts, and complaints from adjoining farmers about game damage.

The moon was in its last quarter when the lion left the Mkuze game reserve and made its way farther south. The lion had an uncanny knowledge of where to expect the most trouble. Instead of going due south from Mkuze game reserve and into the white-owned farmlands, it went east until it was on the edge of the Mkuze swamps, then turned south and wandered into tribal location no. 1, which included the Nibela, a long peninsula making up the northern bluff of False Bay in Lake St. Lucia.

News of the lion reached the native commissioner at Ubombo, after five head of cattle had been killed in as many nights. Some of the tribesmen claimed to have seen the lion, and others said their dogs had chased an *isilwane* (animal) that had a growl worse than any leopard. The cattle killing worried the local tribesmen, who reported what was happening to the native affairs commissioner in Ubombo. He considered it a Parks Board matter, although legally the lion was not on any game schedule. He phoned Peter Potter, the chief game conservator at Hluhluwe, who instructed my old friend from Ndumu, Ken Tinley, to go with the native affairs commissioner and "inspect the damage." We all used this phrase when we didn't know what to do. It had the effect of calming tempers and giving us time to consider what action to take.

Ken and the native commissioner were shown the remains of the dead cattle, and every footprint was pointed out to them. The job of the native commissioner was uncomplicated: he had to take the part of the tribesmen. Cattle had been killed, and the lion would have to be shot. That was the beginning and the end of his duties. For Ken Tinley it was different. We had lived with the Tonga people in Ndumu game reserve and other parts of Maputaland. From not liking them initially, we had grown to admire them and their ability to live in the heat and sand of a harsh environment. Debilitated by malaria and bilharzia, suffering from malnutrition and alcoholism, they were nevertheless cheerful. They would sing and dance at the drop of a hat and as a group their knowledge of the world of natural history was probably unequalled in Zululand. When crops failed, a frequent occurrence in Tongaland, they had to rely upon what they could gather from the land: wild honey, termites, caterpillars, grubs, water-lily bulbs, barbel, tilapia, eels, the fruit and nuts of the marula and the garcinia, monkeys, small antelope, shellfish along the coast, and the lala-palm wine. They were so close to the land that they knew instinctively where to go to survive.

The dead cattle and the obvious suffering this caused the local people concerned Ken, but he was a game ranger with a deep sense of loyalty to the wild creatures of Zululand. The game reserves were small. The big herds of game had been eliminated, and cattle had taken their place. The arrival of the lion was an exciting event. It was the first time since we had been in Zululand that a lion had come so far south. Ken studied the footprints, measuring them against his own big hands. He examined the dead cattle and noticed how the necks had been broken. He looked, too, at the black faces that surrounded him, watching every movement he made.

"Hau, inkulugabi le ingonyama" (A very big lion), he said.

The people echoed and repeated what he had said. Children, potbellied with flies around their eyes, sucked their fingers and stared at him. Food was hard to come by here. Ken wondered if there was a ghost of a chance of the lion surviving.

"I really wanted that lion to live. It epitomized the kind of freedom we all wanted," he confided to me later.

Wherever he and the native commissioner had gone there were *imizi* and people. No one patrolled the area, so it was full of snares. Every *muzi* had its quota of dogs: lean, mangy, half-starved animals relying on the scrapings of the three-legged pots and the occasional bones. They caught lizards, locusts, rats, and mice – anything to stay alive. They were excellent hunting animals. The absence of game except for the ubiquitous grey duiker was proof of their ability. How had the lion managed to escape detection from these hunters? Ken wondered about it and decided that the smell of lion might have acted as a deterrent. If their masters had set them on anything they would not have hesitated for an instant. They were loyal to their owners and would die for them. Ken solved his dilemma by promising that he would recommend compensation for the cattle killed. Later he told me that he had been astounded by the size of the cattle the lion had tackled and the ease with which it had killed them.

"That spoor is big, man. I felt the hair rising on the back of my neck, That lion is a special lion, but I'm afraid someone will kill it. I don't know how it has escaped so far," he said.

The newspapers phoned the native commissioner, who said, "The massive spoor and the claw marks on the dead cattle indicate that it is an old lion. The marks show that the claws are blunt and cannot penetrate the flesh properly. It is evidently a fussy old brute with a sweet tooth and prefers the soft meat of cattle to the tougher flesh of buck and other game. Anyway, the old fellow is probably too slow to tackle game." He didn't know what he was talking about.

Ken, obeying orders, had nothing to say to the press, but Nick van Niekerk, the warden at False Bay, talked quite cheerfully. Nick was an excellent ranger and a disciplined man. He had left a responsible job as a mine captain to take a very low-paid position in conservation. He obeyed instructions, but if they were silly orders he ignored them, and he saw no harm in telling the press what he thought.

"The tribal people are worried about their stock because they are so tame," he said. He commented on how easily the cattle had been stalked, and in each case the neck was broken. No doubt sensing the reporter's wish for more dramatic comment, he said, "The lion is probably an old chap that has been turned out by his pride. These wanderers are dangerous and often become man-eaters." I have no doubt he smiled broadly and chuckled over it when having his nightly brandy with his wife.

Colonel Vincent was telephoned by the reporter. He could, as the director, make any statement he liked. He said that no lion had actually been seen in Zululand since the war, although spoor had once been reported. He repeated that the last lions killed in the Mkuze area were shot by air force personnel stationed in Zululand during the war.

The press asked the farmers, who said it was the same lion whose spoor had been seen in the Mkuze game reserve.

"They are no doubt psychic," Ken Tinley said sarcastically.

Farmers raised a hue-and-cry and told anyone who would listen that the lion – now termed a marauder – was a danger to the community.

"It has got to be shot. The locals are very nervous about their stock, which is tame and easily stalked. There is also a risk that the lion will take a human next," a Mr. van Rooyen was reported to have said.

The hypocrisy left Nick Steele, Ken Tinley, and me breathless. We thought we had grown inured to the attitudes of some of the Zululand stock farmers. They believed the world owed them a living. They were on government-owned land for which they paid a minimum rent and then put twice as many cattle on the land as it could hold, but this situation never bothered their consciences. Their pious concern toward the local tribal people was hypocritical. The fact of the matter was that this was a chance for a grand hunt in the guise of helping the blacks, saving cattle, and possibly saving a human victim. The law was on their side. The native commissioner authorized a hunt, and if the lion ran onto one of the farms, it would be shot.

Soon a posse gathered, armed to the teeth with rifles modern and ancient. They careered around in Jeeps, Land-Rovers, and trucks, ready to shoot anything that moved. The lion was only the excuse. Signposts, tins, or bottles on the side of the road and any antelope that dared show its body were shot at. There was nothing we could do except pray, but there was little danger to the lion while the hunting was conducted in this fashion. Anything within a radius of two miles would have fled from the din.

What is it in man that is afraid of or rebels at anything wild? No supposedly civilized country has escaped the mass killing of wild animals. The bison in America and Canada, and the game herds in Africa were decimated by white pioneers. Bushmen, Maoris, or Aborigines were hunted, too, because they were wild. The so-called lion hunt that we saw taking place in Zululand had its origins in the dusty recesses of the human mind. There were among the group some decent people, but they were caught up in the blood lust. To them this was a wild and dangerous lion, a cattle thief and potential killer. It had to be killed. The police were there too, turning a blind eye to blatant transgressions such as shooting from a vehicle on a road. The lion had become an obsession that was fed by rumours. The newspapers faithfully reported every move, and there was no shortage of farmers prepared to make a statement. "Marauding Lion Worries Zululand Farmers" was one headline. Others read "Zululand Lion Hunt On"; "Old Lion Roams Native Reserve, Killing Cattle in St. Lucia Area"; and "Zululand Lion Away Again."

The good thing about the publicity was that it had drawn attention, as

Singie Denyer had hoped, to the Mkuze game reserve. Keith Cooper, at that time employed by a bank in Mtubatuba but later to become director of conservation in the Wildlife Society of Southern Africa, wrote a very strong letter to the *Natal Mercury* asking for more support for the Mkuze reserve. It could not have come at a better moment.

The lion moved farther south and killed a beast on the farm of T.E. Harrison at Palm Ridge, slightly north of Mtubatuba. The new kill was more than forty miles from the last known kill in the Nibela and False Bay area. It was possible that other cattle had been killed in the tribal area, which the Africans had not bothered to report. There was hardly any purpose in their walking miles to report a death when they knew that the lion had moved into a white farming area. They probably hoped that the white ranchers' cattle would prove to be a greater attraction than their own.

The press were having a field day, and we were delighted. One farmer made a long statement. He said he "would lie up near the kill during the night in case the lion returned, but it was a risky game as it might tackle a man next." He said he was sure it was the same lion because of the lack of deep claw marks on the carcass. "A large part of the kill had been eaten, which showed that it had not fed for a long time. Its last attack took place a week ago," the farmer said.

Other local farmers complained that they were worried about the situation because of the danger to their cattle and because their workers were turning up late because they refused to walk in the dark with a lion about. There was a lot of laughter among the Mfolozi game-guard force when I told them what I had read in the paper about people turning up late for work. "It was too good an excuse to be missed," the guards said.

The chairman of the Hluhluwe Farmers' Association made arrangements for another hunt. The newspaper said that thirty farmers and their staff would take part. "We do not expect the lion to move any farther south and have a good idea which direction he took. With luck we should be able to shoot him," the chairman said.

He was wrong on all counts. The lion did go farther south, but they had no idea in which direction it had gone and they never fired a shot, to our great joy.

One evening it was reported to us that the lion had been seen lying up on the edge of the Dukuduku forest, not far from Mtubatuba. We now had to take action because someone would see it, and the posse that had been organized would kill it. I sent Nick into Mtubatuba and told him to phone me and say the lion had been seen near Mtunzini in a sugarcane field. I could hear the phone being picked up along the line and people listening, as usual; the giveaway was all the background sounds. The plan had worked. A posse went roaring off to Mtunzini, and a donkey was shot as it came out of a canefield. That night the lion walked on the outskirts of Mtubatuba and headed west toward the Mfolozi game reserve. We kept abreast of its movements from tribesmen who had seen the spoor. Then one afternoon Magqubu and Masuku Mzwabantu told us that the spoor had been seen on the old Gome road. Nkosi – the Chief – had come home. What a journey it had been for this magnificent animal.

Six months later, one early morning, we heard it roar for the first time. It finally felt safe.

In July 1963 Metro-Goldwyn-Mayer were making a feature film called *Rhino*. One of the local stuntmen brought a lioness and secretly released her into the park. She turned out to be from either a circus or a zoo. A few nights later she appeared at Nick Steele's house at Gome. She was so hungry she began eating the laundry on the veranda. Nick had to shoot her.

In March 1965, lionesses there were darted with tranquillizers by Ken Rochat in collusion with rangers in the Kruger National Park . Giraffe were then brought into Mfolozi to provide cover for the entry of the lionesses. Ken Rochal, a taciturn man, told in his quiet, dry way how on the way back to Zululand the lionesses began to recover from the drugs. He stopped at a petrol station, and one of the attendants asked what the noise was. Ken said, "Lions." The attendant laughed, so Ken said, "Have a look." The man stuck his head into the back, and staring at him was a huge mature lioness.

John Clark, the ranger in charge of the rhino *bomas*, relates how he looked after one lioness while she was settling down. He fed her in her crate for two days, and on the third he found she had torn apart the tough Oregon pine planks and had escaped. He could hear her calls being responded to by Nkosi, the male who, John said, was "roaring on the run." Two more lionesses and three cubs were brought into Mfolozi. One cub had its back broken by a buffalo and died, but the survivors met up with Nkosi at the junction of the Mpafa and the White Mfolozi rivers. John Clark said you could not have put a hand down without touching a lion spoor, so frenetic was their mating. Any human bumping into the group on that day would have been killed.

So Nkosi's long and lonely six-year vigil was rewarded with three beautiful females. Another saga and circle of life had begun. The lions had come home, and the rangers protected them with a pride as fierce as any lion's.

12

Journey to the Snake

My plans for establishing wilderness trails in Mfolozi had received official approval, and Magqubu and I now needed to find the right places to establish the tented camps. October is always a hot month, and yet even in the burning heat there is a beauty about the Mfolozi landscape.

With my dog Lancer we set out from the Mpila hill past the game-guard barracks with the open parade ground and walked to the top of Momfu, the krantz that overlooked the White Mfolozi River. We stopped for a rest, and I lay on a warm rock looking at one of the most spectacular bushveld views in southern Africa. Many profound changes to the landscape had occurred because all the people who lived there in the 1890s and early 1900s were either driven away by the tsetse fly or rinderpest, or killed in internecine wars, or had been removed by government decree. Human action, more than anything else, had been responsible for keeping the grasslands open. I could see Nqabaneni hill, where old *imizi* sites were being encroached upon by the invading bush.

The sun was hot, and the mass of acacia trees in full bloom shimmered in the heat. The scent was overpowering. Dark-green sycamore figs lined the banks, remnants of the 1957 flood that swept away huge groves and changed part of the face of the landscape. The growing population of humans, cattle, sheep, and goats surrounding the game reserve had begun to take a toll on the land. The thunderstorms in the hinterland pounded the bare earth, carrying off thousands of tons of dark alluvial soil. There was no grass barrier to prevent the waters flooding down the hills and sweeping away everything in their path. I lay looking down on the river winding its way through the white and golden sand and I remembered Hugh Dent's description of the fig trees uprooted as though they were saplings, "Taken away like matchsticks," and swept downstream on the waves of rolling dark water. I visited him a day after the main storm and remembered the sound of the water filling every little watercourse. In the game reserve, where there was an abundance of grass and tree cover, there was little soil loss, and I recalled the cleanness of the water. The difference between inside and outside the game reserve could not have been more clearly marked.

"Asihambe," Magqubu said, shouldering his army surplus haversack, his khaki overcoat bound around it. I was reluctant to move because the view kept changing with the light, and down below a troop of baboons played like children on the sands. They chased one another screaming and yelling into the shallow water, then out to the trees, the youngest racing ahead with their loping running action.

"Mfowethu" (Our brothers), Magqubu grunted. He sang a little song, then danced in a circle, his legs moving in a slow rhythm. "Woza," he sang, and began leading the way down a narrow path along the western edge of Momfu cliff. Soon we were clambering like baboons, hanging on to branches as we slid down the steep slope. The path ended at a ledge, and we walked along it to the entrance of a big overhang.

I glanced about the cave and thought that this would be a good place to sleep overnight for the people who were on trail. But when I looked at the end of the cave there was something odd about it and, looking more closely, I noticed a wall. It seemed out of place. I said to Magqubu, "There is something wrong here, why have the people built a wall?"

My curiosity was aroused, so in the gloom and the semi-darkness we crawled forward and I started to remove the stones blocking up the back end of the cave. I pulled them out one by one, wanting to know what lay behind the wall that had been so carefully laid. I pulled the rocks away and saw ancient Stone Age implements on the floor of the cave. I picked them up, wondering what the people were like who once had had them in their hands. Eventually I removed the wall.

"Hau. Ini lokho?" (What is this?) Magqubu exclaimed.

There on the rocky floor lay a perfectly preserved human skeleton. I put my hand in and grasped the skull. The bone was whitened by age, and I held it in the light to examine it. Magqubu sat next to me and pointed to the back of the skull. His keen eyes had spotted a hole. Someone had killed this person by bashing his head with a knobkierie stick.

Magqubu was an expert on anatomy. He looked very carefully at it, and I asked him, "Magqubu, how old do you think this is, how many years?" It didn't take him long to answer, "This was a boy of about sixteen."

Who had killed him and why had he been killed? How long ago was it? These were the questions I asked Magqubu, and he could not answer. Perhaps it was because they needed *muti*. It could have been in the time of the tsetse-fly campaign, which would account for his being in the cave and walled up: someone had murdered him. On the other hand, it might have happened long before that, in the time of the Shaka and Zwide wars, but why had the people put the body behind a wall and built it up? The more he deliberated the more Magqubu became convinced that this was a boy who had been murdered for medicinal purposes in the time of the *nagana*.

We took out every piece of the skeleton, and Magqubu started to put it together – the finger bones, the bones of the thigh and the knee – until he had it laid out on the ground. I asked him what he thought we should do, and he said, "Why don't you just put it back and build up the wall and leave it?"

I thought that this was perhaps a more recent murder, and I decided that when I got back I would call the police, and I did.

A sergeant from Kwambonambi arrived at Mpila a day later. He was disenchanted when he found that he had to walk from Mpila to the cave at Momfu. It was a hot day, but he plodded along with us, sweating heavily. We took a sack and put all the bones in it. The skull was last to go. I picked it up, and with a Shakespearian pose and accent said, "Alas, poor Yorick. I knew him well, Horatio." The policeman looked at me in absolute surprise and said dubiously, "He's been dead a helluva long time."

Magqubu and I left the cave and climbed down to where the Mpafa stream runs into the White Mfolozi River. It was a dry riverbed but the sands were full of spoor, and Magqubu with one quick glance knew all the animals that had been there. He was about to walk off but I called him back and said, "No, Magqubu, just tell me what has been here, and what is the story."

He looked at the spoor and said, "Well, there've been impala here and nyala, and the waterbuck have come down, and then there is *icamu* [monitor lizard]." Bending down, he pointed at a spoor where claw marks and a tail had dragged along the sand. Then he pointed at the *ufudu*, the tortoise tracks, and at the tracks of another monitor lizard that had crossed over the dry sand to drink at a pool in the shadow of phragmites reeds. In the corner alongside a bank a leopard had walked to the same pool. In a few minutes Magqubu was able not only to read but to explain which animals and birds and reptiles had been down to drink at this small pool.

We left the maze of tracks and walked along a sandy, well-beaten rhino path that followed the bank and went into the tall trees. The reflected heat made me thirsty, but I knew that if I succumbed to the temptation to drink I would suffer for the rest of the day. Magqubu strode on, the backpack bouncing slightly on his broad shoulders. A flock of hadeda ibis, the green on their wings shining brightly in the glaring sunlight, took off in front of us. Their harsh screaming call alerted a black rhino, and I heard the powerful high-pitched snort of this dramatic beast. A surge of adrenalin drove away my fatigue, and I looked anxiously for a suitable tree to climb.

Magqubu kept walking, not even stopping to look up.

"Did you hear *ubejane*?" I asked.

"Yes," he grunted.

"Well, shouldn't we take care?"

"No," Magqubu said. "The birds have warned him about us."

I heard the animal crashing around in the euclea bushes on our right. I loosened my backpack straps and was ready to run. Magqubu looked back and saw my movements. He laughed.

"*Ubejane* is running away," he said. His acute hearing told him exactly where the rhino intended to go. The sound of the body hitting branches, vibrations from its feet on the ground, its breathing and snorting, the wind direction, bird sounds, and other even more subtle signs, as well as his highly tuned intuition enabled him to know exactly what the animal was doing. He pointed to branches that had been browsed, and dung full of little sticks. There were deep scrape marks in the sand.

"This *ubejane* lives here. It is his home," Magqubu said, pointing out the difference between the black rhino and the white rhino spoor. For Magqubu it was like reading a map, and once he had grasped the main points, he knew the animal's movements. His grasp was a holistic one, mine was of individual details. I could not, as he could, rise above the land like a bird and see it all laid out below me.

"*Ubejane* knows we are here," Magqubu repeated. He stomped around, making the sharp snortlike sounds of the black rhino. My dog Lancer lay on the sand, his tongue lolling out and saliva dripping everywhere. "He wants water," Magqubu said. I called Lancer and took him to the White Mfolozi, where he drank, lapping loudly. I fought hard against the temptation to drink. Magqubu squatted in the shade of a tree and watched us. "Donsa, Donsa," he said softly, his name for Lancer. Magqubu was not particularly fond of dogs, but he tolerated Lancer.

We walked slowly for another half-hour to Mahobosheni, The Place of the Puffadder, the name given to this particular bend in the river. Steep cliffs, dark now with shadows in their clefts, rose up on the other bank. Redwing starlings called, and the mocking chat imitated their soft cries. A Natal robin followed the mocking bird, and a small predatory bird swooped from a rocky ledge and flew with great speed downstream. Afternoon was upon us, and I was glad to hear Magqubu say we should sleep the night beneath a big sycamore fig tree. It had been a hot day and I needed a cooling swim.

I stripped, and Lancer followed me to the river where it ran most deeply, below the cliffs. His barking startled a bushbuck, which ran, then stopped to peer at us from behind some foliage. The peace of the late afternoon descended over the land, and I became aware of the change of colours on the leaves of some of the trees, and the change in the atmosphere of the surrounding hills. The three of us were alone in a small remnant of the once vast wildness of Zululand. There were no other extraneous sounds or sights of so-called civilization. We had all this to ourselves, and the warmth of the land, its shapes and contours, seemed to well up enough to dwarf and overwhelm us. Magqubu for me was a link with the ancient spirit of this place. He knew and understood it from a Zulu perspective. I thought and felt it too, but more from Stone Age man's existence and that of the Bushmen. Stone artefacts were everywhere. Our early ancestors had loved this place for its abundance of game, wild fruits, and tubers. The climate was benign, too. I wondered about their pattern of life and imagined them gathering around the fire to talk over the hardships of the day and the fear of the night.

Magqubu, never idle, scraped away the fallen leaves, and we laid out our overcoats. He made a fire – a few sticks, leaves, some dry grass, and one match and the fire was blazing. Later he picked up *umThombothi* logs, put them on the fire, and kept some in reserve. We were ready for the night. Lancer lay next to me, waiting for his food. Magqubu took his pot, went down to the river, dug a hole in the White Mfolozi to allow clean water to filter through the sand, came back, and started to cook *puthu* for the two of us and the dog. The wooden spoon clanked against the iron, and I heard a baboon across the river grunt at the intrusive noise.

When it was dark and I could see the Southern Cross shining in the sky, Magqubu started to talk about the *umKhiwane*, the fig tree we were lying under. He called it *siza abantu*, the tree that helps the people, and he told me that in earlier days when people were starving they came down to the river, collected the figs from the *Ficus sycamorus* and crushed them on the same stones that they used to grind the mielies. Then they laid the crushed figs out in the sun and, when they were really dried, mixed them with *amasi*, finally adding it to their porridge.

"I know this tree well," Magqubu said, pointing upward to the trunk and canopy. "In 1914 I camped under here with Mfohloza" (the Zulu name of Vaughan Kirby). Magqubu told me how he had walked to Mahlabatini, where the game conservator had his office, and waited for Vaughan Kirby, who arrived on a motorbike. From his description it sounded like a Harley Davidson, which Vaughan Kirby rode while Magqubu walked, carrying the camping kit with Mali Mdhletshe, to the Mtunzini hills, where they would leave the motorbike and walk over the top of Ngqolothi, following the course of the White Mfolozi past Itshentega and Nqabaneni to Mahobosheni and this fig tree. Here they would camp for the night.

Magqubu stirred the porridge, scraping the spoon against the rim of the pot and singing quietly to himself, "Siza abantu, siza abantu." He allowed scraps of the porridge to fall on the ground near the fire: food for ancestral spirits, a ritual he never omitted.

A loud snort shattered the peace of the evening. Lancer was on his feet instantly and ran forward, barking. Magqubu shouted "Suka, ubejane," but we heard it coming and we ran for the nearest and easiest branches to climb. Lancer rushed off into the darkness, snarling, growling, and barking in excited yaps. I heard the pounding of the rhino's feet and Magqubu yelled again, "Yeka inja" (Leave the dog). Lancer was far too quick for the black rhino. He had been with me for six years, so he understood the bush. Only at Ndumu in 1954 was there a bad incident, when he was trapped on an island after plunging through the Pongolo River in pursuit of baboons. They attacked him, ripping his shoulder and his stomach open. It was a lesson he would never forget, and he had learned to stay out of range.

I heard the black rhino exhale a long burst of air, and Lancer was barking again. The rhino must have charged him, because we heard Lancer's barking coming from different directions and a short yelp when he probably got too close. Magqubu kept up a barrage of verbal attack on the rhino. "Xosha, Donsa, xosha" (Chase him, Lancer, chase him), he shouted.

It was a strange scene, with us sitting on a limb of the great fig tree, the firelight shimmering on the trunk and reaching into the darkness. Only our ears could tell us what was happening. I think the rhino was becoming confused. We were shouting and Lancer was worrying at it from all directions. We were perfectly safe, and the rhino had every reason to be angry. We had invaded its space, but it had its revenge by giving us a big fright. Lancer came trotting back and stood at the foot of the tree, looking at us quizzically. There was no sound of the rhino, but I could smell it, so it must have been close. Magqubu laughed as he climbed down the branch, saying, "Siza abantu, siza abantu, the tree that helps the people." Honour was satisfied: the rhino had treed us.

We settled down near the fire, gave Lancer an extra dollop of *puthu*, which he swallowed in two mouthfuls and then he looked anxiously for more.

We sat talking at the fire. Hyena were calling from the surrounding hills, their whooping echoing among the *umThombothi* woodlands and down the kloofs from Gome and Tsojkwane hills. The fire crackled, and Magqubu scraped the *puthu* remains from his little three-legged pot, filled it with water, waited until it boiled, and carefully washed it out. This too was a ritual he never failed to follow, no matter how far we had walked or how tired he might be. The pot had almost become part of him, and in the years ahead we had some hellish rows about it. Needless to say, he inevitably won.

This night with the black rhino incident animated Magqubu, and he started to describe early days in the reserve. He had just begun when there was a strange sound from the reeds on the riverbank. Magqubu grew silent and cocked his head. He listened intently. "Ini?" (What is it?) I asked. The sound was a quick pattering, then silence. The reeds were moving but so faintly it could have been the wind. Lancer sat up sniffing the air and a growl began in his throat. Magqubu put his finger on his mouth and indicated I should silence Lancer. I grabbed his collar and tapped his nose. The ridge on his back had risen, the brown and black hairs standing up stiffly.

Magqubu put his ear closer to the ground, and I heard the quick *pat-pat, pat-pat* sound again. It was staccato, like someone playing a game of quick clap-hands, as we did when we were children. In the firelight I saw Magqubu's face relax, and he smiled. He whispered to me, "Ingwe" (Leopard).

I looked at him in astonishment, and he laughed out loud. Lancer was now agitated, and he barked in a menacing way. He had picked up the scent, and he reacted to the old animosity between cat and dog. Now the noise had stopped. Magqubu indicated with his hands and arm that the animal had moved off.

"How do you know it is a leopard?" I asked.

Magqubu shook his head in a gesture of mild amusement. "I know it is a leopard," he said firmly. Then he stood up and demonstrated what had happened.

The leopard had been in the bed of phragmites reeds hunting big cane

rats, delicious eating for all predatory animals, including humans. The pattering sound we heard was the leopard beating its paws in quick succession on the ground, like a man making quick taps on a drum. The noise frightened the cane rats out of their hiding places, and once they were in the open the leopard pounced. Magqubu had worked out from the sounds what had happened in the darkness.

The hyena began screaming, giggling, and laughing in their maniacal way. It is a chilling sound that gives one gooseflesh and a prickling of the hair on the back of the neck. Other hyena answered from the hills, and one big animal padded along the rhino path below us. I walked to the edge of the camp and peered into the night and saw its long sloping back and big head silhouetted in the faint beams of the moon. It began calling, the long, deep reverberating *whooooop* cry. The noise was so close to me that my sternum seemed to rattle and my whole body was filled with the vibrations of the sound. There was a quickening of fear in my blood and, as the noise died down, I could hear my heart thumping. Yet it is a conversely thrilling sound, and one is caught in conflicting emotions when hearing it. The hyena are part of Africa and, in their way, much more exciting than the white wolves of the Arctic.

We sat near the fire, Lancer spread out next to me, his warm colouring glowing in the firelight, his beautiful luminous eyes reflecting the flames. What a wonderful companion he had been to me and how he had put up with all my bad moods, irritability, and loneliness when I was transferred to Ndumu game reserve in 1954. I used to talk to him as to a human being. I knew he would have died for me without a moment's hesitation and I loved him dearly.

Magqubu put another *umThombothi* log on the fire, and the black pungent smoke spiralled up into the darkness, its heavy scent penetrating everywhere.

When the fire had died down, Magqubu gathered small twigs and a handful of sticks, carefully placed them on the *umThombothi*, got on his knees, blew at exactly the right angle, and in seconds the sticks had burst into flame. He moved the *umThombothi* log, which had burnt into two separate pieces, on to the sticks. Oil oozed out of it, and it burst into flame too.

"UmThombothi," Magqubu said in a tone of deep appreciation. I knew what he meant. In the bushveld it was a godsend when you were camping because it burned well for such a long time. A few coals under a three-legged pot were enough to cook a good dinner, and the heat could easily be regulated by removing or adding coals. In the middle of a thunderstorm it was possible to get a fire going using small pieces of *umThombothi* placed in a wigwam shape with a raincoat held over it, and with a few matches the *umThombothi* caught fire. By slowly adding more strips of *umThombothi* the fire was built up. I had to do this many times in the early patrols in Mkuze, Ndumu, and Mfolozi game reserves.

Magqubu began telling stories about men who were unaware that cooking where *umThombothi* smoke touched the food caused terrible diarrhoea. He acted out the gurgling sounds in the stomach, the effect of the shooting pains, and the simultaneous retching and defecating. He pantomimed the careless person not watching where the smoke was going, and talking away instead of concentrating, then eating the food, a pained look coming over the face, then the clutching of the stomach and all the different sounds, the running into the bush, hastily pulling the trousers down, and the noise of the splatter of diarrhoea hitting the ground. He was by now convulsed with laughter at his own story. He wiped his eyes, then laughed again when he mentioned names and described the characters of the people he had seen suffer these indignities. To him it was as good as a movie.

I kept quiet because I had been caught myself many years before. I knew those shooting pains in the stomach and the feeling of the bowels giving way, the groaning when there was nothing left to either puke or shit. My mouth had been burned too because I had eaten a potato that I thought was safe because it had been wrapped in foil, but the *umThombothi* had penetrated right through and contaminated the whole potato. I should have known after the burning sensation with the first bite, but I was extremely hungry, having had no food all day. It was a painful and embarrassing experience and a lesson well learned. Magqubu's act was real.

In earlier days in Zululand scores were sometimes settled with a handful of dry black rhino dung. Magqubu described men at a beer drink – laughing, talking, shouting and singing, and slowly becoming intoxicated. An enemy was identified. The opponent, with a pocketful of dried black rhino dung containing small sticks of *umThombothi*, because the black rhino likes the tree, sat next to the marked man.

"Say Mthembu wants to kill Ntuli and not be caught: he slips the rhino dung into Ntuli's *khamba*," Magqubu said, imitating Ntuli sitting and swaying, talking, laughing, and gesticulating while Mthembu edges closer and closer, bluffing that he, too, is drunk. At the critical moment, when Ntuli is not looking, the rhino dung is added to the beer together with a poisonous plant. Mthembu then slowly moves away and watches Ntuli from a distance. Ntuli drinks more beer and becomes more and more intoxicated, and as the poisons begin to take effect he clutches at his stomach, rolls in agony on the ground, and tries to call out, but the words die in his throat. Hours later he becomes unconscious. The men at the beer drink think he has collapsed in a drunken stupor and they take no notice. In the morning he is dead.

"There are many other poisons even more effective than *umThombothi*," Magqubu said. He knew them and how long you would live once the poison entered your system.

A bushbuck barked on the other side of the river. The towering Ncoki krantz acted as an amphitheatre, and the sound was magnified. From a prone position and fast asleep, Lancer was on his feet instantly with a low growling that rumbled in his throat. I patted him, calming him. The bark is so similar to a dog's that Lancer thought there was an enemy about. He lay down with a sigh, putting his head on my lap, and I stroked his velvety soft ears.

Bullfrogs sang in unison. The earth was parched after the dry season, and it waited for the rain. Streams that were in raging flood in May 1957 were now dry sandy beds. But this was the natural law of this part of Zululand. What most people described as a drought was merely another cycle. Mfolozi had an average of twenty inches of rain a year, whereas Hluhluwe game reserve, twenty miles to the north, had over thirty inches, and the forests along the high ridges, like the Uvive, were lush.

I put the billy back on the fire to boil more water for tea. I was thirsty again. Magqubu looked at me with amusement. He had had his quota of liquid and needed nothing until the morning.

I never ceased to be impressed by the bravery of the guards. When I had taken over Mfolozi game reserve we were using Lee Enfield .303s, and they were in short supply. Only one rifle was available for each outpost, and the senior man, a corporal, carried it. The other guards were each armed with a spear and knobkieries, no match for an opponent armed with a firearm, and such assailants were on the increase. Some of the local white farmers complained about our arming the game guards and reported the matter to their local member of parliament and the provincial councillor in the Vryheid district, a National Party stronghold. One of them had been to see me, demanding to know what our legal rights were. Fortunately, we were covered in the provincial ordinances, so I politely told him to go to hell.

Sitting near the fire in the secluded area of Mahobosheni gave me time to think, to plan, and to look to the future of the game reserve. There were many priorities to be tackled: more game guards, firearms, better living conditions for all the Zulu staff. Tourists in motorcars would be allowed in soon; the roads needed upgrading; and we had to get wilderness trails started.

The fire had died down to a glow. Magqubu dragged a log of sycamore fig while I fetched some small sticks and a thick branch of an *umThombothi* tree. The scent of the two species of wood blended to a sweet fragrance in the evening air when they burst into flame. Lancer woke up and lifted his head quizzically, as though asking if we were about to walk again. I patted him and said, "Go back to sleep." Magqubu and I went to our respective places under the fig tree, rolled into our ex-army overcoats, and were soon asleep.

Dawn spread over the land and a rumbling growl from Lancer woke me. Magqubu made a *tsk tsk tsk* sound, a noise that, strangely enough, did not frighten animals. He pointed with a crooked index finger toward the river. Three mature white rhino followed by two big warthogs were walking along the rhino path. They plunged down a bank, white sand spraying in all directions, the small grains caught for an instant in the soft early morning sunlight. We were perfectly camouflaged in the dense shade of the giant sycamore fig tree. I held Lancer's collar and tapped him on the head, a sign he knew meant that he had to keep quiet. There was no wind, and the dew had obliterated our scent from the sands when we had collected water in the evening. We were apart, and yet also part, for a brief time, of the animal world.

I glanced at Magqubu. He was staring at the animals in a way I had already grown to know well. His eyes acted like a camera: no detail was missed, and all the information was stored for future use. Some red-billed oxpeckers appeared from nowhere and swooped onto the backs and necks of the rhino and then moved up and down in their quick movements, churring loudly, but it was not their warning call.

The sun climbed higher, and more light caught the tops of the *Acacia robusta*, the sweet smell of their remaining flowers lingering in the still morning air. The three rhino padded toward the water flowing beneath the steep cliffs. With their heads close to the ground they stopped periodically

to smell something on the sand, and one rhino snorted loudly, the sound striking the cliffs and echoing upstream. The oxpeckers took off churring loudly, in alarm, and alighted on the warthog, which were standing with drooped heads, absorbing the morning sun. Through my binoculars I could see a cluster of ticks near the anus of one warthog: the oxpeckers hovered and in quick pecking movements de-ticked the warthog. The birds wiped their beaks on the warthog's hide, rested awhile facing the sun, then flew to the rhino and stayed on their backs while the rhino drank. The sound of rhino sucking up the water was magnified by the rocks of the Ncoki krantz.

The vulnerability of the animal was touching. Humans were now the only dangerous predators of these prehistoric beasts, but paradoxically they were dependent upon us for their survival. Since 1895 their future had been in the hands of men like Vaughan Kirby, who fought against great odds to ensure that they remained part of the wild animal heritage of southern Africa. He deliberately underestimated their numbers because he knew that the lower the number, the greater would be the concern for their safety. He understood only too well that without the white rhino, Mfolozi game reserve would soon cease to exist. The white rhino were the aces in the pack, and had remained so until this day. The responsibility of the earlier conservators had been firmly placed in my hands.

My first impression of the white rhino, apart from its ancient appearance, on the misty day that I saw it was associated with a personal identification in its rejection. Here was a beast that once roamed in tens of thousands in southern Africa, then was ruthlessly slaughtered to the brink of extinction. In fact, it had been thought to be extinct. Some part of me had felt rejected by the world; life had placed me in a position where I had to swim upstream. So I believed the rhino's plight was my plight. I knew that without the rhino, Mfolozi would not survive.

We sat watching the peaceful scene of the rhino and the warthog as the hot Zululand sun appeared above the line of krantzes. The acacia and *Euphorbia tyrucalli* trees were clearly outlined, and I knew that anyone living in a city in South Africa or the rest of the world and experiencing this would be touched. A flight of trumpeter hornbills with their long, wailing cries flew overhead. The noise startled the warthog, and they ran up the bank, then stood still, listening with their heads near the ground. The rhino lifted their heads, but the oxpeckers gave no alarm calls, so they stood drowsily content near the water's edge, their tails swishing and their bodies shuddering periodically when the heavy cluster of flies on their shoulders caused discomfort.

The dawn of this new day, with the white rhino, oxpeckers, warthog, and trumpeter hornbills, the light on the trees and the grass, the scent of the fire, the river, the dust and the reeds, was about to deliver a new experience that would become perhaps the greatest step I had yet taken on my outer and inner journeys.

13

The Snake Rises

A gust of wind swirled above us, carrying our scent to the drinking rhino. They whirled about to form a star, backside to backside, in a 360° defensive position. Large ears moved sideways, listening intently for a sound. The warthog took off and disappeared into the *umThombothi* woodland. Their running was too much for Lancer, and he lunged forward, yelping with excitement. I had to stand up to restrain him, and the oxpeckers saw me and started churring frantically, then flew off. The three rhino ran in their fast trotting motion, tails erect. They crossed the river with loud splashing, reached the other bank, and followed the rhino path that went along the contour, then up behind the Ncoki krantz. I could hear their thudding feet on the hard ground for some distance; then it grew quiet.

We ate our breakfast of *puthu* sprinkled with sugar, made coffee, rolled our army coats into a bundle, tied them onto the old backpacks, and Magqubu said, "Asihambe." Time to move.

The heat of the October morning was already shimmering over the bush, and I could feel it burning through the back of my khaki shirt. We crossed the river at the narrowest and deepest point, where the rhino had run. The coolness of the water was refreshing and the thought of stripping and lying in it all day and getting Magqubu to tell stories was tempting. But we had to explore other potential wilderness-trail camping sites, and there was my wife and our six-month-old son at Mpila, to say nothing of piles of reports, pay sheets, and other administrative chores.

From my childhood, rivers had fascinated me, and from 1950 and my exploratory journey down the 110 river miles of the Msunduzi at Pietermaritzburg to the Mgeni in Durban, I was aware of a mystical attraction to these arteries of the land. It sounded trite but was nevertheless true that every time you crossed a river you were a different person. As one gets older, dreams of crossing rivers become more frequent, the last one being the Styx of the ancient Greeks: "O ferryman of souls, beware lest thou be left on the wrong shore" (Robert Johnson).

African rivers where crocodiles lurk have a special atmosphere, and I was

always filled with the sense of pioneering something new when I crossed one. Sheer romanticism perhaps, but it had been this way in Mfolozi from the time I began working there. Perhaps rivers were such formidable barriers to our early ancestors that we have inherited their combined feelings toward them, of fear, love, and admiration. For me today was no exception, and, as we reached the rhino path on the other bank, clambered out, and put on our socks and boots, I was filled with exhilaration. What lay in front of us was a mystery, and anything could happen.

Lancer hung back, running up and down in the water, and lapping when he stopped. I whistled and he ran to me, taking up his normal position at my heels, his pink tongue lolling. Magqubu walked ahead, his stocky body and powerful legs moving with ease as we left the now silent cliffs behind us and steadily climbed the rhino path heading eastward. Magqubu's knowledge of the paths of Mfolozi was unparalleled. He knew every twist and connecting path. When I wanted to follow a well-defined path he shook his head and said it would peter out in five hundred yards. I said it was impossible. He shrugged his shoulders and continued along the path, and almost on the five-hundred-yard mark the clearly defined path vanished into a tangle of scrub and disappeared. I became irritable because of my stubbornness, and he smiled, which made me more angry. He turned right and walked over the veld until he found a faint path made by antelope and warthog. The path gradually became clearer and soon was a broad rhino path following the land's contours and leading down to the river again to cross below Esiwasamanqe.

We rested in the shade to take our boots and socks off, and Magqubu told me how all his life he had walked over the Mfolozi paths, first illegally as a boy poaching, then with the old game guards, Mali and Mankenke Mdhletshe, and during the tsetse-fly campaign he accompanied the paymaster Willie Foster to every one of the tsetse-fly camps. This stopped my arguing, but I was miffed. He passed it off by telling me we should sit and watch the vultures, which would soon be coming.

He asked the time.

"Ten o'clock'" I said.

"One hour, one hour," he said in English.

"How the hell do you know, Magqubu?" I asked, again somewhat irritated by his certainty. He patiently explained how for over forty years he had tramped over this land, and the vultures came to bathe at the heat of the day. I knew he was right, and I was arguing for the sake of arguing. I had come to these cliffs with Ken Tinley when we followed the river from Nqabaneni in 1955. We had arrived at midday and seen the vultures, the crows, and a bateleur eagle bathing, then resting on the sands with outstretched wings drying in the sun.

Presently, as Magqubu had predicted, vultures began circling above the krantz. The wind whistled through their primaries, and Magqubu sang the sound, turning it into a chant of praise. More and more flew above us, their shadows passing in long dark movements over the white sand with the heat waves creating mirages. Crows flew at a lower elevation, cawing loudly and drowning out the eerie sound of the wings. Soon the sky was full of vultures, some only tiny specks in the blueness of the sky. A big lappet-faced vulture, the bright red on its neck shining in the sun, circled above us and glided down, landing with a short hopping run, and staring imperiously at the other vultures and crows as they landed. A magnificent bateleur swept in, the rich red and black of its feathers highlighting the dullness of the white-backed vultures. The beach was soon crowded with vultures and crows and the single bateleur. Bird after bird made its way to a pool on the edge of the main stream of the river, flapped around in the water, emerged with feathers glistening, and lay with wings outstretched as Ken Tinley and I, gawking with excitement, had seen them do three years before.

Magqubu and I finished tea and left the vultures and crossed the river higher up so as not to disturb these "birds of the king." Magqubu stopped to point out the enormous imprint of Nkosi, the lone lion, and the place where it had killed a waterbuck bull with long curved horns. Bits of skin dried out by the heat lay scattered near the bleached skull and the horns. Magqubu pointed to the small piece of nose lying on the sand.

"That is where the lion grabbed this *ipiva*" (waterbuck), he said, and he traced out the killing in the sand.

The range of the lion was incredibly wide. It moved round in a great circle through the reserve and along the perimeter of the Crown lands, its progress marked by spoor in the sand or mud and the occasional kills we came upon during our patrols. Only recently had it begun to roar. At night or in the early hours of the morning Ann and I could hear it calling from our bedroom. The baboons screamed, the troop leader keeping up a barrage of sound until the lion had passed. In the amphitheatre of hills the sound was magnified and echoed against the krantzes and down the river, a thrilling sound after so many years without the lion. His presence had also become a deterrent to poachers, but, regrettably, not for long.

Magqubu walked south following a rhino path, then he turned and we began climbing the ridge toward Dengezeni. We toiled up the hill, Lancer panting heavily, saliva slopping in a frothy mass over his lower jaw. He ran ahead and lay panting in the shade, his whole body shaking with exertion. Distemper had weakened him. The Saint Vitus's dance he had been left with took up a lot of his energy. Magqubu walked up the steep path with ease, and I glanced at him to see if there were any sweat stains on his shirt: not a drop. I was fit and probably at my physical peak, but the hot tea had opened my pores, and I kept wiping the perspiration off my face because it attracted the irritating biting flies. They got onto my neck and up my nostrils, biting viciously where there was even a pinpoint of moisture. I cursed them aloud. Magqubu turned and laughed, saying, "Ziyaluma izimpukane" (The flies bite). But I noticed that none bothered him. He was immune to the little pepper ticks, too. My legs were covered with the minute pests from when we had passed through a cluster hanging from a thin stalk of themeda grass. The hot north wind was howling down the slopes of Dengezeni, and I was now so hot I could not even be bothered to stop and pull the ticks off, not that it was possible. I comforted myself with murderous thoughts of watching them die when the paraffin took effect.

Three-quarters of the way up Dengezeni, Magqubu turned off the path to urinate. I plodded on, the sun beating mercilessly down and the north wind blowing in furious gusts. Lancer padded behind me, flopping into the shade, then getting up, panting deeply, and following me again. The sun was blinding, and my bush hat was tipped over my eyes to lessen the glare.

I looked back and saw Magqubu was taking off his *ncetu*, the little cod-piece the Zulu men used. This was a relic from the days when their only clothing was the *beshu* and *isinene*, the equivalent of the sporran and kilt. Walking in the long grass could irritate the head of the penis.

I looked back again, and Magqubu was a good two hundred yards behind. He was fastening his fly.

I walked on, conscious of the reflected heat from the bare ground. We were in an open patch with little grass, and scattered *Acacia karoo* and *nilotica* trees. Out of the corner of my right eye I saw some heaped stones. The only thing that registered in my mind was that it seemed strange to have a pile of stones in so isolated a part of the game reserve. The thought of the cave, the rocks, and the skeleton of the previous day at Momfu flashed through my mind, but I dismissed it and plodded on in the sun, my mouth dry and a thirst for cold water reminding me of my home on the top of Mpila hill.

I heard Magqubu coming up behind me and he called out. I turned around and said, "Yebo, Magqubu. What do you want?"

He pointed to the stones, which he called an *isivivane*, and he said that I had walked past without paying my respects by picking up a stone, spitting on it, and throwing it onto the cairn. I was hot, tired, and becoming increasingly bad-tempered. Sweat was running off my forehead, the backpack was sticking to my back, and the flies were giving me hell. I was carrying a shotgun in a canvas bag and it felt like a ton of weight. I had only one thought in mind, and that was to get to the top of Dengezeni and take the easiest path home. Lancer had run on again and lay spread out in the shade of a marula tree three hundred yards ahead.

I looked at Magqubu. He was calm and there was no sign of sweat. He watched me and repeated what he had said about picking up a stone, spitting on it, and throwing it onto the cairn.

"Yes, Magqubu, that is interesting, but I am too tired to walk back." He stared at me in amazement and did not need to say, "But you are only a hundred yards ahead." What he didn't understand was that it would mean retracing my steps, and this I had no intention of doing. It was difficult enough going forward.

We were in the hottest part of the day, and the veld was silent except for the wind gusting through the grass and the acacias. Behind Magqubu mirages danced in the heat waves. October days in Zululand could be hell, and today was one of those days.

Magqubu cleared his throat and spoke slowly and clearly. "It is the law, it is Zululand, and did you not say you wanted to learn about Zulu beliefs?"

"Yes," I said, "but I do not consider this to be important."

"Hau! Hau!" Magqubu said. "You say this *isivivane* is not important? No Zulu would pass by without paying respects. The cairns were put here for a purpose. They mark the place where something happened. Perhaps a man died here, or someone escaped being killed by a lion, or rhino, or elephant, and the stones were started to honour the *amadhlozi.*

"My father told me that if a man broke the law of the chief by not carrying out instructions while being sent with others on a mission, the *indunas* were told to hit and kill him. He would be laid down, not buried but covered with stones next to the path they had been walking on. The *indunas* and the other travellers would go and wash themselves, then return and throw another stone, after spitting on it, onto the heap, showing that they did not break the chief's laws on the journey. From then onwards anyone passing would pay their respects by putting on a stone after spitting on it. If they did not do so they were breaking the law of the chief and they would have bad luck on their journey. Everything could go wrong. There would be no food and perhaps they would be attacked and robbed. The cairns are known as the luck of the path. It was bad not adding to the heap, this would bring ill fortune upon themselves. It is like finding a small green snake in your hut. If you kill it, God will take away your good luck. Better to take it outside and let it go.

"When Mtwazi [Captain Potter] was at Hluhluwe, I saw the bones of a man who lay beneath that big *isivivane* on the road just before you reach the camp. That proved what my father had told me."

Magqubu was arguing with me. His eyes were boring into mine, not wavering for a second. I looked back at him, all the while becoming increasingly irritable. It made no difference to Magqubu's demeanour. He was polite but firm.

We argued for what seemed an age, he continuing to urge me to come back and carry out the ritual. I said that I appreciated his beliefs but that mine were different, but this was simply an excuse for not walking back.

"Your beliefs have nothing to do with me," I said angrily.

I saw his jaw set, and he kept repeating that this had to be done. The heat of the sun grew more intense, and even to talk was an effort, but I had become aware of Magqubu staring at me. It was not Zulu custom to stare into a person's eyes, particularly if that person is a senior officer. I began to feel uneasy. This was uncharacteristic of him.

Magqubu's eyes did not waver, and he was insistent that I comply with the law. Had it been a cool day and I not irritable, I would have carried out his wishes just to be polite. But today in the broiling sun it had become a test of wills. I was in an arrogant and unrepentant state. After all, was I not the senior ranger in charge of this reserve? I was the one who gave orders, and Magqubu could not dictate to me.

His attitude reminded me of a confrontation we had had a few days after I had come back to the Mfolozi. Nick Steele reported to me that Magqubu had refused to take warthog as his meat ration. I said, "Leave him to me," and I went down to the barracks, determined to make him accept the warthog meat ration.

At that time there was a heavy overpopulation of these animals, and everyone, labouring staff, game guards, camp staff, the white camp superintendent and his female assistant, as well as any of the visiting builders, was given warthog. It was excellent meat, an opinion shared by many people. Everyone looked forward with eagerness to the weekly meat ration. My wife found ways to cook it that were never forgotten by the numerous visitors who came to our house. Sometimes, thirty years later, people would write or stop me in the street and speak of the warthog meal they had had in our home. It was not a meat to be refused, and I had it in my head that no Zulu would turn it away. This was an unheard-of event.

I confronted Magqubu. "I hear you have refused the warthog ration."

"Yebo."

"But it is good meat."

"Yebo. But I do not eat it."

"Why do you not eat it?"

"I am a Shembe."

The word meant nothing to me, and I was preparing to override Magqubu and order him to accept the meat.

"I eat bushbuck," he said firmly.

We did from time to time have a bushbuck shot for rations, but it was not common.

"*Ntibane* [warthog] is a pig. Shembe people do not eat pig meat. We do not even touch it," he said.

The penny slowly began to drop. I knew Jewish people did not eat pork because of their beliefs. Magqubu's aversion was a religious one. I tried nevertheless to force the issue, but he just shook his head, smiled politely, and repeated that he was a Shembe. He started to explain what being a Shembe meant and how he had become a follower. I cut him short, turned, and walked away.

Magqubu called out in a firm but quiet voice, "I eat bushbuck."

I stood for a few moments, stunned by what in any other man would have been unwarranted cheek. I distinctly remember being aware of everything that was going on around me. The tinker barbets were calling in their monotonous clinking single notes. Hadeda ibis flew overhead, red-billed hoopoe cackled, and there was the smell of *Acacia nilotica* pods that had been crushed by passing animals, their sweet smell hanging in the air.

There were other guards standing nearby and watching. Magqubu was the sergeant, the most senior man in the game-guard force. I knew I had already made a mistake in this public confrontation. In my haste to assert my authority as the officer in charge of Mfolozi game reserve, I had overlooked the correct etiquette of summoning Magqubu to the office and arguing with him alone. I was now caught in a public confrontation.

A bateleur eagle swept overhead, gliding and tumbling in the thermal currents. I felt a relief watching it fly like a huge bat, twisting and turning, showing dark red and black feathers. Then it called, *cor cor de cor*, the sound echoing over the parade ground and the white-walled thatched rondavels of the barracks. The autumn sun was hot, and I could feel it burning through my khaki shirt, and there was the faint tang of my own sweat and that of the guards who were standing nearby, watching and listening to Magqubu and me. My ego was overriding my good sense, but the other part of myself was conscious of the elements, the birds and trees and the scent of men and the earth, and my hubris.

"I eat bushbuck," Magqubu said again in his clearly enunciated tones.

I felt a surge of anger and was about to reply, "If you don't eat warthog you can go without meat." Before I could speak, a bushbuck barked from the edge of the cliffs overlooking the White Mfolozi River. The bark was repeated successively, and the sound seemed to bounce against the krantzes. There is no mistaking the dog-like bark.

I looked at Magqubu, and he smiled as though to say, "There is the sign. It will be all right." Then he pronounced in his matter-of-fact way that the bushbuck had called. He talked about the animal, the bravery of the male, and how if wounded it would not hesitate to attack a man.

An image came to my mind, an old story of a man and a bushbuck who had died in a wooded Natal kloof. The slightly spiralled horns had penetrated the man's chest, and neither the hunter nor the hunted was able to get away from each other. Man and beast were locked in a deathly embrace.

"You can shoot a bushbuck, Magqubu," I said.

He nodded, and moved his shoulders as though to say it was his due, a right he deserved, which indeed he did after his lifetime of service.

I realized later how Magqubu had gently put me in my place. It had been done in such a way that there was no loss of face for me in front of the other guards. I was still the man in charge, but Magqubu had clearly established his own authority. There was a subtlety in the whole incident that totally escaped me at the time.

Magqubu had never been to school, was unable to read or write, and did not speak English. Whites conversed with blacks in their own language, and in this way maintained what they believed was their superiority. This incident with Magqubu was the beginning of many lessons. I was given an insight into his character. He came from warrior stock and obeyed all orders except those that touched on or interfered with his religion. He always retained his independence, and I was never to see him lose his dignity. Self-control and will were as much a part of his nature as eating and breathing.

Sweat dripped into my eyes, and the memory faded. He had won the warthog-eating argument, but that was different – he had good religious grounds. Today it was his superstitious beliefs based on something his father had told him. This had nothing to do with me, and in any case I was white. Yes, a white man, and a senior one in this game reserve.

In my raw state I knew that a lifetime of racial conditioning had come to the fore. The realization was a jarring but unavoidable reality. No matter what I thought or how I tried to rationalize my prejudices away, deep down they were there and had now come to the surface under the duress of my fatigue, thirst, and the unbearable heat. At that moment, without doubt the most critical in my life as a white English-speaking South African, and in an event that has been branded with the searing heat of the day into my memory, Qumbu Magqubu Ntombela, a descendant of a long line of Zulu warriors and people who had never been afraid to fight anyone, said "Uthi qi," in unmistakable tones.

I stared at him in shock, but his eyes did not waver. I stood stunned. Everything around me ceased to exist. I grew cold in the heat of the sun and felt goose bumps burst out on my skin. It took a few moments before I breathed properly again. "Uthiqi" means "You come here and you do so immediately," a phrase that would never be used by a subordinate to a senior.

I recovered with a surge of anger and was about to say, "Who the bloody hell do you think you are talking to?" Magqubu stood watching me with a faint but respectful smile on his face. I thought, "What is going on here?"

Magqubu was motionless, and we stood in silence. Then under a compulsion beyond my conscious understanding I walked back the hundred yards or more, and picked up a stone, which instantly brought me back to the moment because it was burning hot. I spat on it, watched the spittle begin to evaporate, then tossed it onto the old cairn and heard it clatter down the opposite side. Everything was taking place in slow motion. Magqubu followed suit, picked up a stone, spat on it, and threw it onto the cairn. He walked past me, taking the lead, and said over his shoulder, "Asihambe."

We set off following a narrow path the mountain reedbuck used. Slowly I became aware of my surroundings again and felt the sun burning down. The path widened into a rhino path that led toward a pan partially hidden by a screen of trees. Magqubu stopped and pointed, and I saw the broad backs of white rhino that had been wallowing. I took my camera out and snapped the rhino as they heard us and came bewildered out of the pan. Magqubu grinned and said we had had a good view. The rhino moved off in their quick horse-like trotting action, making their *humph, humph, humph* sounds, a continuous repetition as they ran over the brow of the hill and disappeared, but I could hear the sound until it too faded.

"Mkombe," Magqubu said, his way of bringing that little incident to a close.

His attitude was the same as it had been before the *isivivane* encounter. I did not feel uncomfortable, but neither was I too happy. There was a feeling of change inside myself, but I would not have been able to say precisely what had happened. I had been confronted with an aspect of myself that was decidedly unpleasant and come to terms with it in a shorter time than it took to say. I was not the superior person, and my white skin meant nothing. Like the trees that partially hid the white rhino in the pan, my skin was a screen stopping me from seeing the real person within, someone I did not really know or like.

I looked down at the grass growing over the path and thought that October was the Zulu month of *izibandhlela*, the season when the paths begin to be covered by grass. The Zulu way of life is so much more in rhythm with the earth. Each season merges into the other, not in a sharply defined way but more like changing music. My spirits were slowly being uplifted, and we tramped on with Lancer loping at my heels. I could hear his heavy panting. I was feeling better, almost as one does after being involved in a boxing match where your opponent has let you go with honour. Glancing back for a moment I caught like a photograph the White Mfolozi River and the pattern of hills surrounding the White Mfolozi valley. Soon we would be over the Dengezeni ridge, and below us would lie the Black Mfolozi River and its adjoining hills to Siyembeni, the junction.

I felt a surge of fatigue and kept my eyes down, concentrating on Magqubu's boots so that I could forget about the steepness of the hill. I was aware of the bright white flowers of a dombeya tree, or *iNhliziyonkulu* of the Zulu, the "Big Heart." They believed that when the tree burst into flower it was time to plough. It flowered more or less at the same time as the red-chested cuckoo, the Piet-my-vrou or *uPhezukomkhono*, appeared from the north. I wondered whether in the heat we had experienced that month the ground would be soft enough – but did it matter, with the deep ploughs pulled by oxen or, worse, by the tractors that the Zulus now used? So much of the beauty and mystery of the planting and reaping seasons had been destroyed by our modern inventions. With the Zulu people the names of the seasons still survived, and, evocatively, they brought back the rhapsody of the land. I was now acutely aware of the scent of the acacias and of the earth reflecting the sun's rays, and sweat poured off my face.

We walked on. I was tired and did not want to look up, and I stared at Magqubu's boots moving up and down. It was at this moment that I saw below me the thick tip of a snake's tail just behind Magqubu's heels as it passed partially hidden by the grass. *Izibandhlela* – the time of year when the grass begins to cover over the paths. I could smell the hot grass, and before I could shout there was a noise, a rushing whirr, and in an instant a black mamba was next to us, but taller than us both. We froze into stillness. The snake began making a high-pitched *tsi, tsi, tsi, tsi, tsi* sound.

Magqubu and I stood motionless, the black mamba hovering above us. We knew that one movement on our part meant death. I have never been so terrified. The black mamba can strike with chilling swiftness, and we would soon have died on this mountain slope because after our strenuous climb the blood was rushing through our veins, and the venom would quickly have been carried to the heart. Mamba poison attacks the nervous system, a most unpleasant way to die.

I stared at the mamba, totally unaware of anything else, mind and body focused on the menace swaying above us. Then the word *ndhlondhlo* entered my mind. The scales on the back of the snake's head had reminded me of the Zulu mythical crested mamba. I could see why: the scales stood out like feathers. Somehow this realization calmed me.

The snake was within touching distance. Magqubu and I stood for what seemed an eternity looking at it, nothing moving except our eyes. I have no idea how long the incident lasted, but it seemed a lifetime before the snake went down and began to glide away on top of the grass with the most beautiful movement.

At that moment Lancer saw it, and he barked. In one blinding black flash the snake whipped around with the sound like a piece of tin vibrating in a high wind. It came straight at us, and I put my hand down and grabbed Lancer's leather collar and tightened it to a point where he gasped. By now the snake was right next to us again, standing above us. Once more we stood staring at this dark menace, and another eternity seemed to pass. By this time so much adrenalin had gone through my body that I was unafraid. My mind was calm, my body coiled and ready for flight, although I knew that any move would lead to an attack by the snake.

Slowly the snake dropped again, the upper half of its body going down in a near-toppling motion. It moved off with speed downhill. I realized I had my shotgun in my hand. I was about to unzip the canvas carrying case, pull out the gun, and blow the snake's head off. I was angry at it for giving us such a fright. Magqubu stopped me, and something inside myself stopped me too. The snake had let us go. Now we had to respect its life and let it go.

I saw the black tail of the mamba disappearing into the brown grass, then I glimpsed its thick body in an open patch until it vanished, and the long grass stems quivered with its movement down the hill.

Magqubu was standing looking at me with an expression on his face of mingled anger, concern, and anxiety. He stared at me silently, and for a moment I had a terrible fear that he may have been bitten. I was the first to speak and asked shakily if he was all right, but the inner part of myself that knows everything told me that Magqubu could not have been bitten. The snake was so close to all three of us that none of us would have been spared. The mamba moves like lightning, and in our exposed position we would have had no chance of escape or, if bitten, of survival. We had been extremely fortunate. Who knows how it is determined who shall live and who shall die at any given moment? We had been saved for something else. There was other work in store for us.

African snakes are universally feared, and there are arguments and stories about the potency of the various species. However, there is no doubt that the mamba, both the black and the green, is the most dangerous. There are countless stories of mambas moving through a homestead and being attacked by dogs. The mambas kept going, turning and biting the dogs and any people who happened to be near. Horsemen in the early days of exploration in Zululand had been bitten while riding through the long grass. Great legends have grown up about the snake and its speed, and after what I had seen today, I needed no convincing. Everyone agrees about the virulence of its poison. A full bite of a mamba means death unless you can get to a hospital within half an hour at the most.

Magqubu brought me to my senses with the word, "Asihambe." I was shaking, the effect of the adrenalin having worn off. Magqubu walked ahead, and after a short distance he turned and said in a commanding voice, "Hlalapansi!" (Sit down).

He was now very much the leader. I had spurned his requests to put a stone on the *isivivane* and pay my respects in the proper fashion, in a way that generations of passing travellers had done. In my white arrogance I had dismissed the beliefs of Magqubu until he had to command me to return, pick up a small stone, spit on it, and throw it onto the *isivivane*. I now knew how wrong I had been and linked the appearance of the mamba with my recalcitrance. My inner voice had already said, You are very lucky only to get a warning.

I sat down, my back against a rock, Lancer panting in the heat of the day at my side. His pink tongue slobbered saliva over his lower jaws.

Magqubu began to talk, repeating what he had said in our earlier confrontation about the *isivivane*, and how it came to be there. It could have been a place where something bad had happened: someone had been attacked and killed by a lion, or attacked by a rhino, or bitten by a snake, or, alternatively, something good had happened there, so the earlier people had marked the place with a cairn and then had let the word out. He explained that many of the cairns were within view of the chief's *muzi*, and he would have men watching to make sure that travelers would *hlonipa* the *isivivane* by going through the ritual of picking up a stone, spitting on it, and throwing it on the cairn.

Magqubu gave me the lecture of my life, but I was still in a mild state of shock after the encounter. Something had certainly taken place between us, but the full extent of it was only going to become evident after many years of contemplation. Magqubu talked on, and I sat watching him but not listening properly. He pointed in Zulu fashion, with the crooked index finger.

"This is the land of Jobe," he said, his arm sweeping over and pointing toward the junction of the White and the Black Mfolozi rivers. "It is Dingiswayo's land too." And he repeated a history lesson he had given me many times before. It was not a hectoring lecture but a continual statement of fact coming from a man who had spent his whole life in this landscape. I was anxious to get home to Ann and our son, Kenneth, so I politely nodded while Magqubu talked, and yet some part of me was listening and would eventually understand.

On this day Magqubu gave me example after example, pouring his heart out, as it were, to this young white man with whom he had had this close encounter with the snake. He had seen something in me. My prejudice, my rejection, my lack of understanding and appreciation of everything that had been going on around me during the time that we had worked together – he understood this, but he knew somehow that I wanted to learn, and even though I did not speak his language with any degree of fluency, there was the other language of intuition and of unconscious understanding that could take place between two people. This he saw and understood. Many years later I used to listen to the stories he told, and bits and pieces would come back to me of the time when we sat on the hill and he expressed himself about the great importance of *hlonipa*, of respect, because with respect came understanding. It was an understanding that was not only an exterior understanding but an interior understanding too. We were reflected in the landscape, and the landscape was reflected inside us.

Magqubu talked on. He spoke about the need to learn from the animals. He knew that he had to continue talking to teach me and that my thirst would make me concentrate more. I looked at him, and he appeared as a mirage in the haze of the heat. I could smell the red grass, the dust coming off it, and in the distance I could hear the tinker barbets calling, and still Magqubu talked.

"Let me tell you one story of man and animals," he said, "the story of Njonje Nyande. This is a man who tried to steal honey from the honey badger. He did not respect it and it almost cost him his life.

"Njonje Nyande had seen the honey badger digging in a hive and carting the combs away and putting them on a rock. Njonje watched until the honey badger had a pile, and then he thought that this was enough for himself, so when the honey badger went back toward the hive, Njonje went forward and took the honey and ran away. He had gone about as far as that hill," and Magqubu pointed to the crest of Dengezeni hill, "when he decided that this was far enough, and he sat down and started to wipe off all the bees, blowing them off the combs. In the meantime the honey badger had come back, found that the honey was gone, and started to track Njonje. Njonje was sitting comfortably with his back against a rock when he heard a rustling sound, and he turned round and saw the honey badger coming straight at him. All the Zulus know that this is one of the bravest animals in the bush," Magqubu said. "Not only the bravest, but also one of the toughest.

"Njonje sat up and grabbed his knobkierie, and as the honey badger came at him he beat it, and he kept on beating, but it had no effect on the little animal. Eventually the stick slipped out of his hand and the honey badger jumped and bit a hole in Njonje's stomach, and he was lucky that time because honey badgers always go for the testicles. You know the *isinene*, the *mutshi* that we wear, that is made out of skins? Well, fortunately for Njonje the honey badger, in trying to get hold of Njonje's testicles, got a mouthful of the skin from the *isinene* and began chewing it. Njonje then remembered he had put his shield and his assegai down on the ground some distance away and he turned and ran to get them, but the honey badger followed him. He managed to get to the assegai and pick it up, and the honey badger came at him again. He tried to stop it, but the spear glanced off its back and went into the ground and bent. He was now left with another knobkierie, and he hit the honey badger on the side of the head and stunned it. The following day he came back with a friend to collect the badger, but it had gone.

"This man Njonje was very lucky not to have lost his life. But you see," Magqubu said, "he did not respect the animal's right, and instead of only taking a few combs he took everything, and this is why the honey badger came after him."

Then Magqubu laughed and said, "Of course, everyone knew about this story because his friend who'd gone with him to try to find the honey badger the next day saw that in the struggle Njonje had defecated on the ground in his great efforts to keep the honey badger from grabbing him by the testicles. There were faeces on the ground and also on the back part of the *mutshi*. So the friend told everybody, and Njonje was very humiliated by all of this."

For Magqubu, this was the lesson to be taught: You can take from the animals, but if you take too much, then you could be killed, and if not killed, then you could be humiliated. Everything that Magqubu had seen or heard in his life from his father, grandfather, and other elders was a lesson in how to live with the natural world. If you lived well with the animal world, then you lived well within yourself.

"You like birds," Magqubu said. "I've watched you take out your binoculars and you are always looking when the birds fly over. And I see that you listen, too, but how carefully do you listen to the birds?

"My father taught me to look and to listen, and I learned from Mali and Mankenke Mdhletshe, who were old game guards who worked here when this place was just beginning, and they showed me many things that are now being forgotten, but when you came, you said to me that you wanted to learn. I said I would teach you."

14

Magqubu's Conversion

The afternoon shadows had begun to lengthen, and Magqubu fell silent and stared toward the distant hills of Umendo. Down near the river from the top of the sycamore figs a purple- crested lourie called persistently. Magqubu murmured the bird's name, *iGwalagwala*. He told me how the red and black feathers were prized by the Zulu kings, but he spoke without enthusiasm, and I could see that his mind was occupied with something that was more important to him than the purple-crested lourie feathers. He sat silent for quite some time, and I could hear Lancer breathing and the wildebeest flies buzzing round my ears and eyes, trying to reach the sweat drops. Then the call of an *uFukwe* (Burchell's coucal) floated up from the valley and the liquid notes echoed again and again. The bird called repeatedly, and I saw something stir on Magqubu's face. It was a bird he was deeply attached to because it always announced the coming of the rain.

Magqubu looked at me intently and said, "Today we had a lucky escape from the mamba, but I must tell you how I was once bitten by a snake and went on a long journey that took me to Shembe, the Zulu prophet."

Amos Shembe founded a religious sect in the 1930s. It was designed to incorporate Christian and Zulu beliefs. The retention of tribal dress played a big part in the ceremonies and had done a lot to ensure that the tradition of *beshu* and *isinene* was kept alive.

In 1940 Magqubu was in charge of one of the groups of guards employed to shoot animals in the southern Crown lands at Gome. Once a week each man was given twenty-five rounds of .303 ammunition and was expected to bring back both the empty *doppies* and the tails of the animals he shot. If a man missed with all twenty-five rounds, he was dismissed. Wounded animals had to be followed and killed. The guards were told to leave the snakes except the pythons, which were killed and sent to Durban to make belts.

"The government ordered us to shoot all the game," he said. "Only at Hluhluwe where Mtwazi [Captain H.B. Potter] lived and looked after the reserve were the animals left alone. But everything was shot outside the game reserve, at Nqabateki, Ntabamhlope, and the hills around Mashiya."

(Mashiya was named for the thick bush along the ridge, which looked like eyebrows.)

"The game was shot at Mkuze game reserve too – mainly wildebeest; the impala were spared. In Mfolozi, black rhino and white rhino and the baboons and monkeys were not shot."

"What happened to the meat?" I asked.

"The animals lay in the bush after they had been skinned. The government would not allow the people to come and get meat for themselves. It was left for the hyenas and jackals, the vultures and the marabou storks, or it just rotted on the ground. Many zebra were shot, and only the tails were taken. Wildebeest skins were collected and sent to Durban. Buffalo carcasses and skins lay in the veld. We who were doing the shooting were allowed to eat the meat, but it was nothing, there was so much. Sometimes after talking to the guard in charge, one would hang meat in a tree, hidden away. It would be fetched in the dark and taken home for the family to eat. Buffalo meat is the best and we were sad to see it lying on the veld until only the white maggots were left. If the family of the guard were caught taking the meat, the guard would be fired by Mashiya (William Foster). This was the law from the government."

The enormity of the constant killing must have caused a psychic shock to a man like Magqubu, who had grown up alongside the animals and spent half his life protecting them from poachers. The killing defied logic because, as Dr. George Campbell said, why kill the game when it is the tsetse fly that is the problem? But the cattle ranchers had a powerful political lobby, and their hatred for the game went far beyond the bounds of reason. Blood lust lay just below the surface. I was to see it repeatedly in my career, even in those who were in charge of the game reserves. Few people could resist the temptation to find a reason for killing. In the small game reserves selective culling would always be necessary, but some scientists became obsessed with their own discipline and thought nothing of authorizing killing.

Magqubu was camped in a cave with other guards on the Gome stream, and one morning he saw a snake, but it was a mirage. Symbolically, the cave and the snake are extremely important in ancient healing rituals. Magqubu was in a disturbed state of mind with the constant killing, and he was now forty years old and still subservient to his father. Unconsciously he was trying to break away and be his own man, but it was a painful struggle against tradition and a deep love for his father. Shembe, the Zulu prophet who combined Zulu custom and Christian beliefs, had become known then and was gaining converts, but as a result of his father's influence Magqubu had rejected both Shembe and Christianity. The appearance of the imagined snake was probably a psychological signal of imminent change. Magqubu's character was too strong for him to remain subservient to either his father or his father's beliefs. He had to find his own way. C.G. Jung once said, "If you do not deal with your problems internally, you will meet them externally as fate."

A day or two later Magqubu saw a real snake in the cave and struck at it with a stick. In all probability it was a boomslang, although he called it a mamba. He said it was green, and the green mamba does not occur in the dry country. He struck at the snake repeatedly. He severed it, and half the body and the head fell on his head, biting him in its death throes. Magqubu called out, and the other guards came to help him and they squeezed blood out of the punctures. They gave him the rough antidotes they carried with them and made him swallow them with water. Magqubu said he was in intense pain right round his head, except for the place where he was injured during a faction fight at Ongeni. The guards took him into a hut, stripped him to his *beshu*, and laid him on the floor.

"I heard a loud noise as though it was thundering and then I became unconscious," he said.

Magqubu now described his long internal and archetypal journey. He walked downhill to a river and a voice said, "Get into the water." He obeyed and was carried downstream, being turned over again and again by the water. After an interminable time he was thrown out onto a sandbank and found himself below a high cliff. The waves in the river were trying to draw him back. He looked around, and the way he had come was no longer there. He could not return, so he began climbing the cliff, with difficulty. Near the top he looked back, seeing the river dimly in the distance.

"Something came into my mind that I was already dead and it would be better to throw myself backwards into the river," he said. But a girl appeared, wearing a short white dress. She held out a stick and pulled him with ease to the top. He followed her for about fourteen kilometres along a small path in beautiful grassland savannah and trees. They came to a big building and the girl knocked on the door, and when it was opened she called Magqubu inside. There before him were row upon row of people, all wearing white robes. No one was talking. Then he heard a voice say, "Let us pray," and everyone knelt down and "the whole building thundered," Magqubu said. They sang a hymn and Magqubu sang it now, and his voice floated on the hot wind. He remembered every word.

His story continued with the people descending, all in their white robes. He remained alone, clad in his *beshu*.

The girl reappeared and told him to follow her, and she led him to a place where there were fire holes in the ground. She told him about the evil, then took him to other holes where black and white smoke poured out. She again warned him about the dangers of evil. Another girl appeared, and the two of them said they had been instructed to take him back to his children. They walked back to the high cliff above the river. The two girls jumped and he followed, landing in the river, where he was thrown about, but eventually he reached the other side. After a long walk through familiar country they came to the hut where his body was lying, but before entering the hut and returning to his body, Magqubu was instructed to pray below a particular aloe. "If you do so, you will live," the girl said.

"That's why I pray every night," Magqubu declaimed. "My spirit now entered my body and I became conscious. I picked up my blanket and put it over my shoulders. I was very weak. The two girls knelt at the door. I joined in the prayer because after crossing the river and coming back I was now a member of Nazareth. The two girls stood up, and I saw them going away and my heart was sore when they disappeared," he said sadly.

It was early in the morning. Magqubu had been unconscious for a long time. He gathered some grass and sticks to make a fire for tea, and this woke the other guards and one exclaimed, "Ntombela is back."

The guards boiled the water and made tea for Magqubu, who was still shaky. He tried to explain the journey he had been on, and some of his companions seemed to understand.

When Magqubu had sufficiently recovered he went home. He was ill for a long time. His father pressed traditional medicines on him, but they made him no better. His father, although sceptical, eventually agreed to let him see a white doctor at Nongoma. Magqubu was injected several times. By the end of a year he was no better.

"I continued going to doctors and *sangomas*," he said. "They told me I would get better, but I got worse."

In 1945 the government moved all the people, including the Ntombela clan, out of the corridor of land between Hluhluwe and Mfolozi. The Ntombelas had been there for four generations. Magqubu couldn't walk at the time, and he was taken to the new Macibini *muzi* by wagon.

"My father walked behind the wagon with the women and children and what remained of the cattle and goats after *nagana* attacks.

"We did not feel bad about moving because we were told that after they had eradicated the tsetse fly we would be allowed back." Their stock losses had been heavy. Of their 208 head of cattle, all except two had died.

In 1946 Magqubu confronted his father. Inwardly he knew he was suffering from a soul sickness. He told his father that he had been through three years with traditional medicines but that he was still no better. "I think if I had been with Shembe for these three years I would have recovered. Could you allow me to go there?" Magqubu pleaded with his father. In some irritation his father said, "Go to Shembe and become a Nazarite. If you become better, I will also be a Nazarite." This was the turning point.

Magqubu's children carried him eighteen kilometres to the chief's house at Mtubatuba, where Shembe was due in the next few days. Some time lapsed before Shembe actually came, but Magqubu said he had already begun to feel better. He chopped wood and built a small hut for his family. When Shembe arrived, people rushed out to greet him. Magqubu was afraid and found his legs were trembling, although it was a moment for which he had longed for years. An assistant minister told everyone who was sick to assemble in a nearby house and to think about their illnesses. Magqubu thought about the snake bite and all the difficulties he had encountered over the past three years. He heard a voice shouting out loud, and saying, "All sickness must quickly disappear," and people began to cry.

"I felt cold air moving toward me," Magqubu said. "In fact it was Shembe with one of his ministers carrying a big cloth. He was putting it over the rows of people. My whole body became hot, and I felt his hand on my head. My insides were churning and something in my chest went down my intestines. It rested on my bladder.

"When it moved I felt my intestines moving upwards in my body. My head felt heavy. Suddenly, while I was feeling all this, my arm shook vigorously. Then I felt the lord from Ekuphakameni coming nearer. He put his foot on my chest where this thing had entered and had gone down to my bladder. I felt like urinating.

"Then he stepped on me with his foot, and my leg began jumping. He forcefully moved it to one side, together with an arm. One of the people had vomited pus from his stomach, and my head fell onto it. Some people had given him poisoned liquor to drink. It smelt terrible and I was rubbing my head in it until I lost consciousness.

"Later my children came and took me to my hut, and they carried outside the man whose vomit I had fallen into. There were many people scattered about, and others were farther away, crying of their diseases.

"When I was in my hut, I cried until morning, and my legs were jerking, out of control.

"At about half past seven in the morning two of my wives came. They led me outside, took my clothes off, and washed me thoroughly, holding me because I was still shivering. They put on a better *beshu* and gave me a new shirt. When they had finished, my children brought me porridge.

"This gave me strength and I walked by myself to my hut. That's when I realized that Shembe is an agent of God. I, Magqubu, ought not to have recovered, and walked on my own feet after the three years of suffering.

"I had never spoken of my disease to Shembe, or told him that something in my chest went down my intestines and got into my bladder. This is why we say that God is manifesting himself in Shembe, because he was able to see something within a person.

"In the afternoon, all the sick were again called. We went back and I could now feel I was going to be healed. Shembe and his ministers prayed for us. I could walk unaided for the second time. I felt like going down to the river, so I called my son to accompany me. When we were at the river I bathed and rested. Later, I went back to the hut and arrived in time for the evening service, which began, 'O Lord, be with us when we sleep, through your kindness save us this very night. Protect us from dangers, and be our resting place. Cover us with the blanket of your kindness.' When we had finished evening prayers we went to sleep.

"In the morning we had prayers again. The morning prayer was: 'May the grace of the Lord be with you holy ones, and the preacher must increase it, Amen.' Then the congregation started singing, 'Be with us on this very day, during our rising moments.' I felt better now. Then the service was over and we left.

"While we were relaxing we heard somebody shouting out, 'Tomorrow there will be celebrations for everybody.' I said, 'Will I be able to dance, because my whole body is painful?' The following morning everybody went to put on the traditional dress. I thought to myself, 'You know, I must try and dance because I'm much better. I can walk, and I am not shaking.' I made an effort and dressed in my skins and feathers and went to the dancing.

"I was among these people as an invalid, with no hair. Because of this snake disease, I had horns all over my head. When I came to the people who were dancing, some stopped. I was no longer a person – I was like an animal who no longer needed to dance with living people. Some looked at me and laughed while others looked at me and were sad. I saw others shaking their heads, saying, 'This person shouldn't be here.' In the midst of the festivities, I saw my wife bringing me food. I had had nothing to eat. She had brought me porridge. When I had eaten twice, Shembe sent somebody to tell me not to return to the dance because I was sick. I rested and watched the dancing instead.

"That's where I first met with the Shembe way. I saw that it had life because I woke up from the dead. I felt that this must be better because I became healthy without taking any medicine. I didn't even take a tablet from Shembe. After having been ill for such a long time, I had faith and I was healed.

"The following day after the festivities, the Shembe ministers announced that all those who believed in him were to be baptized in the Mgqogqweni River.

"I knew that Shembe was my leader and I would follow him for the rest of my life. The next day I saw Shembe going right into a pool in the river. We were all afraid to follow because this pool contained crocodiles. Shembe went in until the water was right up to his chest. He pushed his staff into the mud and called us. We entered and he baptized us one by one. We could see the crocodiles' heads, but they did nothing. Those who were beating the drums were standing there and singing.

"I myself entered, although I was afraid of the crocodiles. When I reached him, he asked me my name and I told him, 'My name is Magqubu.' He put his hands on my head and dipped me into the water, pushing me backwards with his left hand, and others followed.

"When he had finished baptizing us he said, 'All those who have been baptized must come and pay for the soap to wash my clothes.' We all paid the number of shillings we could afford.

"After all that, I was healed. The meeting lasted eighteen days, and on the nineteenth day Shembe packed his belongings and went to another place, together with his ministers and the other people he had come with in a lorry. When Shembe left he blessed us and said we must go with blessings to our homes, and be devoted to the Nazarite religion.

"I sang until I reached home, and my father, who had been very worried about me, was now very happy. He shouted jubilantly and came to meet me. I was singing a song I had got from Shembe's: 'Those who come sad, leave rejoicing, to the generations of Dingane and Senzangakhona, for the deliverer has arrived. Truly I have seen the deliverer, freeing all of us who had come before him. When we left we had been healed.' When I heard this song, it was as though they were saying that to me, I who came a sad person to be a Nazarite; but when I left, I left rejoicing.

"I could definitely see that the deliverer had arrived, because he relieved me of all the pain I had. I became a healthy person, when it was thought I would not live. I used to sing this song with feeling, for I was a sinner in the sight of Shembe, but when I returned to my house I was happy, being a healthy man with no ailment. My healthiness started in 1946 and has continued until now.

"Even today I believe in what Shembe said because I was saved without taking any medicine. Only the word of God from Shembe saved me. I used to frequent *izinyanga* who tried to treat me, killed my animals, sheep, goats, cattle, and took my money. The *inyanga* would demand five pounds or ten pounds, and steam me with his medicines. I would give him ten pounds and he would say that he was removing the wizardry that was in my body after having been struck by the snake. Nothing would come out. Ten of my sheep were killed, fifteen goats and four cattle – but I didn't get better. I didn't even have any clothes left."

I knew, when we got up to walk back to Mpila camp, that the encounter with the mamba and the lecture that Magqubu had given me were the beginning of a profound change. I could not have explained what had happened in words, but intuitively I knew my world could never be the same again.

It was late in the afternoon before Magqubu was finished with the story that has lingered with me all my life. In the many years that we were together, Magqubu was to tell me the story again and again, but I did not understand its full significance until I became interested in Jungian psychology.

We began the return trek, back to Mpila hill, to my office and to my home, following the path running through the large dolomite rocks and then over the ridge and down toward Mdindini and the steep path to the top of Mpila.

I remember walking into my office, and the first thing that caught my eye was an official envelope on the desk. I opened it because I knew it would be from the local magistrate. Magqubu had killed a poacher in self-defence in July and a trial had been held, but the judgment had been reserved and the letter was to say that he was not guilty.

When I told Magqubu about it, he said that if he had been guilty, then the snake would have bitten us, or would certainly have bitten him.

The lesson with the snake and the long talking-to that he had given me were not subtle because there were no witnesses, yet they were in no way disrespectful. Our roles had been reversed. He was now the authority and the leader, but with a different leadership, one by example. He was now the teacher and I was the pupil. It was forever to remain that way. In actuality it had been like that from the beginning, but I had not been ready to accept and understand it.

15

Wilderness

Both my parents were from Natal. Economics had forced their parents to leave the green hills of the province and move to Johannesburg. My paternal grandfather went to the diamond diggings on the Vaal River, following in the footsteps of my great-grandfather, who died on the Kimberley diggings. My maternal grandfather was a Scot, and he bought land in Kew, where he grew flowers and sold kikuyu grass. My father trained as a miner on Crown Mines and later became a shift boss on Robinson Deep gold mine, a few miles from the centre of Johannesburg. I worked on the same gold mine when I returned from the Second World War. My parents met, fell in love, married, and I was born in 1927.

My earliest memories are of sterile mine dumps, slimes dams, scraggy gum trees, turtledoves and sparrows calling in the early morning, and day and night the constant rattle of mine machinery.

My parents moved to the smallholding owned by my maternal grandparents when I was five years old. Immediately I was conscious of the contrast between the noisy mine machinery and the singing of the Cape robin and the spring call of the hoopoe: two entirely different worlds. We drew water from a well with a windlass, and had no electricity or bathroom. We heated water on the coal stove in a four-gallon *isigogo* (the onomatopoeic African name for a Laurel paraffin tin full of water). There was an outside pit toilet. There was no telephone, but we had a wireless, and this kept us in touch with the world. We were surrounded by farm dams, a wonderful habitat for the red and the yellow bishop birds, turtledoves, herons, migrant waders, and crowned plovers.

But one of the most dominant memories is the night-time chorus of frogs. In the spring and in the summer they sang like a great symphony, the earth vibrating in the waves of sound floating out from the dams and the natural ponds fed by underground springs. I remember, too, riding my pony to school and seeing white-backed vultures feeding on a carcass that lay half hidden in the tawny thatch grass.

My wilderness initiation began when I was six years old. I went with my father on a fishing trip to the Wilge River in the Orange Free State. There were dawns and sunsets, mist on the river, smells of the campfire, the clanging of a billycan, the plop of fish rising, crowned plovers calling, the silence of the night and then the dawn again, or the few moments before the first flash in the sky when the whole world seemed to stand still with its scents, sounds and the different colours. This was the introduction into the archetypal world when the earth was a paradise for mankind, perhaps even a glimpse of a time when we first became aware of what lay around us.

Later I carried a hidden air gun to school, shot doves and sparrows on the *koppies* opposite St. John's College, and cooked the kill on an open fire in a hidden cleft. There was a sense of intimacy with friends, and seclusion.

When I was a teenager I once watched a meerkat crossing the road at sunrise, and spent days and nights in the Kruger National Park hearing the lions roar and having the car chased by a lioness and cubs late one afternoon. We came back to Skukuza rest camp in the early evening and saw impala antelope grouping together. At night we sat around a fire in the wattle-and-daub rest camp, with the smell of burning acacia wood, *boerewors* cooking, and ground coffee boiling in a kettle on the open fire. There were the sounds of the night: hippo grunting in the Sabi River, water gurgling over the rocks, and the scream of an elephant on its way to drink.

After the war I visited Rhodesia (now Zimbabwe), and I will never forget the first time I saw the Zimbabwe ruins at sunrise – the numinous glow on the bush-covered hills and the first light shining on the stone walls of the mysterious buildings. The light touched the human soul, bringing human being, the land, and the universe into one. When the moment of transformation had passed, I knew I could shout out and be understood, "Praise be to God." This was a religion I could understand, and be at one with.

These were my first contacts with anything wild. Some part of me was touched by the various experiences. The wilderness of Africa had begun to spin the first strands of its web.

Thirty years later I began reading the works of Carl Jung and his associates. I was stunned when I read in Jung's *Memories, Dreams, Reflections*: "That is why the sun's birth in the morning strikes the natives as so overwhelmingly meaningful. The moment in which light comes is God. That moment brings redemption, release. To say that the sun is God is to blur and forget the archetypal experience of that moment."

16

Wilderness Trails

Magqubu and I had surveyed all the wilderness trail routes and completed our planning. He knew what was at stake because he would be the eyes and ears of the trail party, and if anything went wrong on the first trail, in bureaucratic language we would be for the chop. There were, however, still officials who opposed the trails. The Natal Parks Board head office reported that no one in the public had shown any interest in making a booking. There were the usual stories too of how we were stopping development of tourist camps.

Roy Rudden, a newspaper friend on the *Sunday Times*, took some beautiful photographs in the game reserve and wrote a story called "Adventure at a Pound a Day." Placards emblazoned with these words appeared throughout South Africa on a Sunday morning. On Monday the switchboard of the headquarters of the Natal Parks Board was jammed with calls from people trying to book trails. Wilderness trails had arrived. For the first time in the history of modern South Africa, people were going to be able to walk inside a game reserve among wild animals and sleep out on the veld. This was a revolutionary concept, because heretofore visitors to game reserves and national parks throughout most of eastern and southern Africa were required to stay in a vehicle. The concept of walking trails in the wilderness drew scorn from many professional wildlife conservationists, who predicted disaster.

On March 19, 1959 Magqubu and I led the first official wilderness trail in the Mfolozi game reserve for the Natal Parks Board. It was the culmination of many years of hard work and the start of a new dimension in wildlife conservation. Magqubu led the trail party of six people along the steep path down from Momfu cliffs to the Mpafa River, then followed the rhino paths south to Mahobosheni, where the donkeys had taken the kit and the tents. It was getting dark, and we all relaxed because we only had a hundred metres to walk to the camp.

There was a faint sound in a nearby wallow, and I turned to see the glint of light on the horn of a black rhino. Before I could even shout, the black rhino came storming toward us, snorting and crashing through the bush.

The trailists performed undreamed-of physical achievements, pulling themselves up into trees with one hand, or scattering in all directions, shouting at the top of their voices. When the rhino had gone and everyone was together again, unhurt beyond a few scratches and a sprain, Magqubu said, "The *amadhlozi* were with us today."

I knew he was right, because if the rhino had killed anyone, the bureaucrats who were against the trails would have ensured they died an early death.

Later in the evening Magqubu laughed and laughed. He showed how the rhino charged and the acrobatics of the people going up the trees, their shouting and their running. I was to witness this many times. It was for him hilarious to see white people scatter when a rhino charged. This was his cinema.

Magqubu was animated by this kind of excitement and, in later years when we were on trails, he liked nothing more than to see people running pell-mell for the trees when a black rhino threatened. It was even funnier if in their haste they climbed a thorn tree. His stomach would bob up and down and his hand would slap the ground. He elaborated on all the sounds the people made, the stifled "yips" of fear, the swear words when thorns hooked into flesh, the different actions when running. He missed nothing, and his nuances bit to the bone. If anyone ever farted in fear, he really had a field day. His descriptive powers were used until everyone was screaming with laughter, and he would walk ahead of the group making the farting noise with his lips, his shoulders shaking with mirth. He was never crude, but he was very basic. I did not dare tell some of the people the names he gave them – they would have been mortally offended. Magqubu's eyes and ears missed nothing, and the names were often unpalatably true.

When the fire had died down and everyone had a mug of coffee in their hands, I asked Magqubu for a story. "Yebo, lungile," (Yes, all right) he said, and he spoke about Vaughan Kirby, the first game conservator for Zululand, who had camped in this very place. Vaughan Kirby, a soldier and hunter, got the job in 1912 and by the end of the First World War he had become embroiled in desperate administrative manoeuvres to save the game reserves. He had to endure vilification, official contempt and indifference, and, what was worse, isolation and treachery from some of his colleagues. But his true worth was recognized by the Zulu game guards who worked with and for him. The called him Mfohloza, an onomatopoeic name from the sound of his long khaki trousers moving through the grass that was wet with dew: *fohla, fohla, fohla* they went, and so he became Mfohloza. It stuck for the rest of his life.

Magqubu recited Vaughan Kirby's Zulu praise names: Umjingoqo isiyengayengane esayjenga amabhumu eNgonyamaneni. He explained that the name related to a story of the early 1920s, when a group from northern Natal had come hunting in the shooting zone between the Mfolozi and the Hluhluwe game reserves. They shot a buffalo and decided to make biltong, and they asked Vaughan Kirby to give them a few packets of salt. He gave them alum and said they should sprinkle it all over the meat, and this they did. By the time the meat was dry all traces of the alum had gone, but it had firmly penetrated the raw flesh. When the people started to eat it they had severe diarrhoea.

Vaughan Kirby had been besieged and beset by hunters who were actually killers concerned only about making biltong. He grew to loathe the sight of them because they wounded animals and even destroyed the herds. The game guards Mali and Mankenke Mdhletshe watched Vaughan Kirby's grim pleasure when he was told by the guards how the hunters were squatting and groaning in the bush. He had some small revenge for his years of unhappiness at seeing the wild animals he had such an affinity for being killed.

Magqubu had great respect for Vaughan Kirby, and whenever he had the chance he loved to tell stories about him. One of his favourites was about Vaughan Kirby and a black rhino.

Magqubu said he and Mali Mdhletshe frequently patrolled the Hluhluwe game reserve in the early 1920s and camped at a place which they called iStairs. They gave it this name because every evening a black rhino came, and Magqubu swore that the rhino was actually looking for Mali and himself. It always appeared just as it was getting dark, and on seeing the guards it would charge, scattering the blankets, the pots, and the clothing, and treeing the guards. It happened every time, so they made a long ladder and used it to construct a platform in the trees. Here they were safe. They reported this to Vaughan Kirby, who pooh-poohed the story and said they were exaggerating. But every time they camped in this particular place the black rhino would come.

On one of his periodic patrols to the Hluhluwe reserve, Vaughan Kirby walked with them to the particular camp. In the afternoon he told them to pitch his tent, and they did. He put up the stretcher and prepared to settle down for the evening. The guards warned him that it would not be long before the black rhino came. He ignored what they had to say. When it got dark the two guards climbed the ladder to their platform. They invited Kirby up and warned him again that the black rhino was dangerous.

Vaughan Kirby rejected their invitation with a laugh and a reference to panicky old women.

Magqubu giggled. "We had no sooner laid out blankets on the wooden platform in the trees when we heard the *ubejane* snort across the valley," he said. "Slowly the black rhino came toward the camp, pushing over saplings and feeding on branches. We knew it would not be long before it reached us."

Vaughan Kirby was now in his tent, and Magqubu heard him lie down. The stretcher creaked and moved as he tried to get comfortable.

"We shouted a warning to him again that this black rhino was coming, and that it would be wise to come up and join us on the platform, but Mfohloza just laughed," Magqubu said.

When the rhino was about thirty metres away it realized that Vaughan Kirby's tent was in its path. It stood looking at this strange apparition for quite some time. Magqubu cocked his head like the rhino slowly sniffing the air and looking intently at this white tent.

"Then it came," Magqubu said. "We mame!" (My word!).

Magqubu made the sound of the feet pounding on the footpath and Vaughan Kirby's surprise as the rhino came crashing toward him.

Magqubu laughed and described Kirby's ungraceful exit. The rhino stopped at the tent and with quick movements of its head it uprooted the pegs, smashed the poles, and ripped the canvas. Vaughan Kirby in the meantime had hidden behind a tree; then the rhino saw him and charged. Kirby dodged behind another tree and swore profusely at the rhino. Magqubu wiped tears of laughter from his eyes at Vaughan Kirby's language.

"After that we had no trouble, because whenever Mfohloza was in doubt about anything, we reminded him how he had ignored our warnings about the black rhino at iStairs," Magqubu said. But there was an important moral to the story: white rangers ignored the advice of the game guards at their peril. With all his experience Vaughan Kirby thought he knew better, and the two guards, having warned him, allowed events to take their course.

In my six years of service I had witnessed incidents where white rangers did not appreciate how much the Zulu game guards were contributing to the cause. White rangers who made an effort to cultivate a friendship were rewarded a thousand times by loyalty of the biblical kind, where guards were prepared to lay down their lives.

The game guards, being Zulu, enjoyed the dangerous parts of the anti-poaching work and the possibility of a fight. Their lives were by no means easy. They lived in rough conditions – a hut and adjoining kitchen – for weeks at a time. The sergeants inspected the camps at irregular intervals to ensure the guards were not being subjected to outside pressures. Family and relatives could make their lives a hell. Requests for meat could tempt a guard to steal a .303 bullet, secrete it, and then, at an opportune moment, kill an antelope or warthog. Much depended upon the white officer and the game-guard sergeant. I had to dismiss some men who poached game, a most unpleasant task, but they took the punishment without complaint. This was before Magqubu and I worked together. He would not allow me to employ anyone he did not know. We had had words because I did not consult him about some new recruits. He warned me emphatically that they would be troublesome, and he was quickly proved right. Like Vaughan Kirby, I had to learn a lesson.

There was much publicity about the trails and word-of-mouth descriptions too, and the consistent demand changed what began as a trail every fortnight to a trail a week. The people varied on each trail, and some of them could be extremely difficult to deal with when they arrived. They complained about the colour of the water or its taste, but a long walk in the burning sun soon changed their minds. One group were so thirsty they flopped into a rhino wallow, scraped the faeces aside, and drank deep gulps. They simply did not care that a good percentage of the water was urine. Then they lay in the water fully clothed and rolled in the mud, like rhino. Magqubu stared at them in disbelief. When we reached the river after more hours of walking over the sun-baked veld, they plunged into the water like mad cattle. I asked sarcastically if they approved of the colour and the taste.

Some people verged on hysteria when Magqubu explained that the tiny insects crawling up their legs were not lucky spiders, but minute ticks.

Within a few days they began scratching, and they de-ticked one another like baboons.

One moonlit night the trail party was awakened by the most terrible screams from a woman. I thought a hyena had grabbed her, and we all rushed over to her tent. She may have been dozing and seen the shadows from the fig tree, which had evoked some monstrous vision. She soon calmed down, and by the last night of the trail she was weeping because the wilderness journey would be over the next day. Women always had a deeper appreciation of the trail experience.

Magqubu's stories and his being able to see or hear game long before anyone else made him a focus of attention. He was forever being photographed, and this could have turned the head of a lesser man, but he was unmoved. His sensitivity made a deep impression on the trailists and I was amazed at his politeness in answering the same question repeatedly, and at how he turned a tense situation into one of great humour.

The days of apartheid were very much with us, and once when it began raining and we all crowded into a tent, a male trailist complained about Magqubu's presence. Magqubu understood the gestures and the intonation and began getting his kit together, preparing to move out. I stopped him and told the trailist that there was a simple solution to his problem: if he didn't like Magqubu in the tent, then he was free to leave. After a few hot words the trailist backed down. Magqubu displayed all the great qualities of his race. He neither gloated nor sympathized, nor did he give a hint that there had been unpleasantness. The following day on the trail he excelled in the finding of game and in his historical knowledge, all the time behaving impeccably to the offender.

On another trail, when the moon was full and we were sleeping around the fire, Nkosi the lion walked to the edge of the clearing and roared. The people leaped up in their sleeping bags and jumped around in the way we used to do at school in a sack race. The shouting and the yelling continued long after Nkosi had fled from the racket. Magqubu shook with laughter at the sight of everyone tumbling about, yelling and shouting, banging the cooking pots or heading for the fig tree. The lion encounter was a good opportunity to bring everyone to earth, and the next night he re-enacted the whole scene with heavy emphasis on the way people's stomachs churned when the lion left. I don't think I have ever heard people laugh so much, and in the end they were begging him to stop, but he carried on until they were weak from laughter.

Magqubu's fame spread. Journalists came to write about him, and Sven Persson of the South African Tourist Corporation made a television documentary that was distributed all over the world. None of it fazed Magqubu. To him it was part of his work, in the same way as catching poachers or disciplining guards.

There was other work that cropped up too. Late one summer evening a game guard from the Masinda outpost reported to Magqubu on Mpila that a white rhino was bogged in the mud. Magqubu brought him to my office and questioned him further. The guard described the rhino in the mud with all its legs completely covered. "It will die," the guard said. Magqubu asked how long he thought it had been trapped in the Tjevu River. "Two days," the guard said.

I spoke to Nick Steele, who had come over from Gome outpost, and we agreed we had to make an effort to extricate the animal. This had happened once before at Siyembeni, the junction of the Black and the White Mfolozi rivers. A big white rhino bull had got caught in an old cattle dip. We tried hard to get it out but we failed, and the poor beast died. Nick said there was nothing we could do until the next morning, and the unfortunate animal would have to suffer until we could get to it.

We set off early the next day with two vehicles and all the men we could find. There was an old road that led through the corridor, built when huts and materials from the original area camp had been moved to Masinda camp, which then became the tsetse-fly campaign headquarters. The road was terrible, and the Land-Rovers rattled and bumped over the stones and broken stumps. The cab of the vehicle smelt of petrol, burning rubber, and dust, and the men on the back hung on tightly. The steering wheel jolted my shoulders, and my foot ached as I tried to keep it steady on the accelerator. It took a good hour of travelling to do no more than three miles. We eventually had to cut a track through thick acacia tree encroachments to reach the Tjevu–Black Mfolozi confluence. The day was overcast and sultry.

Spades were off-loaded, and Magqubu led a gang of labourers to the rhino, which lay deeply embedded in the mud and incapable of moving an inch. The men became excited, and soon everyone was yelling and shouting about what needed to be done. Magqubu's and Nick Steele's voices rose above the din, and slowly order reigned. Magqubu, always leading by example, grabbed a shovel and danced toward the rhino. I called out to him to let someone else do the heavy work, but he feigned not to hear me. He sang a loud Zulu chant, making up verses as he and the other men dug into the mud. *Thump*, the spades would hit the clay in unison and piles of mud would come flying out. The overcast weather was stiflingly humid, and everyone sweated profusely. For an hour without rest the men shovelled the heavy mud away from the white rhino's withers until enough had been removed to place a cable around its backside.

Magqubu gave orders and pulled the heavy cable, attaching it around the rhino, then hitching it onto the vehicle. I noticed that he had faint traces of sweat on his face and shirt, whereas the other men were sweating profusely. Magqubu waved his spade, prancing and singing, and ordered the men onto the back of the Land-Rover. When the cable was taut, Nick Steele revved the engine and I shouted, "Go." The cable strained and the Land-Rover shot forward. The rhino squealed in pain and terror. We all bounced up and down on the back of the Land-Rover, which moved forward in a series of jerks. Above the high-pitched revving of the engine I heard Magqubu alternately singing and urging greater effort. The vehicle inched forward, dragging the animal to the edge of the mud.

"Woah, woah," Magqubu shouted as the rhino moved its big legs. Nick reversed the vehicle, and the cable was slipped away. I thought the job was done, but that judgment was premature. We were going to suffer in the hot humid weather for the whole day. A purple-crested lourie called from the dark-green sycamores laden with green figs, and a black-collared barbet repeated its loud and familiar call. Everyone was silent, staring at the rhino lying on its side and breathing heavily. Cicada beetles screeched, and that agile raptor of the African skies, a male bateleur eagle, soared overhead, caught up in the thermals, moving without flapping its wings.

The rhino lay jammed on the lip of the hole, and the Land-Rover could move it no farther. There was still a long stretch of oozing mud ahead, and the rhino would get stuck the moment it tried to walk. The labour gang grabbed their shovels, and with Magqubu leading and singing another chant they danced in slow motion, working up the energy to attack the mud again. One man jumped forward and the others followed, and Magqubu increased the pace of the chanting. Mud was shovelled out and landed with loud *plops* on the ground. There was a burst of laughter when Magqubu said it sounded like diarrhoea.

Everyone became quiet again for a few moments, and I heard the coucal in the thick reeds above where we were working. The notes descended down the scale, a liquid sound that gives the bird one of its alternative names, bottle bird. Another name is rain bird, because it calls frequently before rain sweeps in on the southern clouds. The hot, humid conditions were strong indicators of rain, and the bird's call confirmed it. Magqubu knew I liked the bird, and he looked at me as the liquid notes echoed over the slow-flowing dark waters of the Black Mfolozi. "*Fukwe, fukwe*," he said, giving a perfect imitation of its call. We had often been together waiting in reed beds and on river banks for poachers who had entered the game reserve. The *uFukwe* – Burchell's coucal – used to be part of our camouflage, because once we had settled down it took no notice of us and called uninterruptedly, and poachers assumed that no one was there.

The labour gang shouldered their shovels like game guards carrying rifles, and Magqubu led them in a slow dance that resembled men drilling on the parade ground. I admired the way Magqubu could turn a serious situation and hard work into a game. I said to Nick Steele that when we were hot and bothered we became extremely irritable, and this just added to the Zulus' amusement, and they indirectly poked fun at us. Magqubu did it in a direct way, by imitating me, and it was so hilariously funny I couldn't take offence. He had a wonderful understanding of the fine line between insulting humour and a joke that gently poked fun at someone. The guards and labourers loved it when he limped around mimicking me, giving orders on the parade ground or swearing at someone who had incurred my ire. His sense of humour took over whenever meetings became too heated, and he could calm everyone down with a few remarks and gestures, but it did not stop him from making fun of himself or me, and this always defused hostile situations. He could, however, be quite a tyrant and work men until they were ready to drop. On this particular day he could see how the humid weather was affecting the men, so he was firm but gentle.

The labour gang steadily shovelled the mud away, but whenever anyone approached too near the rhino's head it would lunge forward, trying to hook the person with its horn. The men scattered, laughing and yelling. A honeyguide was attracted to the noise and flitted in the large yellow-and-green fig trees, trying to entice someone to follow it. Two men walked to the river, drank, and washed the mud off their hands. I noticed that it was a hurried motion, for they were concerned about the crocodiles. All was quiet while everyone took a rest, then the Christmas beetles started their screeching, and Nick Steele said, "Let's try again, we must get away from here."

The cable slipped through the sloppy mud and the men tied it to the back of the Land-Rover. "Qapela" (Look out), Nick shouted, and everyone ran for cover. The Land-Rover roared, but above the noise I could hear the trumpeting and the snorting of the rhino. I also saw sweat pouring from the nuchal hump. The trapped animal laid its ears back in rage and terror. The horn was covered in mud, and it was just possible to see the eyes. The rhino moved slightly, then its head was jammed below the mud.

"Pull," I shouted, "it's going to drown." Ranger Ken Rochat had now arrived with another vehicle. He jumped out, and with the help of one of the men rammed a log under the rhino's neck. One nostril showed above the mud, and the rhino breathed slowly, gasping for air. It was a terrible sound, this long choking and rattling in the throat. Quickly and silently the men unhitched the line, dragged it out, and relaid it behind the animal's hindquarters. The Land-Rover started once more and churned up loose wet sand, and it moved the rhino far enough out of the mud so that it could breathe again. We all sighed with relief, relaxed, and wondered what to do next. A faint breeze floated downriver, and we were cool for a few blissful moments. The heat was overpowering. Black oozing mud, rotting figs, rhino dung, the tang of the brown river and wet sand, and sweating bodies were a strong combination.

At eleven o'clock we hitched the cable onto another vehicle. We now had two Land-Rovers pulling. In one dramatic moment the rhino was pulled to the edge, and the front legs came out of the mud and the back legs gripped onto the slippery bank.

"It's out, it's out!" we all yelled enthusiastically. The noise of the engines and our shouting was too much for the rhino, and in one moment it lunged sideways, then turned and ploughed back into the mud hole. This was a moment of bitter disappointment, and I thought it was the end. I remembered the rhino that died at the Siyembeni dip. The memory gave added energy to our efforts to save this rhino, because we were determined it was not going to be eaten by the vultures and the long-legged marabou storks.

We got the gang going again and battled with little rest until just before four o'clock. It then struck me that we had not made full use of the large quantities of sand lying close by. Every available shovel was now used, and within fifteen minutes we had piled a mountain of sand around the rhino. Then someone would shout at it, and as it moved we rammed the sand under its body, and slowly the rhino was lifted. I had forgotten Archimedes' principle. We got the cable out, and with both Land-Rovers pulling we moved the rhino to the edge. It lay there for a few minutes and then lifted its front feet up. I had a camera and crept round to get a picture of the men behind the rhino. My movement spurred the rhino into action, and with a few frantic heaves it pulled its body out of the sucking mud, walked onto the hard ground, and then turned around and faced us for a full two minutes. We in turn stared back and the world about us was silent.

Magqubu said quietly that the rhino had turned to say thank you. The rhino took a few staggering steps, climbed the bank, and disappeared.

"Hamba kahle, mkombe" (Go well, white rhino), Magqubu said, raising his arm in a Zulu salute.

For the rest of the year Magqubu and I took the trails, but the added work meant that other duties suffered. The increase in the white rhino population urgently needed attention. The capture and translocation to other national parks and game reserves was becoming a priority, but first the board had to be lobbied to take this unprecedented step. Poaching was increasing, with the number of displaced people on our borders growing daily. We had not yet secured the extra land on the south and western Crown lands. The trailists who now arrived every week were given insights into our problems, and they were becoming the nucleus of an important lobby. This was particularly so with the journalists whose articles were stirring up government departments, and we had visits from officials about boundary demarcations. Some of these men taunted us with impossible boundary lines, but we retaliated by walking them up the steep Masinda hill at midday. The hint of more walking up even steeper hills made them more generous with the promised allocation of land. However, it was not until 1962 that the final boundaries on the south and west were finalized by proclamation.

I persuaded my seniors to send me another man, and in 1960 my friend Hugh Dent returned to the Parks Board as the wilderness trails ranger. His superlative bush skills, knowledge of the Zulu people, and love of wilderness made him the ideal person.

Meanwhile, at Lake St. Lucia, Jim Feely was leading trails, and with his ornithological and general ecological background trailists gained knowledge about the rhythms of the lake and the value of this unique estuarine system.

Wilderness trails had been well and truly launched, and the concept of wilderness was on its way to being accepted, but long and bitter battles still lay ahead to have the concept accepted by our colleagues in the National Parks Board and other conservation agencies in South Africa. The concept was still far too radical for people in my own organization, let alone in others. I had seen enough of development in game reserves and national parks to know that if wilderness areas were not set aside, the parks would become like city suburbs. Wildness frightens most people, and they want either to eliminate it or tame it.

17

Wilderness Leadership School

From 1958 until 1964 I worked on an almost daily basis with Magqubu. In 1963 Metro-Goldwyn-Mayer came to Mfolozi to make a film called *Rhino*, and for two months we had to deal with some Hollywood stars who could, to put it mildly, be quite temperamental. But again it was Magqubu who was always ready to smooth ruffled feathers and make an apt comment.

In 1964 I was promoted to chief conservator of Zululand. This put me in charge of all the game and nature reserves north of the Thukela River. From being a field man I became increasingly involved in administrative and political work. Magqubu decided he wanted to retire, and he went to live at his *muzi* at Macibini. I visited him whenever I passed his homestead, and we discussed the multiplicity of game-reserve issues.

In May 1964 I visited America for the first time, as a guest of Metro-Goldwyn-Mayer. I arrived too late to meet Howard Zahniser of the Wilderness Society, who had died just before my arrival. I have always deeply regretted not being able to shake his hand and say thank you for all he did for wilderness. When I was catching a plane in New York I saw Hubert Humphrey walking toward me. He was obviously in a hurry, so mentally I sent him a message of thanks for all he had done. During a visit to Washington, D.C., I met Stewart Udall and had an immediate rapport with him. In 1977 I was able to invite him to be a keynote speaker at the first World Wilderness Congress in Johannesburg, a part repayment for a debt of honour. Ira Gabrielson and Lloyd Swift, two prominent biologists and wilderness men, were present when I met Udall, and I thanked them too for what they had unknowingly done for African wilderness. Lloyd Swift later visited Mfolozi game reserve, and I was able to show him what we had created.

For five years our home was in Hluhluwe game reserve; then in 1969 I was transferred to the Natal Parks Board headquarters in Pietermaritzburg. My brother Gary's generosity allowed us to acquire a small farm in the Karkloof district, where many of our early forebears had once lived.

In early 1970 Magqubu came to live on the farm and took control of all the farm affairs. His bearing, forthrightness, and wisdom won him the respect of our white and Zulu neighbours, and his counsel was frequently sought. For me it was an opportunity to spend time with him after work, talking and recording much of the early history of the game reserves.

I resigned from the Natal Parks Board in April 1974, after twenty-two years' service. It was not an easy decision to make because an attractive senior post had been offered to me, but I knew that I had more to contribute to wilderness and wildlife conservation outside the Parks Board than in it. My experience with Magqubu in the wilderness had brought me to a new understanding about life, and I really could say that my life had been saved. I felt compelled to make it possible for more people to have wilderness experiences so that their lives could be changed, and then they too would become advocates for the fast-diminishing wilderness and the parks, which were under constant political threat. I knew, too, that important work lay ahead for Magqubu and me as a team.

On my last day of work, as I gathered my papers in my office at the Natal Parks Board headquarters, I wept. So much of my life's energy had gone into serving the board and wildlife conservation. The political battles had been unending. A victory always preceded a new threat, but we could be proud of and thankful for our achievements. Ndumu and Mkuze game reserves had been saved from deproclamation, and additional land had been added to Mfolozi game reserve. Operation White Rhino had been an outstanding success, with the animal translocated to all its former habitats and significant gene pools established in Europe, the United Kingdom, and the United States. The species was down to about fifty in 1895, and we had enabled it to recover and be put back on the hunting list. Hunting on game ranches had become a growth industry, and a white rhino trophy was eagerly sought after by American, German, and Spanish hunters, who were prepared to pay large sums of money to kill the unfortunate animal. However, even in death the white rhino has contributed to conservation by saving land from being turned to sugarcane or gum and pine trees. There are now millions of acres in South Africa that are being managed as private game ranches.

Wilderness trails were being accepted, and the concept of wilderness was making some impact on the thinking in government departments. In 1971 South Africa's department of forestry attached an amendment to the Forest Act empowering the minister of forestry to set aside state forest land as a wilderness area. This was a giant step forward, but unfortunately the department never took the next step, of having staff lead wilderness treks. Had this been done it may well have turned the tide in favor of a more general understanding of the wilderness concept. Many years were to pass before the

National Parks Board accepted the idea of wilderness areas and wilderness trails.

I had learned that among the professional ranks of wildlife conservation officers there were two distinct groups: those who believed in the wilderness concept and the value of having land set aside for wilderness areas, and those who did not. The idea of wilderness being a sacred place and beneficial to the mental health of human beings was better understood by the general public than by officialdom.

Mfolozi and Lake St. Lucia game reserves were the crucible of the wilderness movement in South Africa, and had been since 1955. When Colonel Jack Vincent left the Natal Parks Board in 1963, I was told that not another acre would be added to the wilderness areas that had been established, and that those of us who were wilderness advocates wanted to "lock up land." The opposite was true. We were trying with little success to unlock the official mind-set of developing more and more buildings within the parks. I explained all this to Magqubu, and his answer was most apt. "Those men enjoy sitting on their office chairs and giving orders. They will never understand what we are doing until they sleep on the ground and hear the hyena cry," he said.

When I shut my office door for the last time I felt like a monk who was leaving a monastery. The world outside was not going to be easy, but I would have more freedom of movement and of speech.

My pension amounted to a three-thousand-rand cash payment, nothing more. This was a shock, but I had never worked for the money; I believed passionately in the cause.

I left the Natal Parks Board with a heavy heart. The severance of this particular umbilical cord was painful. I now moved out into a world where I had to find my own income. The Parks Board salary was minimal but it was regular, and the accounts department would hunt you down to give you your cheque. Now I had to do the hunting.

Through friends in America I had been given the opportunity of establishing the International Wilderness Leadership Foundation. I spent two years travelling to and from America raising money, which enabled one senior Explorer Scout from each state to come to South Africa and participate in a Wilderness Leadership School trail. In 1976 Barry Clements, who was running the Wilderness Leadership School, resigned, and I was asked to take his place.

It was in 1957 that I conceived the idea of the Wilderness Leadership School. I was stationed at Charters Creek on Lake St. Lucia, and six boys from my old school, St. John's College, came to visit us. I took them on patrols along the eastern shores among the hippo, crocodile, pelicans, and flamingo. When they returned home they all wrote to say how the experience had changed their lives. They had been smitten by the moods of the lake and the spirit of place.

On their last evening we sat around a fire with the sounds of the hippo grunting and the Tonga people playing their drums in the distance. I listened to the excited talk of the boys describing their boat rides and walking along the lake edge, and I recollected how difficult it had been for me when talking to magistrates, policemen, farmers, and politicians, because they had such little understanding of the environmental issues facing South Africa. The future did not look rosy. All the game reserves were threatened in one way or another. Every day I had problems implementing the wildlife ordinances. The very people who should have been upholding the law were some of its biggest violators.

Listening to these youngsters talking made me realize that the future lay in their hands. Problems were looming up everywhere, and human populations were exploding. No one had done anything to make the black people of our country aware of the importance of parks as their historical and cultural assets. We were in the vice-like grip of apartheid administration, and every effort was being made by the government to erect more barriers between white and black people. My concept of the Wilderness Leadership School was to bring individuals of all colours together in the wilderness, where they would see one another as people and together appreciate the sacred nature of wilderness areas. Wilderness and wildlife conservation had become my politics, and I believed that every person we could take into the wilderness would become an advocate for the cause. I wanted them to feel the soul of Africa through the soles of their feet. I was not naive enough to think that wilderness politics would supersede national politics, but I was certain that a wilderness experience could influence our political future for the good.

I saw the role of the Wilderness Leadership School as choosing people with leadership qualities and having them sponsored by commerce and industry. Initially it was to be schoolboys and girls, but I knew that their stories would spark their parents and other adults into wanting to participate.

We had no money or equipment, but I put a pound on the table when talking with Hugh Dent and some other rangers and said that if God wanted the idea to prosper, this would be the beginning. Shortly afterward my brother Gary won the Transvaal Open golf championship and donated his winnings to the fledgling Wilderness Leadership School. We had begun.

There was no staff, so we simply took off our Natal Parks Board uniforms, put on different clothing, called ourselves Wilderness Leadership School field officers, and took the young trailists into the wilderness area. They had to carry their own kits, unlike the Natal Parks Board trails, where donkeys carried everything.

We needed a symbol, and I had been impressed with Grey Owl, the Englishman who became an Ojibwa Indian in Canada. He was one of Hugh Dent's heroes, and Hugh was always quoting Grey Owl's last statements to his biographer after a lecture tour in England. "You are tired with years of civilization. I come and offer you – what? A single green leaf." So I asked Magqubu to find a leaf. He came one day with a leaf of the *Erythrina caffra* tree – *msinsi* in Zulu. "Take this leaf," he said, with an almost biblical injunction. "The tree is found in the wild and also in the settlements. The work of the Wilderness Leadership School is to take people from the settlements to the wild and back. This is a different tree too, the leaves are bright green in summer and the flowers bloom red in winter. Other trees flower in spring and summer."

So the erythrina leaf became the symbol of the Wilderness Leadership School, with the three points of the leaf embodying the philosophy "Man to God, Man to Man, and Man to Earth."

After my experience with the Natal Parks Board trails I was determined to introduce other features into the Wilderness Leadership School trails. Keeping watch at the fire was one ritual. Not only was it important that someone kept an eye open for rhino or lion or a too bold hyena, but there were religious reasons too. In my early days at St. John's College in Johannesburg we kept watch in the crypt at Easter, and this was by far the most important experience I had had in the Christian church. I was only ten or eleven years old, but it gave me an opportunity for a glimpse inward and left a profound impression. I realized that there was another part of myself that was of an unknown world. Watching the flickering candles and the shadows dancing on the great stone walls brought a deep sense of inner peace. So despite the scorn of some ranger colleagues, who thought keeping watch at the fire was not only unnecessary but was for sissies, I persisted.

To this day the fire watch continues, and there is no doubt that it served two functions admirably. Nearly everyone who has participated in the Wilderness Leadership School trails has commented how the time spent alone at the fire was enriching. For many on their first watch it was a terrifying time. There were, after all, lions, rhino, hippo, leopards, and other wild animals that under certain circumstances could be dangerous. Yet it was fascinating to see that most trailists, desperately afraid as they might have been, stared into the fire, where there was no danger except from an emerging scorpion. This showed that it was the inner wild animals of which they were afraid. The danger lay at their backs and beyond the fire. By the time they had done their third watch fear had dissipated, and this was for many the beginning of the inward journey, a sense of being one with the world – a primordial experience and a connection with the ancient part of humanity that still lies within us all. I had often lain in my sleeping bag watching people sitting alone at the fire, their shoulders hunched and a far-away look in their eyes. A breaking branch or cough of a leopard might disturb them, but soon they would settle down and stare once more into the fire. The smell of woodsmoke helped, too, to take them back into the evolutionary world.

With the administrative training I had received from Colonel Vincent in my Natal Parks Board career, I was able to manage the Wilderness Leadership School in my spare time, gradually expanding its work. In 1963 a trust was formed and a board of governors was appointed. Carl Erasmus, a hotelier in Durban, became the first chairman and allowed his office to be used as the school's headquarters. Barry Clements, Hugh Dent and Jim Feely, all Natal Parks Board wilderness trails officers, later joined the school and brought with them their expertise. In 1970 I made a presentation to Chris Saunders, chairman of the Tongaat group of companies. He advised me to take Anson Lloyd, a senior executive of the Sugar Association, on trail and sell him the concept of the school. I did this and was able to persuade the Sugar Association to donate fifteen thousand rands a year for three years. This established the school. Later, when traveling to international congresses I was able to tell the story of the school and raise funds from organizations such as the San Diego Zoological Society and the Texas-based Game Conservation International while at the same time recruiting Americans and Britons to come on trail.

With the other field officers of the Wilderness Leadership School, Magqubu and I broadened the scope of the school internationally, and, slowly, by word of mouth and editorials in the press, the trails attracted some outstanding people. Documentaries were made by British, American, and German television. Wilderness as a concept in Europe received a stimulus.

In South Africa more and more people from all walks of life participated. Schoolchildren from the township of Soweto, businessmen from the commercial centres of Johannesburg, Cape Town, and Durban, engineers, doctors, schoolteachers – all walked the trails.

One of the other rituals on Wilderness Leadership School trails was the *indaba* held before leaving the wilderness. Participants gave their opinions about the trail, what they had seen, their feelings, the impact of the night watch, and criticisms, if they so wished. When it came to Magqubu's turn he first thanked Nkulunkulu for the safe passage, then added comments about the people or a close shave with an animal. On one trail he spoke about the need to have an *indabankulu* (big gathering) of all the people over the last twenty years who had trekked on the trails. This gave me the idea of having a world wilderness congress, and it took place in 1977 against opposition from various scientists, who complained that the money being raised for the congress could be better spent. The total budget was approximately two hundred thousand rands, and it included the airfares of thirty international speakers.

My reply to the critical scientists was that the South African Defence Force spent over a million rands buying a tank, a weapon of destruction. The World Wilderness Congress was a step towards bringing people from all over the world to tell us South Africans their story of what was happening to the environment in their own countries. Laurens van der Post was a proverbial tower of strength and defended the congress in every available forum. He was *persona non grata* with the South African government because of his longstanding anti-apartheid opposition. Television and radio were instructed not to quote him, but we defeated the bureaucracy, and Dr. Piet Koornhof, then the minister of sport, participated in a Wilderness Leadership School trail and was extremely helpful.

The eventual success of the First World Wilderness Congress lay in the variety and sincerity of the speakers, who came from as far afield as Thailand and Alaska. Politicians such as Lloyd Brooks of Canada and Dr. Piet Koornhof of South Africa rubbed shoulders with the banker Edmund de Rothschild, artists Guy Coheleach and Bob Kuhn from America, and writer Robert Ardrey.

A Bushman from the Kalahari attended, along with hunters and anti-hunters, oceanographic and elephant experts. My longtime friend Ken Tinley, now a leading ecologist, spoke on the diversity of wilderness. Dick Roughsey, an aboriginal from Cape York in Queensland, told the delegates that the Aborigines in Australia were a unique people. "Over the millennia," he said, "we have flourished sufficiently to produce a race of philosophers who developed a civilization of high degree based on spiritual and not material values."

My proudest moment in the congress week was when my friend Magqubu Ntombela walked up the stairs to the podium. This was the first time in the history of South African conservation that a black game scout had spoken to an international audience. Magqubu began with the Zulu greeting of *sanibona*: "I see you, and I greet you all, and all of those who have come from afar to see this land of mine." He gave a brilliant description of the Zulu months of the year. The audience sat mesmerized as he spoke in his poetic Zulu, interpreted by a close friend and neighbour, Maurice Mackenzie, an outstanding Zulu linguist.

"Nhlangula," Magqubu said, "is the month of May, when winter starts, the leaves fall, and we feel the first pinch of cold. The days grow shorter and a great stillness falls upon the land."

On the last day of the congress Magqubu commented that although he was unable to speak English he could see that the speakers were people of great ability who spoke from their hearts. It showed that there was a stewardship of conservation beating in the hearts of many people all over the world. He also voiced what many had said, that those who attended the congress should take personal action.

Magqubu was complimented by Chief Mangosuthu Buthelezi, a principal speaker at the congress. The compliment, coming from so important a Zulu leader, meant a great deal to Magqubu. In his address to the congress delegates, Chief Buthelezi made a most pertinent remark. He said that politicians of the world should periodically gather in the wilderness, for he felt that this was the way they would resolve their differences.

An old American friend, Ray Arnett, president of the National Wildlife Federation and a former director of the fish and game department in California when Ronald Reagan was governor, summed up the congress. He said, *inter alia*, "How fortunate we are to have taken advantage of this once-in-a-lifetime opportunity to attend the World Wilderness Congress 1977. It is indeed unfortunate that the whole of mankind was not able to participate with us. The world would soon be a better place in which to live if all human beings were direct beneficiaries of the same exposure we have received at this congress."

The proceedings of the week had been a great reward for all the hard work that had gone into the planning, the raising of money, and the difficulties of dealing with bureaucracy.

For me this congress was to be a unique effort. I had no intention of ever being involved in another. My stamina and nerves had taken a severe pounding. However, forces much more powerful than my human ego decided otherwise. The Australian delegates under the leadership of Percy Trezise wanted to stage a Second World Wilderness Congress in Cairns, Australia, in 1980. Malcolm Fraser, the prime minister of Australia, did not want to open the congress because South Africans were involved. But through the lobbying of Laurens van der Post and Edmund de Rothschild the congress took place, and many Australian environmental issues were brought forward.

Laurens van der Post spoke with extraordinary clarity about wilderness and the human spirit. He said, speaking of people who had been into wilderness: "Somehow they emerge from the wilderness transformed, as if they were coming from a highly sacred atmosphere. Indeed, wilderness is the original cathedral, the original temple, the original church of life in which they have been converted and healed and from which they have emerged transformed in a positive manner."

Another eloquent speaker was Enos Mabuza from KaNgwane, a leader of the Swazi people of South Africa. We had become friends in 1976, and he had addressed the First World Wilderness Congress as the last speaker on the first day, a most difficult slot, but his humility and depth of feeling made a deep impression. At the Second World Wilderness Congress, he, as an African, paid generous tribute to Stevenson Hamilton, the warden of the Kruger National Park, who was responsible for its expansion after the proclamation of the small Sabie game reserve by President Paul Kruger. Enos Mabuza concluded, "Perhaps the answer to the turbulent Africa of today lies in the re-discovery of the wilderness experience by the African, even if only within the limited precincts of what remains of the African wilderness."

One of the delegates to the Second World Wilderness Congress was Vance Martin, a young American who was working with the Findhorn Foundation near Inverness in Scotland. I took an immediate liking to him, and by the end of the congress we had become friends. I had read stories about Findhorn and the miraculous vegetables the community had grown. I was keen to know more about the people who formed this group. We agreed that a world wilderness congress was needed in the United Kingdom because it was by far the furthest behind in the English-speaking world in appreciating wilderness values. We resolved on behalf of our two organizations, the Findhorn Foundation and the Wilderness Leadership School, to have the Third World Wilderness Congress in Scotland in 1983.

Little did we know what we were undertaking. If the first two world wilderness congresses had been difficult, the third was a nightmare. Raising funds seemed impossible, and the conservation establishment looked with horror at a congress at Findhorn among the "New Agers." For the first time in my life I was on the point of giving up. Then I had a dream about an old game-ranger friend who did not have a negative bone in his body. He had died some years before, but I dreamed of him alive and well and a passenger in a car I was driving. I was going fast in reverse and he said, "Why are you reversing? You must go forward, not back." I obeyed.

With Laurens van der Post in London

Laurens van der Post again backed our cause and Ray Arnett, by then assistant secretary of the interior in the United States government, agreed to be a speaker. This calmed down some of our more violent critics, but we still could not persuade many speakers to appear at Findhorn itself. So we compromised with an opening ceremony and two days of papers from those who could not, or did not want to, appear at Findhorn at the Eden Court theatre in Inverness. For the rest of the time we gathered at the Universal Hall at the Findhorn Foundation. The spirit moved among the delegates and the whole congress was a delight, ending with Laurens telling African stories to an enraptured audience.

Vance Martin had worked extremely hard for three years, and I was impressed with his administrative abilities and his capacity for work. I suggested that it was time for him to return to America, the land of his birth. The International Wilderness Leadership Foundation, which I had initiated in 1974, had been dormant for several years, so I spoke to the trustees and they agreed that Vance could become the president if he found his own salary. Vance accepted the challenge and returned to America, and straightaway we launched the Fourth World Wilderness Congress. Four nerve-shattering years later it took place in Denver and Estes Park, Colorado. The outstanding success of the congress established the International Wilderness Leadership Foundation, by then referred to as the WILD Foundation. The search for funding continued and does to this day, but as an organization it has made a unique contribution to the world wilderness movement.

18

Fourth World Wilderness Congress

In 1986, while walking along the rhino paths that skirted the Black Mfolozi River, Maqubu and I stopped to make a fire and boil a billy of tea. I broached the subject of the forthcoming World Wilderness Congress in America. I explained that it would be an important affair, and I wanted him to be a speaker. He had of course met many Americans on trail, but he asked me if we could travel via England because he wanted to go where the men lived who had fought against his father (in reality his uncle, but in Zulu custom he was head of the *muzi*) at the great battle of Isandlwana on June 22, 1879. He repeated the story he had told so many times before, how his father (or uncle), fighting with the Zulu army in the Ngobamakhosi (Bender of Kings) regiment under Mnyamana Buthelezi, had killed four redcoats with his spear. It was many years before he had admitted to this because he had experienced the bitterness of the Boers over the killing of Piet Retief at Dingane's *muzi* in 1838. Magqubu said he wanted to make his peace with the spirits of the men his father had killed. This was a stipulation I had no hesitation in agreeing to, but the other was more difficult: he wanted to take his famous three-legged pot, which he never ceased to remind me had cost five shillings in 1925. "Wherever I go, the pot goes," he said.

I knew this to be so, because wherever we had gone together, even to the smartest hotels, he took his pot. He always found a fellow Zulu to replenish his mielie meal and take him to a kitchen where he could cook his own food. This time I had to explain to him that taking the pot could be difficult. For one thing it was heavy, but the other reason was that when it went through the X-ray machine at airports, people might think it was a bomb. He looked at me, smiled, and said reassuringly, "But it isn't a bomb."

"Yes, Magqubu," I said. "I know it isn't a bomb, but the people will think it is and they will get into a panic."

"It is not a bomb, it is my pot. And where I go my pot goes." I was wasting my breath.

We left in the early part of September, accompanied by Bongani Ngubane of the KwaZulu Bureau of Natural Resources, who was the interpreter; Chip

Kamber, a public relations officer for the Wilderness Leadership School; and Ann.

During the long flight I walked to Magqubu's seat to see how he was faring in the middle of the night. He was eating Marie biscuits, had the earphones on, and was listening to country-and-western music, swaying to the beat. When we arrived at Heathrow the next morning, he showed not a trace of jet lag and was as fresh as when the journey had begun.

A friend of mine had phoned Major Bob Smith of the Royal Regiment of Wales in Brecon, and he had at once agreed to a visit from Magqubu and invited us to attend a luncheon at the regimental headquarters. We travelled by early-morning train from Paddington to Newport. Magqubu's new shoes were giving him trouble, so he took them off and walked barefoot in the train. He stared out of the window and missed nothing, a golden pheasant in a field or a rabbit in a copse. His keen senses took everything in, and he exclaimed constantly at the greenness of the land, the fat Friesland cows, the falling rain, and the clear-running streams. I knew we were in for a long day and tried to persuade him to relax, pointing out that at his age of eighty-seven he needed rest. He looked at me and grinned, his polite way of saying, "Don't bother me."

At Brecon barracks there was a mob of television, radio, and newspaper people waiting in the courtyard. I explained quickly to Bongani Ngubane who they were and he told Magqubu, who laughed and said that he had met people like this before. He got out of the vehicle, squared his shoulders, and walked straight up to them. He was photographed from all angles and plied with every conceivable question. Nothing anyone asked confused him, and I stood back marvelling yet again at his enormous dignity and sense of humour.

Major Bob Smith took Magqubu by the arm and led him through the museum to a diorama of the battle of Isandlwana. Magqubu stared intently at the toy soldier figures and the Zulu regiments. He pointed out where his father's regiment had been in the attack. The media people began to press around him, asking more and more questions, many of them political, but he was so hemmed in he could hardly move. He glanced up at the shield and spear hanging above him on the wall and, his eyes twinkling, he leapt up like a cat, grabbed the spear and shield, and adopted an aggressive Zulu warrior pose. The media hurriedly withdrew, then they saw he was laughing and came back with more questions. Magqubu later told me that, coincidentally, the shield and spear were from the Ngobamakhosi regiment.

After the museum tour we were invited to the officers' mess for lunch. We sat down at the long polished table. The meal was about to begin when

Magqubu pointedly asked whether the English did not say grace. I replied that these were not English, they were Welsh. He looked about and said they looked like English to him. I explained that there were some people who might have thought that the Zulus and the Basutos were the same. Again he looked about, and this time said the equivalent of "I see what you mean."

I spoke to the senior officer at the head of the table and told him that Magqubu had enquired about grace, and he at once asked Magqubu to bless the food. I felt apprehensive. Magqubu was known for his extraordinarily long graces, and he was capable of praying for an hour, but he only spoke for about five minutes.

The tableware was confusing: which came first, and for what purpose? I watched Magqubu, wondering how he would cope. He sat quietly until the senior officer picked up the appropriate cutlery, and then he followed suit, and I followed him. He had demonstrated his innate understanding of etiquette and his powers of observation. It was a happy meal, with Bongani interpreting for Magqubu and the officers.

Toward the end of the meal I asked the adjutant if there would be any speeches. He replied that there was a tradition not to have after-luncheon speeches, but he had hardly spoken when the senior officer tapped a plate for silence. He made a short speech saying how nice it was to have a descendant of the warriors who had fought his regiment one hundred and five years ago now sitting in the mess on a peaceful mission. Magqubu responded with wisdom and a sense of the occasion, then he took three pieces of beadwork from a pocket of his blazer. He said that each piece was a reminder of that war fought in Zululand between two brave foes. The snuff box was for the men who died, the bangle for the married women who mourned their men, and the beaded switch was for the girlfriends and fiancées of the men who had died. It was a most touching little ceremony, and the men were clearly moved.

After lunch we moved into the lounge, and Magqubu asked to see the waiters and the cook so he could express his appreciation. An officer was instructed to find everyone, and the waiters appeared. Magqubu gravely shook their hands, thanked them, and took ten pounds from his pocket to give to each man. We waited for the cook, and he was a long time in coming. Eventually a tall black Jamaican came through the door, and Magqubu looked at him in astonishment because up until this moment everyone had been white. Magqubu greeted him in a flood of Zulu and asked where he came from. The man stood somewhat perplexed until we explained to Magqubu that he only spoke English. Magqubu went through the ritual again of shaking hands, giving ten pounds, and politely thanking the man for an excellent lunch.

In the late afternoon we were driven to Brecon Cathedral, and within the silence of the stone walls we read name after name of the dead. We were shown the faded colours that Coghill and Melville had carried from the battlefield and that were washed down the Buffalo River to the rock where they were found a few days later. The wind was blowing outside, and rain splattered down on fallen, yellowing leaves. Dark clouds were visible through the open door. Magqubu knelt at a pew and began to pray aloud. He called on the spirits of Senzangakhona, Shaka, Dingane, Mpande, Queen Victoria, Cetshwayo, then his father and the unknown men his father had killed. He asked God for peace for ever between the Zulu and the British. No one who was there will forget that afternoon of dark brooding skies and the silence in the cathedral broken for the first time with the praise names of Zulu kings.

The sincerity and dignity of this remarkable eighty-seven-year-old Zulu caught the imagination of the British media, and for days there were reports in the papers and on television and radio. Magqubu had travelled a long way to make his peace with the spirits, and when we returned by train to London that afternoon the expression on his face showed that he knew he had succeeded.

During our few days in London Magqubu spent an afternoon with Laurens van der Post in Chelsea. He also travelled on the upper deck of a tourist bus and saw the sights. He exclaimed at the buildings, but when he saw the Thames he said, "This is a working river. We have many rivers at home, but none are like this." He pointed to the barges, the small boats, and the pleasure craft, and he said, "See, this river is working, night and day." Above us jumbo jets came in every few minutes, descending toward Heathrow. It began to rain and I reminded Magqubu how he had said at his *muzi* that it was the aircraft flying overhead that caused the drought. I pointed to the aircraft and the shower of rain and said, "But look at this: here are airplanes and rain." I asked if he was still prepared to cling to his theory. "Of course," he said firmly. "This is England, this is not KwaZulu." Magqubu was not easily beaten in an argument.

We left London and flew to Chicago, changed flights, and carried on to Denver, where we were put up at one of the best hotels, the Fairmount. Within a few days Magqubu complained about the food. I explained that it was a five-star accommodation, but he replied that the food was far too fatty, and that what he needed now was a good pot of mielie meal. I irritably asked him where on earth he thought I was going to be able to get mielie meal, and he calmly replied that when we were flying from Chicago to Denver he had looked down and seen vast fields of maize. We had begun our flight in the early afternoon, and he had identified the maize fields from a height of twenty thousand feet. I said I would do what I could but did not hold out much hope. "I will find it then," he said resolutely.

Part of the congress proceedings included an art exhibition and auction, and during one of the evenings I saw Magqubu talking to a tall, sharp-faced Native American. I edged closer to try to hear the conversation. Magqubu was going full bore in his normal impeccable Zulu, but I heard the word *mpupu* (porridge) repeated many times. Back at the hotel I asked Magqubu what it was about, and he said that he had asked this man – "the one who looks like *ikanka* [jackal]" – for some meal, and the man said he would get it. I subsequently discovered that the man's name was Coyote and that he had spoken to other Native Americans, who had sent a special car down to New Mexico that would be returning with a packet of the most prized blue corn.

Magqubu interacted brilliantly with the delegates and the other speakers. I have clear memories of Magqubu, in his full Zulu tribal dress, walking with Finlay MacRae, dressed in his kilt and Scottish paraphernalia, down the main mall of Denver on our way to television and radio interviews. Finlay and Magqubu had first met at the 1977 World Wilderness Congress in Johannesburg and, instantly overcoming all language barriers, had become friends. It was an unusual session in the radio studio with Finlay talking in his broad accent and Magqubu in Zulu with Bongani Ngubane translating, except when Magqubu imitated the lion, hippo, elephant, and other animals, which needed no interpretation. The radio interviewer expressed what I imagine the unseen listeners must have felt, that this was the most interesting radio broadcast that had been heard in Denver. Magqubu's fame had already spread after publication of an enormous colour photograph before he arrived in Denver. He had no hesitation in singing for the radio broadcast or in doing a slow Zulu dance when Finlay MacRae played his chanter. No matter where he went, he charmed everybody.

Mrs. Harlem Brundtland, then prime minister of Norway, arrived to address the congress, and Vance Martin asked if Magqubu would make a presentation to her. We explained that she was the prime minister of Norway. He was unperturbed and at lunchtime took some beautiful Zulu beadwork, a necklace and a bangle, to Mrs. Brundtland's table. Instead of simply handing it to her, he insisted on placing the necklace around her neck and the bangle on her wrist. I watched the ceremony from across the room and was near to tears, seeing Magqubu's gracious actions and Mrs. Brundtland's response. Again I remembered Disraeli's quote about the Zulu being a remarkable people, and I thought of the great distance Magqubu had travelled, from being a barefoot little boy looking after the goats on the misty Ongeni hills, to joining the game-guard force and spending nearly his whole life defending the wildlife of Zululand and keeping the oral culture alive. I thought of his becoming a wilderness guide extraordinary when we together took more than two thousand people of all races, creeds, and colours into the wild country of his forefathers and the Zulu kings.

Magqubu and I had a row about the subject of his talk. North American Indians were on the programme, and the principal content of their talks had been of a spiritual nature. Watching the audience, I sensed that they had made an impact, so I wanted Magqubu to tell the story of the seasons of the year, which he had done many times before with poetic brilliance. He, however, wanted to talk about white rhino mating, because a few months previously he had done that at a KwaZulu legislative assembly gathering and it had brought the house down. I met Bishop Zulu, speaker at the assembly, shortly afterward. He relayed Magqubu's performance and described how the assembly yelled with laughter and wildly applauded the old man's antics and sound effects.

The experience had impressed Magqubu, and he wanted to repeat it in Denver. With Bongani Ngubane interpreting all the finer points and nuances of Magqubu's exquisite Zulu, the old man was adamant. He twisted a white handkerchief in his hands and I realized with a shock that he was nervous, and this increased his stubbornness. He got his way, and did the rhino performance.

The subtleties of rhino behaviour were lost on the audience because most of them had never seen a white rhino in the field. Bongani Ngubane softened the language in his interpreting, but Magqubu's imitation of the grunting, squealing, and deep bass growls of the rhino bull and the cow's reluctance to accept him painted a very clear picture. It was his presence that captured the attention of the crowd. He was dressed in all his Zulu finery of beadwork, skins, and plumed feathers, but his essential strength and humanness ensured that no matter what he was saying or doing, there was no loss of dignity.

After the opening of the congress in the Denver Convention Center we moved to Estes Park in the splendour of the foothills of the Rockies. Here Magqubu was able to renew his friendship with Edmund de Rothschild after their first meeting at the World Wilderness Congress in Johannesburg, and subsequently on a trail in Mfolozi. The de Rothschilds were astounded by Magqubu's tracking knowledge. Anne de Rothschild had dropped a switch while walking to the camp and was upset at losing it. Magqubu backtracked the following day and returned the switch two hours later.

Magqubu's friendship with Oren Lyons, a Native American leader, grew out of the respect each had for the other's culture, and I remember Magqubu returning one afternoon after having seen a herd of bison and being much impressed by the size of the animals. Oren Lyons asked Magqubu to imitate the buffalo walking, then laughed in amazement at Magqubu's accuracy of detail of the movement. "You have certainly seen our grandfathers today," Oren Lyons said.

One afternoon there was a meeting of all the different Native Americans attending the congress, and they invited Magqubu, Chip Kamber, Nick Steele, Bob Staffeson, and me to attend. When we reached the hut, Magqubu was making a fire and beginning to boil some mielie meal in his little pot. Coyote's promise had been fulfilled, and someone had come back from New Mexico with a packet of the precious blue corn.

At a certain moment I turned to Nick Steele and Bob Staffeson and said that we should leave the indigenous people to their own discussions, and there was a glint of appreciation on Coyote's face. Chip Kamber was part Native American, so she stayed. We had hardly left when they moved the chairs and tables into a circle. I am sure that Magqubu would have exchanged much of his wisdom with the indigenous people of America.

Our other contribution to the congress proceedings was a six-projector audiovisual presentation of Magqubu leading a trail in the Mfolozi. In contrast to the other films presented, there was no commentary. The only sounds were the animals and the birds and one plaintive Zulu lyric. The impact on the audience was staggering, and Magqubu and I were besieged by delegates and speakers offering their congratulations. Magqubu greeted everybody with the same openness, and his behavior won many friends for South Africa and the Wilderness Leadership School.

The finale to the congress was an *indaba* and a prayer circle with Magqubu's little pot in the middle. He gave a long prayer about the coming together of people from all over the world to celebrate our reunion and our re-affirmation of the power of wild country and wilderness to guide humankind on the right path.

A few months after our return to South Africa, Chip Kamber had a phone call from Coyote, who told her that he had had a long conversation with Magqubu in the spirit world. A week or two later I was visiting Magqubu at his *muzi*, and he said to me, "Do you remember that man Ikanka, whom we met in Denver?" I said that I did, and Magqubu went on, "I had a dream about him the other evening and we had a long conversation."

He and the Native Americans had their own way of communicating and the contact came in ways that we, sceptical modern Westerners, would find difficult to believe or understand.

19

Dreams, and Lions in a Glade

The year 1978 was momentous for me, and I was led into deeper paths of the mind. *Venture to the Interior* by Laurens van der Post, books by Paul Brunton, the fundamental principles of the wilderness concept, the American Senate Wilderness Bill, had all been preparation for what was to come in 1978.

Laurens van der Post had been a friend for many years and I had read, or rather devoured, the books he sent me. Then one day the book *C.G. Jung and the Story of Our Time* came in the post. I opened it, read a few pages, saw it was about psychology, and wondered if Laurens had lost his marbles. This definitely was not a book for me. I wanted more on the Kalahari, the Bushmen, the POW camp, and Africa. What had gone wrong with Laurens?

Two years later I was travelling to America via London, and I saw *C.G. Jung and the Story of Our Time* in the Heathrow bookshop. I decided I really owed it to Laurens to read the book, and I needed something to put me to sleep on the long flight to San Francisco. I began reading it after the plane had passed over the green landscape of Ireland. I was enthralled. Two years after receiving the original copy, the book had found me, to paraphrase Jung himself. My life was never to be the same. When I arrived in San Francisco I phoned Laurens's apartment. He was away, and I spoke to Ingaret, his wife, and told her of my excitement about the book. She said she had known Jung and had originally introduced Laurens to him.

The book was another turning point in my life. The dream world burst in upon me and I began to write my dreams down to honour them as Laurens recommended in his book. They came fast and furious and I had no idea what they were saying. I continued to write them all down religiously, hoping something would happen that would enable me to untangle these visions of the night. I was now aware of the two worlds in which I lived – the conscious and the unconscious.

The next step was a visit from my friend Hugh Dent. He had undergone a radical change and I insisted on knowing why. He said he had been seeing a woman who analyzed his dreams. I said I wanted to meet her, and he introduced me to Gloria Gearing at St. Mary's Hospital at Mariannhill. Hugh. Dent had directed me to the only person in KwaZulu-Natal who understood and practised Jungian psychology. She skilfully took my dreams apart, like a woman untangling threads of wool, and explained what the unconscious was telling me. I slowly became familiar with the language of Jungian psychology and was led to the modern literature. The books of John Sanford, *Dreams: God's Forgotten Language*; Robert Johnson's *He, She,* and *We*; Jung himself, *Modern Man in Search of a Soul*; Marie-Louise von Franz's writings – the list grew. My work with wilderness trails took on new dimensions as I understood more about Jungian typology.

As time went on, dreams emerged of paths leading to and from wells, crossing rivers, looking into beautiful and startling landscapes, and of fishing. I was forever fishing, and was not the fish a basic Christian symbol? My deep involvement with the living landscape and wilderness had made me question Christianity, the religion I was brought up in but had only paid lip service to. When I left school and went into the army I said I would not go to church again – seven years at St. John's had been enough. At the first church parade in the army, a sergeant major directed the various denominations to their respective churches – Catholics, Protestants, Jews, and the non-believers. I went with the non-believers, but after having to spend Sunday picking up cigarette butts I hastened to the Anglican church the next week. It was easier going through a one-hour church service than picking up *stompies*. That sergeant major knew a thing or two. It was amazing how quickly the men became converted to a faith.

Later, during the Italian campaign, I went into the Duomo in Florence soon after I had been told of my mother's death. The Catholic service that was in progress, the incense, the candles burning, the choir, and the priest intoning, all created an atmosphere that moved me but did not penetrate to the depths of my soul. The ritual and the dogma had ceased to have meaning, and I attended only weddings and funerals. Yet I knew that Christianity was important.

Later still, on a trail and sleeping on the banks of the Black Mfolozi River, I had a dream that resolved my religious problem. I dreamed of arriving at a Norman church that had a big eucalypt tree growing from it to form part of the church building. I went inside and said, "The roof is fine." Then I came outside and said, "If the tree falls down the church will collapse, and if the church collapses it will pull the tree down." For me the tree symbolized wilderness, and here was the unconscious telling me that the church and the wilderness in me depended upon each other.

This confirmed the work I had been doing for wilderness since 1955. It had, unknown to me at the time, been a religious quest. Now the wilderness and the church had come together in an inseparable bond.

Other healing dreams followed. I had for some time been overcautious about black rhino after a trail party Magqubu was leading was charged twice by an irate black rhino cow and a calf. Each time we had just managed to get the hysterical people out of harm's way. This was playing on my nerves until I had two dreams and saw an unusual sight. In the first dream I was walking out in the open veld and from nowhere a black rhino came charging toward me. There was no place to hide, no trees to climb, so I did what I would have done in reality. I stood my ground, took my bush hat off, threw it at the charging rhino, and shouted as loudly as I could. The rhino stopped, looked at me, turned, and walked away. I awoke with a pounding heart but satisfied that I had taken the right action.

In the second dream I was walking in an ancient landscape and looked down a valley to see a dinosaur-like rhino feeding on herbs. It became aware of my presence and looked up at me. I shouted out to it, "I know you, I know you," and I gave its Latin name. It looked at me again, then ambled slowly on. When I awoke I could not remember the Latin name, but the dream animal was certainly one of the oldest ancestors of the rhino. The dreaming took place in Mfolozi game reserve, and that evening at dusk a black rhino cow with the longest horn I have ever seen and a young calf at her heels walked down a path a few metres from me. I called out to it, "I know you, I know you, *Diceros bicornis*." The cow stopped, ponderously turned her head with its huge horn, and looked at me in the same way as its prehistoric ancestor had done in my dream.

Simply put, the dreams were telling me about the black rhino nature of myself. When I meditated I realized that I had become too aggressive in some of my personal encounters with people and acted like a charging black rhino, and I had projected those feelings onto the actual black rhino.

My dream notebook became as important as my field journal, and I marvelled at how the dream was not confined by time and space. Later I learned that it was possible to have a dialogue with the unconscious, and I realized how much we missed in the madly materialistic rush of the modern world.

The year 1978 also marked the first time we had to shoot an animal in self-defence. Magqubu and I had walked thousands of kilometres in Mfolozi without having to fire a shot; in fact, he was the only one who carried a firearm. My weapon was a red-ivory wood stick.

In October Magqubu and I were leading a group on a Wilderness Leadership School trail into the Mfolozi game reserve. It included Allister Sparks, the well-known journalist of the *Rand Daily Mail*, his two sons, and

Pat Farley of the *Sunday Tribune*, a Natal paper. I had a premonition that something unusual was going to happen. The air was filled with an undefinable foreboding. I was aware of the sounds of our feet moving along the path, breaking twigs and scratching on the gravel patches. The wilderness area was silent, almost like the time of the great flood in 1963, when thousands of warthogs died and white rhino, waiting to go to Zimbabwe, were nearly drowned in the *bomas*.

The birds called faintly, and I heard trumpeter hornbills and black-collared barbets wailing and cackling from the fig trees in the riverine forest. They seemed to call in isolation, as though apart from the land.

We passed through a dense patch of *umThombothi* woodland, where a lone white-browed scrub robin sang its bright little song indicating the coming of the afternoon. We reached the river and sat, taking a breather. Egyptian geese fed on an opposite sandbank, but there was not an animal in sight. Most unusual. The thought of lions came into my head at the sight of big-padded imprints on the sand. Magqubu, aware of everything, turned and, with his eyes, indicated the spoor. I nodded and he smiled. Our long and close association required no words to enlarge on what we had seen. I also liked to walk in silence, and Magqubu demanded it for safety reasons.

Lions dominated my thoughts as we plodded up the path, my distorted knee bending with some difficulty, and my backpack weighing me down. I felt the sweat start to trickle down my face, and the wildebeest flies swarmed around my head. I kept brushing them off with a branch of the *iGqeba-elimhlophe* (*Tarchonanthus minor*), the scent of the broken leaves hanging in the heavy air of the afternoon. Who was the Englishman who said that Africa was a place where the flowers did not smell and the birds had no song? How wrong he was.

The last few hundred meters to Mpika Manqele's old kraal site had me sweating and breathing heavily. I glanced at Magqubu. At seventy-eight he was as strong as a man of forty. His pack was twice the weight of mine. He carried his own sleeping bag, all his food, his famous little pot, a ground sheet, spare clothing, his white Shembe robe, and a heavy .458 rifle. I whistled softly, and he stopped. I pointed to the remains of Mpika Manqele's forge, the pieces of slag, and the earth still hard from the pounding of human and cattle feet.

He showed us the fallen walls of the forge, held an imaginary bellows to his mouth and breathed and blew, then made the noise of the fire burning fiercely and the metal bubbling. He said that the best spear-makers always used fat at some stage, human fat not excluded, and that was why mothers kept their babies away when the forges were lit.

Magqubu picked up some slag and said that his father had taught him to shoot with an *mnqonqo* and that the slag was used as bullets. He showed us how the gun was loaded and made the sound *qon, qon, qon* as the ramrod was pushed down the barrel, hence the onomatopoeic Zulu name of the gun. He told us how his father had made him crawl behind until they came upon a reedbuck and then handed the gun to Magqubu, who fired. There were clouds of black smoke, and as it cleared he and his father ran forward to see the reedbuck kicking in its death throes.

"That is how I learned to shoot," Magqubu said.

He was quiet, tracing his fingers along the outline of the forge. He murmured about Mpika, that he was spear-maker to King Cetshwayo.

I glanced around and saw how the *urochloa* grass was pushing up through the hard pan, and it reminded me of Jim Feely's observations that one always found a white rhino territorial bull near the old forges. They liked the short sweet grass. Here was a case of humans modifying the environment to the benefit of certain species. The subject became Jim's passion and led him to make extraordinary archaeological discoveries.

We left the forge and walked to the edge of the hill and sat looking at the view of the river winding its way up the valley. There were no animals on the sandbanks. I spoke quietly to Magqubu, asking where the game was. He shrugged his shoulders, but I could see that he was looking carefully for some sign. Images of lions flashed through my mind again, and I wondered if the bridge pride had been overly active in this part. I had a twinge, too, when I remembered a statement of Jim Feely's about this particular troop of lions. "They're too damned tame, and *gatvol* [fed up] with human beings," he said.

Tourists passing over the bridge on the way to Mpila camp would stop to look at the pride, and when they didn't move for a photograph, someone would throw a bottle, tin, or stone. This had been going on for a long time. Furthermore, they were frequently called up by tape recordings, darted, and marked. Some of the young males were culled. They were certainly losing their fear of *Homo sapiens*. One of the trail parties had encountered them feeding on a big nyala bull. The lions were chased off and a leg of the nyala was carried into camp. As Jim Feely said, "I don't like that story because we might meet them in a gully in the Tjevu stream and not be able to get out of their way."

We rested and waited until the sun began its descent behind Mpila hill, then we followed the clearly defined rhino path that wound along the ridge of Amatshemnyama to our camp site. Magqubu put on a spurt and jogged jauntily into camp while I limped behind, exclaiming at his prowess. He laughed and said he would last as long as Mpika Manqele.

That evening around the fire of burning *umThombothi* logs with their scented black smoke, he told us stories, bringing past and present together in a coherent way. When the others went to bed and I waited to take the first watch, I sat with Magqubu in the dark and he told me his current problems. Tabete, his old and faithful wife, had complained bitterly about the hyena that were coming in the night and raiding the goat and calves pen. She had had to go out alone with only an old spear and a failing torch to confront the hyena. Magqubu asked me quietly what he should do. I felt helpless to answer because we both knew how we actually loved the hyena. Without it the wild would be soundless at night. Whenever they whooped in the hills he shouted their praise names, then cursed them for coming to his *muzi* to steal the goats and the calves. I was troubled, too, because I knew how hard Tabete had to work to keep their small stock of animals alive. Had I been in her position I would have blown the heads off the hyena. The only thing that made the difference now was that we had a game reserve. In the old days of Zululand there would have been a balance between domestic stock, people, and the wild animals. That era had gone. People and domestic animals had increased beyond the carrying capacity of the land, and wild animals had been incarcerated in pitifully small reserves. It had taken a long time, too, for the game reserves to be appreciated. Even then, in 1978, there were still forces at work trying to undermine the value and integrity of the reserves and find other uses for the land.

The hyena called again downstream and it was strangely comforting to hear them because we had seen no animals in the day. Magqubu raised his hand in a despairing sort of salute, a gesture of love and anger. "*Mpisi, mpisi,*" he said softly. We both knew there was no solution except better fencing to stop animals from leaving the reserve.

He told me about a dreaded group of people in the old days of Zululand, the *inswelaboya*, or Those Who Have No Hair. They were reputed to come out at night from their hiding grounds and ride giant hyenas to different parts of the country, where they murdered people and gathered human fat, which they used in magic medicines. Even today there are men who are said to be able to make a hut full of people fall into a deep hypnotic sleep by burning a concoction of the eyebrows of a hyena and special herbs.

I went to my sleeping bag and lay down, looking at the stars through the canopy of the large fig tree. Magqubu extracted his white Shembe robe and walked down the bank to a smaller tree he always prayed under. I could hear him faintly praising and thanking God, calling him "Baba," and saying how grateful he was to God for conducting us safely through the wilderness.

He asked for protection too of his home and his family, and other things I could not understand or properly hear. Hyena called again as though in response, otherwise the night was quiet. I could smell the heavy ripeness of wild figs.

Magqubu returned from his prayers, and we talked quietly in the dark shadows of the sheltering giant sycamore fig. Our lives had been closely intertwined in the last twenty years, and we kept nothing from each other. I told him of the difficulties I was having to find money to keep the Wilderness Leadership School alive. His white teeth flashed a smile that even in the half darkness lit up his face. He said that nothing was ever easy, but we were obliged to keep going. Knowing all the difficulties in his life I was almost ashamed to voice my concerns.

I told him, "When we were in the Parks Board, the government gave us money. Now I have to go out and ask people for it."

Magqubu cocked his head and said, "Why is that wrong? It is only when we ask that we receive. The work we are doing now is different from the Natal Parks Board. Our main job was to protect the animals. Only when you started wilderness trails did we teach."

The old man was right. He was able to concentrate on what was important. It was the story of his life. For him it had been one long continuous struggle. Children dying, wives dying, cattle and goats dying, a pittance of a salary. From 1914 right through to the 1950s he received no more than four pounds a month. He once said, pointing his finger at me in Zulu fashion, "I did not get money until you came."

It was a compliment but it was true. The moment I took over Mfolozi game reserve I fought with every bureaucratic means not only to increase the number of Zulu game guards but to ensure that they received a decent salary. Colonel Vincent always gave me a fair hearing and then actively persuaded the board to implement the requirements. But it was never-ending. Wildlife conservation was not a priority of the Natal provincial administration. However, Magqubu and the guards knew me and trusted me to fight for their rights.

A leopard began coughing in the reeds downstream, rousing the baboons in the trees across the river. They barked and screamed, and the old dog baboon roared like a lion. I was glad to hear the noise. It seemed to break the spell of not having seen any game on the trail.

"Will we see game tomorrow?" I asked Magqubu, reminding him that we had seen so little on the trek.

"If we see *ufudu* [the tortoise] we will see a lot of game," he said confidently.

The night passed without incident, and at breakfast Allister Sparks and I discussed conservation and politics. Allister had contacts that enabled him to speak with authority. He had always been a fearless journalist and consequently suffered the ire of the Nationalist government. I was able to tell him how conservation in Zululand had suffered as a result of factions within the Nationalist party and some civil servants. The sadism of some of these bureaucrats had been hard to bear. There was one individual in the lands department who boasted that he had recommended to various ministers that the game reserves should be abolished. We got our own back by walking him up the steepest hills in the hottest part of the day so he could point out which areas within the parks were going to be given to cattle ranchers. Allister was able to cap my stories with his tales of the persecution of newspapermen. Our country had gone through a dark period, but Allister predicted that the government would not last. There were too many forces against it.

Magqubu sat at his own fire cleaning his little pot. He rolled up his sleeping bag and oiled his rifle. This was always a signal that it was time to start walking. A strong south wind was blowing as we walked up a well-used rhino path and headed for the Tjevu stream. We had not gone far when a big tortoise showed its head above the grass. Magqubu was delighted and said, "From now on we will see game." He walked carefully round the tortoise, saying its Zulu praise names and humming quietly to himself about the animals we would soon be seeing.

We started walking again, following a game path that led down to the Tjevu stream. We crossed over after looking for a few moments at the mass of spoor in the sand. Magqubu pointed out the imprint of a big lion. We climbed up the bank and walked over the open grassland toward a pan, where we rested for a while under an *Acacia nilotica*.

Later we followed a path that meandered up the eastern end of Ncebe hill until it turned west along the top of Ncebe toward a pan where there was always a chance of seeing rhino. I heard impala snorting and told everybody to keep quiet. We stood waiting, and soon a herd of impala came down to drink. They were nervous and kept looking in the direction opposite us. This was an indication of something unusual. Magqubu grabbed my arm and nodded with his head beyond the impala. I looked and realized that there was a predator about, and expected to see a lion. But a magnificent leopard came out of the bush, smooth and glossy and blending into the background. It walked past the impala, ignoring them, while they snorted and pranced. The leopard walked with grace, and I saw the look of admiration on Magqubu's face as it padded past the pan and then appeared to glide into a grove of trees, where it disappeared. I had often asked Magqubu which animal he liked best, and he was always unhesitating in his reply. The leopard to him was the king of all the predators with its beauty, grace, and skill in hunting. Whenever it called at night he was the first to sing out its praise names. I recalled how he had once woken me when a leopard had walked past, his sixth sense and empathy with the animal having warned him of its presence.

The leopard that had just vanished from our sight was in its prime, and I will never forget the look on its face, its haughtiness and scorn for the snorting impala and barely a passing glance for our little party. We were all silent in our admiration, then Magqubu shouted out the praise names of this king of animals and did a little dance in its honour.

For the rest of the day we saw game everywhere – nyala, kudu, wildebeest, zebra, white rhino. Magqubu had been right about the tortoise.

We returned in the late evening to the camp.

After we had eaten I lay listening to the night noises of baboons coughing and then barking as they roosted on the rocky krantzes at Amatshemnyama. Our trail camp was on a ledge above the river with a steep hill rising behind it. This acted like an auditorium, and all the sounds were magnified. I could hear the figs plopping from the enormous sycamore that gave us protection. Through the branches I could see the Milky Way blazing in the sky with the Southern Cross and Scorpio constellations. This great tree had been a wonderful companion for many years, and it was always a relief to see it at the end of a long day's trek and to make the fire below the canopy and boil the billycan. On rainy days, with a cold south wind, we would linger near the fire and Magqubu told stories. He could talk for an hour or more about the sycamore fig tree itself.

Magqubu liked to describe the monkeys and the baboons, trumpeter hornbills, and barbets feeding on the ripe figs, and how the baboons sometimes roosted in the tallest branches to escape the leopards, only to find that big pythons had climbed up to prey on the youngsters.

Once, when we were chased by a black rhino and quickly climbed into the big branches, Magqubu laughed and said, "Siza abantu – the tree that helps the people." The dark-green leaves and the yellow bark on the trunk and branches made it a distinctive tree that marked the river course. For Magqubu it was a close friend, and he greeted each one we passed. I, too, came to do the same. The tree lived.

We breakfasted the next morning, packed our haversacks, and walked toward the Volkswagen Kombi about six kilometres from our camp. Magqubu carried the .458 rifle in one hand and his tiny three-legged pot in the other. The creaking of the pot and the faint slap of the leather band against the rifle made me focus on the path as we walked in single file up the western slope of the hill. With Magqubu leading, I was able to think freely, knowing that he would give me ample warning of danger.

It was a dull overcast day and we reached a split in the path. The one to the left entered a grove of *umThombothi* trees, then thick euclea bush and scattered acacias until it emerged at a big pan. This was the short route to the vehicle. The path on the right went up the steep back of Amatshemnyama hill through open country, and I normally chose it because it was safer.

As we approached the point where the path divided, I heard vervet monkeys chattering excitedly. Magqubu stopped and looked up into the trees. He indicated with his eyes that I should look too. We were in a hurry, so I glanced up somewhat impatiently. I noticed that the monkeys were staring in the opposite direction despite being aware of our presence. We now talked quite loudly, but the monkeys ignored us. A large one looked once in our direction but took no further notice – something had his attention in the *umThombothi* glade. Magqubu indicated we should take the right-hand path, the long way round to the vehicle. I hissed "No," and tapped my watch, letting him know that we were in a hurry. Magqubu pointed to the monkeys. He knew that something was amiss. I should have known too, because on this very trail I had seen the impala ignore us when the leopard arrived, but I insisted we move off. Magqubu shrugged his shoulders, and we carried on into the semi-gloom of the forest.

We had walked less than a kilometre when Magqubu pointed. "Over there – the lions," he said.

I looked up. A whole string of lions lay across the path; a big pride. Their tawny and slightly spotted skins blended with the background. My heart began to pound, because the lions made no effort to get out of our way. I talked loudly to Magqubu, letting the lions know where we were. They took no notice but continued to stare at us, their yellow eyes glowing. One of the females stood up and slowly began to pad toward us. "Load your gun," I said to Magqubu, and gripped my walking stick, the only weapon I had.

Magqubu put his little pot down, indicating we should move back. I heard the cartridge slip into the rifle chamber and the gun was cocked. We kept moving back, trying to increase the critical distance. When Magqubu put his three-legged pot down this was a sure sign to me that the situation was serious. We backed away and Magqubu shouted loudly, "Hamba, hamba" (Go away, go away), but the advancing lioness paid no attention. She broke into a run and was coming straight at us. Magqubu lifted the .458

and fired. The heavy calibre bullet hit her in the chest and she dropped stone dead in front of us. Jim Feely's warning about the bridge pride flashed into my mind. This was without doubt that pride. They had lost their fear and respect for humans. We were in grave trouble.

The noise of the .458 blunderbuss discharging under the closed canopy was deafening, and the sound of the shot echoed and re-echoed through the bush. I was sure that the disturbance would scatter the remaining lions, but as the shot lioness gave her last kicks, I saw the lions had hardly moved from their original position. Another lioness was on her feet loping toward us in that peculiar manner of the large cats. We had by now backed off a fair distance. Magqubu calmly reloaded the rifle and aimed at the tawny blur coming toward us. If he did not kill her, one of us was going to be seriously injured. My particular concern was for Allister Sparks's young sons.

Magqubu fired and the second lioness dropped, but she rolled over and lay hidden in the dry grass. She was obviously badly wounded and would not live long. The rest of the pride retreated into the shadows. There were now two cartridges left, and we had moved out into the open. Magqubu wanted to return and go after the wounded lioness, but with only two bullets this could have been suicide. The remainder of the pride – and there were twelve or more – were still close to us, grunting and growling ominously. I would never forget how they talked to one another. This is the only way I could describe the sounds coming from the various animals.

Magqubu began to insist on going in to finish the wounded lioness, but I was adamant he should not. Magqubu argued vehemently, but I refused to let him go. Then he remembered his three-legged pot. He said he was going back to fetch it. I exploded.

"For God's sake, Magqubu, forget about your bloody pot. It's too dangerous in there. You have just seen what has happened with the two lionesses."

Magqubu gave me his long, stubborn stare.

"I'll buy you another pot," I said, shouting and using choice adjectives.

"No," Magqubu said firmly.

To argue with him would have been hopeless, to order him unfair, and I knew he would have disobeyed me. I pleaded with him. "Your life is too valuable, you still have so much to teach us."

He was adamant. It was his pot and his life and no true Zulu was afraid to die. A sombre bulbul whistled from the depths of the *umThombothi* glade. Was this an omen?

"I paid five shillings for that pot in 1925." I said he had no right to risk his life for a miserable three-legged pot. He ignored me, shouldered his rifle, and walked off into the bush, talking to himself about his pot.

I was shaking with fear and anger. I loved this man. He had been a father, brother, teacher, and mentor to me. I heard his footsteps brushing against branches and the dry grass, and the light of the afternoon grew gloomier and long shadows spread all over the bush. Magqubu had a firm belief in God, and if his time had come, then God wanted him. I could not see it that way. He was too important to go now.

I was expecting to hear an angry roar, a shout, a dying scream. There was nothing, and Magqubu emerged from the silent bush carrying his precious three-legged pot and smiling cheerfully. "Asihambe," he said, shouldering his rifle as though nothing had happened. I gave a deep sigh of relief, and he looked and smiled again as if to say, What on earth are you fussing about?

We walked quickly to our vehicle and drove to Mpila, where I reported to the duty ranger. A formidable force of two rangers and three game guards armed with 30.06s and .303s was soon put together.

On the way to the lions, one of the guards, settling an old score when he had been a junior under Magqubu, harangued the old man. "Why did you shoot the lion?" he said. "You, Magqubu, you have worked here all your life. You know it is against the law."

Magqubu stared at him stonily. "Is it against the law to save the lives of people?" he asked dismissively.

We approached the glade in a tight group. "You're in charge," I said to the young ranger. "You tell us what to do."

At that moment a terrifying growl came from a patch of bush.

"It is the injured one," Magqubu pronounced.

There were clicking sounds of rifles being loaded, and we moved forward slowly, staring into the bush. I thought I heard a soft cough to our right but ignored it because the wounded animal began snarling and growling continuously, nerve-racking sounds. A shallow depression lay ahead, and Magqubu pointed out how the grass had been flattened by the lioness dragging herself away.

"She is right there," he said.

We halted, the wounded animal moved, and I saw her eyes, blazing yellow in spite of her pain, looking defiantly at us. Four rifles cracked and she collapsed. As the last echo died, Magqubu shouted a warning, and from our right a huge male came straight at us. I was only aware of a thick black mane and, again, blazing eyes fixed on us: this was the source of the cough I'd heard.

Without a second's hesitation the ranger, Chris Freeman, half-turned and shot the charging lion from the hip with his 30.06. It was a brilliant shot, instinctively made, and the lion rolled over, dead.

The other lions in the bush began to cough and grunt, and there was a great tension in the air. We were all on edge, wondering where the next lion was coming from. The shadows of the afternoon had lengthened, too, and it was becoming difficult to see into the gloom. A white-browed scrub robin called from the top of an *Acacia robusta* tree, and it was followed by the soft lyrical song of the white-throated robin. A crow croaked its rattling-marble call near the first lioness. It was waiting to pick out the eyes.

There were two of us in the group who were unarmed. I was one of them, and I felt very vulnerable with only a stick in my hand. Magqubu sensed my concern and indicated a nearby *umThombothi* tree. Hardly was I comfortable on a branch when there was a succession of snarls, growls, and roars, and another lioness charged out of the bush.

The game guards fired a volley of shots, and I saw the dust flying near her; she turned and, in a flash, was gone. We waited, but the bush was silent. Then the two robins began to sing again.

We soberly gathered the dead lions. They lay there in death, still beautiful, their tawny coats gleaming in the late afternoon sun. I cursed those who had tormented them, causing them to attack us. The poor bloody lions were not at fault.

On the way back to the vehicle where we had left Allister Sparks and his two sons, I looked at Magqubu's face. His jaw was set and his eyes had a glint. I knew someone was going to receive a broadside.

He turned on the guard who had harangued and lectured him about shooting the first two lionesses. In the same unctuous tones the guard had used and with his same faint stutter Magqubu launched his attack.

"Why was the male lion killed and why did you shoot at the last female who charged us? Do you not know that this is a game reserve? Are you not a game guard to protect the animals? Perhaps I was not seeing properly, but you lifted your gun and you fired shots. Or was I imagining it?" Magqubu said. The guard looked sheepish and hung his head. "I don't hear your voice now. This morning you never stopped talking. Have you forgotten that you said I should not have fired at the lion? You said I was an old game guard who knew the law. Now you are not talking. You can tell me nothing. I was walking and working here with Mfohloza before you even piddled on your sleeping mat. You were not born. Did your father not tell you to respect men who knew more than you? When I was a man your father was still herding goats. You were not even in his balls." Magqubu did not let up.

The guard raised his hands in a motion of surrender. "Yebo, baba. You are right. I was wrong."

The other guards roared with laughter as Magqubu did the equivalent of a victory dance, then he laughed too. All was forgiven, and he kept smiling as he made his final remark.

"I shot the lions because they were going to kill us. You did the same. Today you have learned a lesson."

The guard smiled shyly. "Yebo, baba," he said.

Everyone laughed again, a release of adrenalin after the severe strain.

When we reached the vehicle I happened to look at Magqubu's rifle. The foresight was missing. I found it in the gun bag. He had shot the charging lioness instinctively.

That year, 1978, was a year never to be forgotten. We had been spared to do other work in both psychology and wilderness, and we eventually helped to bring them together.

20

Drought and Rhino Capture

In the early 1980s I took a group of Wilderness Leadership School trailists to Mfolozi for a four-day trek into the wilderness area. We fetched Magqubu at his *muzi* in a howling northeasterly gale that clouded the landscape in a thin film of black dust. We drove to the park and left the vehicle and began walking south toward our campsite on the Black Mfolozi River. The heat was overpowering, and I had to call for frequent halts. We sat in the shade of a spreading sycamore fig, and I could hear the dust filtering down through the leaves. The topsoil of the country was blowing away. The poor record of South African conservation, the human overpopulation of the high rainfall areas, and too much pressure on the grasslands from cattle, sheep, goats, and donkeys had precipitated a situation that, short of the most drastic measures, was almost impossible to rectify.

I told the trailists a true story of an experience in 1953, when Hendrik van Schoor and I had been instructed to do an aerial count of the white rhino in Mfolozi game reserve. Many counts had been done on the ground with varying results, and the aerial count would be more accurate. Our pilot had done the spraying for the tsetse fly, so he knew the country. We took off and first flew west. The heat threw the plane about, and the smell from the DDT tanks was sickening. The pilot turned round and threatened to give us the ride of our life if we spewed down his neck.

The plane climbed higher. I looked beyond the borders of the game reserve and saw with a shock that the catchment area was collapsing from erosion, lack of grass, and heavy concentrations of people and stock. The reasons went back into our history to the post-Zulu-War period, when a whole culture was overthrown. When we returned to the airstrip with our count of 437 white rhino, I predicted that the Black Mfolozi would soon dry up. Everyone laughed. This had never happened in the history of Zululand. That evening I wrote an article for the Natal newspapers about my prediction. It was returned with a note: "Nonsense." The Black Mfolozi was known as the one safely perennial river. I tried various other publications and eventually had to turn the article into a short story, and it was published in a girls' school magazine.

On this very day, thirty years later, I heard on the radio that the Black Mfolozi had run dry.

Magqubu hoisted his backpack and said, "Asihambe," and as we walked toward the river I told him it was dry. He halted, turned round, and said, "That is impossible. This river has never dried up."

"The river is dry, Magqubu," I repeated.

His jaw set and he stared at me. "This is the river of the Zulu. It does not dry up," he said forcibly. His voice rose, and the trailists moved uncomfortably. "Asihambe."

"You will see and believe me," I replied.

Magqubu walked at a brisk pace, and I knew he was anxious to prove me wrong, but I also knew the radio report was accurate and that the old man was in for a shock. I could hear him muttering. At the nearest hillock to the river he stopped and stared in disbelief. The river, apart from a few small scattered pools, was bone dry.

We reached our camp site in the late afternoon. The heat was intense, and the northeast wind still blew relentlessly. Everyone was affected by it and the swirling black dust. We looked at the shimmering sands of the river and an nyala bull walked slowly toward a pool on the edge of the reeds only to leap back in fright. Magqubu, who missed nothing, said a crocodile was hiding under the bank. A depression settled on the group that could not even be relieved by a cup of tea. To light a fire in this wind was too dangerous.

Darkness fell, and in the distance I could hear shooting and the thump of bullets hitting into hard flesh. "They are killing all the game we protected," Magqubu said in a tone bordering on anger and sadness. The Natal Parks Board had embarked on an extensive culling operation in response to the drought, but those of us who had worked in Zululand knew that "they" had already killed far too many animals. The scientist advising the board did not have the experience to know how quickly the veld could recover after a few good rains. So the killing continued. On a previous trail we had the misfortune to see a herd of buffalo being blasted from a helicopter. Once the killing begins a mania takes over that the Afrikaners descriptively call *bokkoors* – buck fever. This was licensed slaughter.

A hyena passed near the camp, and we heard the deep *whoops* repeated by other hyena on the hills. The sound symbolized the despair I felt at what was happening to the land. The trailists sat huddled under the fig tree, their heads hanging low. Three shots followed in quick succession, and the sound of the connecting thump was carried on the wind. "Nango," Magqubu said. "There, they have killed more nyala." I queried how he knew it was nyala, and he gave a long answer describing the habitat of the animal and the pitch of the sound. Seventy years of listening to the shooting of wild animals with a variety of rifles enabled him to say, "I know." I did not argue.

The wind began to die down, and soon we were able to light a fire and boil a billy, then prepare supper. Food and liquid revitalized our spirits, and over coffee the trailists wanted to know why the killing was taking place. I explained that culling was part of game management and that some removal of game was necessary. However, what angered me was that we had developed methods of game capture in the 1960s which made wholesale culling unnecessary. I told the story of Jan Oelofse, who had devised the plastic-sheeting method that enabled us to catch as many as six thousand animals in a few months. This had revolutionized wildlife management in Africa, if anyone chose to listen. In the 1960s and 1970s we had re-stocked game ranches, and the demand for animals was increasing. One trailist posed the obvious question: "Well, why are they killing animals?" I knew from my old friends in the Parks Board that a group within the service had been caught up in the possibilities of revenue from game meat. This, and the scientist's view that drastic culling was necessary, created the current situation.

Former game rangers and other members of the public had complained to the board and to political leaders, but the killing mania was rampant, and it had to run its course. The same thing had happened in the 1920s, 1930s, and 1940s, but in those days there was no method of game capture. To convey conservation politics and how it interacted with provincial and national politics was an impossible task at this campfire talk. I tried, but there were basic questions that were unanswerable, and soon the group split in two, one side understanding culling and the other against it. The argument was punctuated by the shots in the night and Magqubu's grunts of "Nango" as another bullet struck living flesh.

A silence fell on the group, the two sides considering their arguments. In the silence there was a rumble of white rhino fighting and jostling each other at a pool on the river. Magqubu with his wisdom and good sense saw the opportunity to tell a story. He talked about Operation Rhino and how we had captured this great grey beast. He stood up to demonstrate how he led me to rhino, then with a few gestures he showed the rhino staggering as the drug took effect. The original rhino capture team consisted of Magqubu, John Clark, Owen Letley, Nick Steele, and myself, with Dr. Toni Harthoorn, the veterinary scientist. As senior ranger I had responsibility for a group of the hardest working and most dedicated rangers I had ever been with. I frequently had to order them to stop work. To re-stock the areas formerly inhabited by the white rhino had become a passion. Magqubu was talking, explaining the difficulties we had encountered. "Do you remember," he said, "Malamba [Nick Steele] following the rhino calf that had been darted and the mother turned and charged? Malamba stood on his horse's back and climbed into a tree because they were on a narrow path in thick bush."

We had been following on foot and had found a shaken Nick Steele. He said that as he climbed the tree the rhino cow had hooked his horse and thrown it a good two metres off the ground, and for a split second he had found himself staring into the horse's eyes. We chased the cow off, captured the calf, and injected large quantities of antibiotics into the horse. It survived, and months later was back at work.

Magqubu was becoming animated, and he put more wood on the fire. Rhino capture was for him a miraculous time. He named Toni Harthoorn Mtakathi – The One with Magic. In the first experiments a drug was used that killed the rhino if the antidote was not injected within minutes. Magqubu giggled when he described rangers climbing onto the rhino's back as it staggered under the influence of the powerful drug. His antics of men being flicked off like flies to return and be thrown off again had the trailists in fits of laughter. His memory of the unrestrained bad language was remarkable, and I recognized each voice. The scream of pain when a foot or a hand was stamped on, followed by a stream of swear words, was as realistic as the day it happened.

"Do you remember Ngozi?" Magqubu asked.

Before I could reply he began telling the story of the first black rhino we had caught. Ngozi (Danger) was a cow that had been caught in a cable snare around her neck. The wire had eaten deeply into the flesh. We darted and brought her to the *bomas* at Mfolozi. Unlike the timid white rhino, which took six weeks to tame down, after a few days Ngozi came when she was called. She would stand, her head cocked on one side, waiting for the antibiotic liquid and powder to be poured into her wound.

Magqubu acted out her movements and the appreciative sounds she made when the soothing liquid ran over her wound. Magqubu showed how John Clark climbed into the pen with the rhino. Magqubu showed us John gently running his hand along the rhino's back, then to the neck, and slowly examining the wound and pouring acriflavine into it. I watched the trailists looking at Magqubu, following every movement and gesture with wonder and appreciation.

"What happened to her?" one of them asked. Magqubu understood enough English and demonstrated how Ngozi was coaxed into a crate, fed and watered for days, then transported to Ndumu game reserve and released on the shores of Nyamithi lake. Magqubu wiped imaginary tears away and said that everyone at the *bomas* had fallen in love with this gentle wild beast. We had learned a lot about black rhino behaviour and food preferences from Ngozi, which helped immensely in future black rhino translocations to the Kruger National Park.

The night wore on, with Magqubu putting more logs on the fire and boiling the billy. When he was in full stride, nothing would stop him. I saw the trailists dozing, then sliding onto their backs and going into deep sleep. One by one they passed out until only Magqubu and I were awake. Magqubu had revived so many memories of the pain and the ecstasy of Operation Rhino. It was a story, as he rightly said, that would be told and retold round the fires for a long time to come.

Magqubu reminded me of a previous trail, when we had climbed Ncebe hill and, picking our way over the boulders, I caught a glimpse of a white skull between two rocks. Looking idly at it, I could see it was that of a big white rhino bull.

"This was the one that died over there," Magqubu nodded to the western end of Ncebe. He saw my blank look and said, "Have you forgotten Jonah?" Slowly it came back to me. Jonah was a huge bull I had darted in 1961 and before the new drug, M99, could take effect it had run to the edge of the cliff. Nick Steele and Owen Letley, both brilliant horsemen, had galloped alongside, desperately trying to turn the large animal, but at a critical moment the drug worked and it slid over the krantz. I remember the agony in Nick Steele's voice when he said, "The sound of the body thumping against the rocks made me sick in the stomach."

The whole capture team rushed to the ailing rhino, and Dr. Harthoorn, avoiding the wildly kicking legs, gave it an intravenous injection of the antidote to the narcotic. John Clark ran back up the hill to the vehicle and returned, breathing hard, with a rope. He made a slip knot and lassoed one of the front legs, and four of us hung grimly on, trying to get the animal into a better position. Every time the rhino jerked its leg we were pulled about like puppets on a string, and soon we were drenched with sweat, our palms lacerated by the rope.

The antidote took effect, and Jonah became even more lively, thrashing about and calling pathetically. There was a flurry of movement, he rolled over, and in a flash had heaved himself onto his feet. He stood breathing heavily, staring at us, then took a step forward. We scrambled in all directions for trees or cover. The large posterior horn was too close for comfort. John Clark moved to the right and quickly slipped the rope off the front leg so that when Johah moved he would not trip. It was the act of a brave and dedicated man. Sometimes I had to reprimand him for the risks he took.

The sun had set, and in the half darkness of early evening, Jonah the giant rhino stood, panting, his body dark with sweat and every muscle trembling. All around us were long shadows, upturned rocks, and the silent bush. Hordes of flies hovered about his flanks, biting through the skin and drawing blood. There was the combined smell of human sweat and the heavy dank smell of the rhino, of fresh dung, and the crushed leaves of the trees bashed against the rocks by the heavy body as it fell.

Jonah died that night and we were bitterly upset, but his death was not in vain. It was the beginning of a programme that led to the capture and translocation of thousands of white rhino, probably one of the greatest successes in wildlife conservation.

"You remember it all now?" Magqubu asked.

"Yebo, Magqubu," I said, and picked up the skull and hung it in the highest branch of an *mkia* tree. We placed a few stones as the beginning of an *isivivane* and honoured it when we passed. In time a wind would blow the skull off the tree and it would lie exposed on the rocks. The harshness of the sun and the summer rains would slowly weather it away. Porcupine and other animals would chew it, and ultimately nothing would be left but the story in our own minds.

The fire died down, and Magqubu said that we were fortunate to be chosen by Nkulunkulu to carry out the work of sending the white rhino all over southern Africa and to safe places in Europe and America. I had to explain that all the rhino we had taken to Mozambique had been killed during the war between Renamo and Frelimo, the second time within a century that the rhino had become extinct in Mozambique. Large-scale killing had taken place in Botswana, where the population of one hundred had been reduced to four. The population we had re-established in Zimbabwe had taken a severe pounding, and those in Zambia were wiped out.

Yet, paradoxically, white rhino in South Africa could be hunted on game ranches and provincial hunting reserves. Even in death they were saving land from being turned over to maize fields, sugarcane, or gum trees. Other species on the game ranches owed their existence to the white rhino. Capture and translocation from Mfolozi continued, and subsequent game rangers were as dedicated as our original team. They built on our experience, and where we had used horses, they had helicopters. The demand for white rhino was international, and there was hardly an accredited zoo in the world that did not have white rhino. The phenomenal initial success of breeding at San Diego Wild Animal Park had stopped with the second generation, but at Whipsnade in England the rhino we sent there in 1970 continued to breed. Perhaps the clearest lesson to be drawn was that we had to ensure the species survived on the African continent, especially in Mfolozi and Hluhluwe. New dangers had arisen, with rhino poaching taking place in both reserves. New techniques of protection were vital, but in the end only the ranger on the ground, armed and well trained, could see the rhino surviving into the next century, thus confounding F.C. Selous, who predicted the rhino would not see the twentieth century.

Magqubu and I shared the remaining night hours on the fire watch, and only one black rhino came within snorting distance.

Mfolozi habitat was changing fast, and it favoured this species. Once again, KwaZulu-Natal had proven to be the bastion of an endangered species. The record for the rest of Africa was appalling: ninety-five percent of the black rhino on the continent had been killed. The northern white rhino in Zaire were almost gone. When I was in Uganda in 1960 there were over a thousand northern whites. It is doubtful if there are thirty left.

Magqubu woke me for the dawn watch, a time he described as the sun shining through the elephant's ears. The day was calm without wind, and yesterday seemed a nightmare to be forgotten until I saw the thin film of soil on all our kit. I collected water from a hole in the sand, shaved and washed in a spare billycan, then lit the fire for tea. The trailists awoke, drank tea, and took turns washing. We had breakfast and set out to walk toward the junction of the Mhluzi stream.

We walked slowly over the dry bed of the Black Mfolozi, stopping to examine different tracks. Magqubu interpreted the diary of the night, pointing first at the big imprints of a lion.

"Look carefully," he said. "The lion chased a waterbuck here."

He traced out where the lion had inched forward to the dozing waterbuck, and Magqubu became alternately the lion and the waterbuck. The lion springs, and Magqubu's arms are outstretched, his hands curled like claws. Instantly the waterbuck tries to trot away, and Magqubu moves forward, his head up like the buck carrying a heavy set of horns. For a fateful second the bushbuck looks backward and the lion is on it. There is the loud roar, the stifled snort, and the waterbuck crashes to the ground. Magqubu falls down, rolls, and play-acts the drama, the waterbuck thrashing around and the lion with an immovable grip on its throat. Slowly the struggle subsides and with every move of the waterbuck there is the deep growl of the lion. Soon blood spurts from the neck of the antelope, the body shivers, and the death rattle comes from its lacerated throat. The lion relaxes, licks the blood, then begins to chew the soft stomach. Magqubu stops for a moment, lifts his head, turns, and snarls. Other lions are approaching. The big male chases them off, returns to the carcass, and feeds. Cubs whimper, and there are the soft coughs of the females, but when they crowd too close the big lion rushes forward and swipes the nearest one.

The trailists stood fascinated by the theatre of the wild.

Magqubu stepped forward, glanced around, and picked up a dove's feather. Everyone drew closer, expecting something as spectacular as the lion. Magqubu held the feather aloft, and the sun caught the spots of dew on it from the previous evening. He turned the feather, staring at it intently. Everyone was riveted. The sun was hotter, increasing our body smells, and I was aware of the soap and perfume of one of the women. Without warning Magqubu dropped onto his knees and pointed dramatically. Everyone looked but could see nothing. "Nango, nango," he said softly, touching the sand. He stood up, waved everyone back, raised his arms, craned his neck forward, and made the sound of air whistling through primary feathers. For some reason I was reminded of the players' scene in Shakespeare's *Hamlet*, when they acted out the poisoning of the king. The trailists gasped, "He's a hawk." Magqubu showed the bird hurtling through the sky and smacking the unsuspecting dove feeding on the sands. For a second or two the dove struggled, and there were the faint lines on the sand. Magqubu pointed at each mark until, like one of the psychological photographic puzzles, the whole picture became clear and the group almost simultaneously voiced an "Aha." Magqubu beamed and congratulated his class.

Everyone was eager for more, but I could feel the sun burning exposed skin, and the reflections from the sand grew sharper, dazzling our eyes. Around me the birdsong was growing quieter, and only a trumpeter hornbill kept up its wailing, baby-like chant. All the other bird calls were intermittent. The scent of the newly flowering acacias, particularly the robustas, came in waves over the riverbed like a prehistoric aphrodisiac. It evoked something in Magqubu, because he sniffed the air and talked of the Zulu women in his youth and how they used a mixture of herbs and the bark of selected trees to make their powder. He told us that the young men used to lie in wait near the river for the girls coming down with gourds on their heads to collect water. He moved his body like a teenage girl, accentuating the swaying of the buttocks and the bobbing of the breasts. To the amusement of everyone he said that Zulu men were far more attracted to hips and buttocks than breasts, not like the white men.

The deep consecutive barks of a kudu bull attracted our attention, and Magqubu moved slowly toward the middle of the river. He stopped to point out black and white rhino spoor and explained the difference in meticulous detail. A woman asked the age of the white rhino tracks. Magqubu got onto his knees and pointed to a tiny spider's web in the corner of the spoor. The dew still sparkled on the strands. He plucked an insect from the web and said that from all these clues he was able to determine it was more than three days old.

We reached the middle of the river, and Magqubu talked of the history of the people who had once lived on both banks of the river. He pointed to the rising hill of Amatshemhlope (White Rocks) and said that the great King Dingiswayo, mentor of Shaka, once had a big *muzi* on the lower slopes. He swept his arm in a semicircle, naming every hill, and sang out the praises of prominent early inhabitants associated with this important Zululand landscape. This was history being taught in a different way. The sun was higher, and people were thirsty and licking their lips in the heat. Magqubu talked about the great floods that had swept down this river, in 1918, 1925, and, in my time, in 1957 and 1963. A fish eagle called from high above, and shadows of circling vultures moved across the sand.

Magqubu stared at the birds, and everyone was quiet. Only the sound of the wind through the primary feathers of the vultures floated overhead. For a few minutes I had a feeling of great apprehension. The middle of a river is always a vulnerable place. This was where kings and armies were attacked because they were not sure whether to go forward or return. I allowed my mind to drift, and a vision of a raging flood floated before me. I could hear the water churning and roaring and saw trees and dead animals bobbing up and down. Magqubu broke the spell with his urgings for us to rest under the trees. We spent the rest of the day dozing, looking at passing animals, and listening to Magqubu's stories. This was the world without time, the once-upon-a-time world where there were no watches, only the sun's passage across the sky and the diurnal and nocturnal rhythms. This was a world we could retreat into from the modern, frenetic, and materialistic madness of our twentieth century. Still, there were people in charge of the parks who saw it as underdeveloped land, and they wanted to build lodges. I kept all this to myself because I did not want to spoil the magic of the moment.

In February 1984 my vision of the flood came true. The cyclone Demoinia brought deluges of rain in the upper catchment of the Black Mfolozi, and almost every sycamore fig was washed away to the sea. Pools were filled, and the character of the river changed. Nothing could ever bring it back. It had become a storm drain, but life would go on. People who never knew it would look upon it and say how beautiful it was, because as long as the park remained, the animals would cross it, leaving the spoor, making their calls, and showing themselves in the sun. So all was not lost, and the work to save the parks was not in vain if the wilderness areas were left where humankind could walk in the footsteps of our ancient ancestors, in the landscape of the soul.

21

The End Approaches

Magqubu was seldom ill. He had a strong aversion to any medicines because taking them was contrary to his Shembe beliefs. In the early 1980s there was a prolonged drought, and with the lack of water a cholera epidemic spread through the Macibini district, where he lived. Magqubu became a victim, but while he was conscious he refused to allow any of his family to take him to the clinic. Ikonamangele, his son, and Tabete, his senior wife, pleaded with him, but he was adamant. They had to wait until he lost consciousness, then they rushed him to the clinic, where his life was saved.

Toward the end of 1988 I was in Hluhluwe game reserve waiting for Laurens van der Post and a German television film crew. I had an intuition that something was wrong with Magqubu, so I drove to his *muzi*. I noticed that the women and children were huddled in little groups, and the cattle and goats were unattended. I went quietly into Magqubu's hut, and in the light of the late summer afternoon I saw the old man lying on the floor. This was a sign that he was dangerously ill. He was so still that I had to look closely to see if he was breathing. His face was drawn and his eyes had rolled back. I sat next to him and whispered his name and he replied, "Yebo, Madolo, yebo, Madolo."

Ikonamangele came into the hut and described Magqubu's symptoms. It was obvious he was suffering from gastro-enteritis, but he was again refusing to go to the clinic, expressing his faith in Shembe with a passion that made lesser believers feel ashamed. I could see that he would soon lose consciousness, and I told Ikonamangele to prepare a vehicle. I sat watching him and listening to his shallow breathing. The suspense was overpowering, and I had to stop myself from picking him up and putting him in the truck. It was dark before he passed out, and we raced him to the clinic. A competent nurse dosed him intravenously and he lay back sleeping. I returned to Hluhluwe game reserve and told Laurens van der Post what had happened, and that I was afraid Magqubu might not live.

The following afternoon Laurens and I called in at the *muzi*, wondering what we would find. In the big maize field the tractor was turning over the black soil and white tick birds were feeding on exposed grubs. A knot of people followed a little way behind. A figure in brown overalls waved and came walking over to us. It was Magqubu.

"My God, Magqubu," I exclaimed. "Yesterday you were nearly dead. I can't believe my eyes."

Magqubu laughed. "Yes," he said, "that is true, but now I am alive and there are *madumbies* [an edible tuber] to be planted."

It was not long before we went out on trail together again, but I knew that our trail days were coming to an end. Magqubu was eighty-nine, perhaps even ninety. He wanted more time to himself to pray and to meditate.

I had a warning of what was coming a few years previously at the trail camp at Amatshemnyama (Black Rocks). I was sitting a little distance from the camp in the early morning listening to the song of the white-throated robin, which for me is the most sensitive sound of the wilderness. Magqubu came forward in a determined manner, knowing that he was breaking in on a moment when I wanted to be alone. "I had a long dream in the night," he said. I listened to his account and it seemed to me to be the unconscious warning him against going out on trail on a Saturday, which was his Shembe sabbath. I spoke about what I thought the dream was saying. He agreed volubly about breaking the sabbath. "We must stop or Jehovah will punish me," he said.

For a while we avoided Saturdays, and he conducted his services within the circle of white stones under the erythrina tree at his *muzi*, but the pressure of work caused a drift back to incorporating his sacred day on our trails. Magqubu said nothing, but I could sense his uneasiness as we continued trekking through the Mfolozi toward the sabbath, which, for Magqubu, began on Friday afternoon.

In June 1989 we took a trail that included the American consul general and two Johannesburg businessmen. We began on a late Thursday afternoon and arrived at the camp in the evening. I sent Magqubu with the three men to collect water from the Black Mfolozi and stayed behind getting the fire going and unpacking the food. The group returned half an hour later, and I heard Magqubu shouting about lions. I don't know exactly what happened, but it appears they surprised a pride of lions in the reeds, and in keeping his eyes on the lions Magqubu fell into an antbear hole and twisted his knee. He limped into camp and sat disconsolately near his fire.

I knew I was in for it when he called me over and showed me his swollen knee. "You see, Jehovah has now shown he is angry. I told you many times that we should not violate the sabbath," he said over and over again.

Trying to break the tension, I joked that perhaps Jehovah had made him realize how he made me suffer when walking down steep hillsides or among boulders. "My knee looks like yours the whole time. That's why the Zulu call me Madolo," I said. I could see that this remark got under his skin, and I was repentant. I knew he was too low in spirit to respond immediately, but later I would feel his wrath. I helped him to apply hot water to his knee. He refused any kind of ointment. That was his way.

The next day Magqubu stayed in camp with Tex Harris, the American consul general, while I walked out with the other members of the group, and we returned in the evening. Magqubu sat nursing his leg and saying little. The following morning was Saturday, and he appealed to me not to leave because it was his sabbath. I could see that he was depressed, and this deepened when I explained that the men on trail had to catch a flight in Durban.

At the *indaba*, where we sat in a circle and discussed the events of the trail, he let me know that I had transgressed. With the white-throated robin whistling softly in the background and an emerald-spotted wood dove singing, Magqubu pointed out that I had endangered his life by flouting God. No explanation of mine satisfied him, and the walk back to the vehicle was long and painful for him. I could see his knee was now badly swollen, the ligaments probably torn. We walked over the hills covered in red themeda grass. In the distance were rhino and buffalo, and I hoped that this would not be the day we were charged or it would give Magqubu more ammunition to fire at me. Worse, it would endanger his life.

We left him at his home and he looked me straight in the eye. "You have tempted God and I have to pay the price. I will see you later," he said. He was angry, and I did not blame him.

The next time I saw him Magqubu lectured me at length about how I had annoyed Jehovah by making him go on trail on the sabbath. He remembered all my faults, dragging them up from the past and elaborating as only he could in every detail. I knew better than to try to argue, so I kept quiet, bit my tongue, and nodded my head.

"You are not listening properly, I can see by the way your eyes are staring into the distance," he thundered. I snapped back to attention. "That's better," he said, then he burst out laughing and imitated my embarrassed body movements. I knew I had been forgiven. He shook his finger at me and said with a smile, "Even you must not go out on the sabbath."

This confirmed my feeling that his trail days had come to an end. The Lord and Magqubu's Zulu ancestors could truly say that he had worked harder in his lifetime than a dozen other men put together. He fulfilled and exemplified his creed of having to sweat a little each day. For him not working was a sin, and he led by example. From the day he was old enough to look after the goats and throughout his long service in the game reserves he was always the first to report for duty and to volunteer for any dangerous tasks. When I left him late that afternoon he sang the Shembe hymn he heard on his interior journey after he had been bitten by the boomslang in the cave at Gome outpost in 1940. He waved goodbye, and in my heart I knew that he had forgiven me, but I knew too that he was planning for his last days. The mere thought of him not being around depressed me immeasurably. That night I had a dream of him and in it he gave me a stick. He had handed over the power. The stick to the Zulu is important both literally and symbolically.

In 1992 I went often to see Magqubu. We were still in a punishing drought. The state of the land reflected the aridity of our political and environmental crises. Not only were the rivers low and in some cases dry, but weeds were growing prolifically on the sandy beds, indicative of the severity of the desiccation. The land was drying up because of human overpopulation, the historical and political mistakes of land allocation and plain misuse. The monoculture of exotic trees and sugarcane was the biggest culprit.

I arrived at Magqubu's *muzi* one weekend when the hot winds from the mountains howled over the parched countryside, blowing dry sugarcane leaves into piles on the sides of the roads. Droughts were growing worse. In my many years in Zululand I had learned to know the smell of them. Magqubu had taught me to read the early signs. Drought had become known to us who lived close to the land, anticipating the seasons and looking for the clouds of hope, the dark rain clouds. I sat waiting for Magqubu to emerge from his hut, and I reflected, as all South Africans were doing, about the fate of our country. I thought how ironic it was that the heavy dark clouds were the ones that would bring relief from the relentless sun. So it is with politics. The dark clouds looming over us politically were, paradoxically, pregnant with great possibilities of renewal. Perhaps we needed the drought to remind us that we are dependent upon the land for our water and our food. In good times we took it all for granted and seldom said thanks when the rain came. Similarly, for too long our political complacency has blinded us to the cruel world of inequality of opportunity. In the same way that we have to go through the drought to make us appreciate the sound, the scent, and the benefit of rain, so with politics. But a dam was about to break. South Africa was in the process of dramatic change. I sat in a pensive mood at the gate of the *muzi* of my friend, now in his ninety-third year. We had known each other for forty years, and my life had been enriched beyond adequate description by our association.

It was a very sad meeting, because age had suddenly caught up with him. That incredibly strong body of his, forged on the Ongeni hills as a boy then tempered as an *udibi* to the early conservator Vaughan Kirby and as messenger, paymaster, and game guard to Captain Potter, was ailing.

He invited me into his hut, and we talked in the language that we have communicated in since we met: my poor Zulu and his exquisite Zulu, repeated with infinite patience, and the telepathic understanding of the non-spoken world.

He had been very ill, he said. He had been to see a white doctor in Mtubatuba who had injected him and given him pills that had relieved his pain. I knew he must have been in a bad way to have gone to a doctor. He saw the incredulous look on my face, smiled, and said he had been to the Shembe church for a special dispensation.

His face was drawn and his eyes were beginning to cloud over with the bluish tinge of age; yet when he smiled, I saw that except for a few back molars he had all his teeth. I remembered how he had told me, while we were on trail and walking past the faint remaining marks of Mpika Manqele's *muzi,* that Mpika could eat a mielie cob when he was ninety years old. Magqubu could do the same, which says much for wood ash and massaging the gums.

We talked of old times and of the men we had worked with, a fortunate band on whom the gods had smiled. There were the wilderness trailists, too, who had been touched by this remarkable man. He had spoken to them of the spirit of the land and shared his deep knowledge of history and the interconnectedness of the natural world and ourselves, ecopoetic descriptions of bird, animal, plant, and tree drawn together and presented holistically.

I was overcome with grief at the thought that his time was limited. He was always so indestructible, and we had been through so much together. I tried to choke back the tears that began welling up, because I did not want to upset him. I loved him too much to add to his distress. He saw my grief, held my hand, and began talking to make me laugh. He made a joke of his ailments and imitated his laborious moves in the night to get to the door in time to pass water. He did not tell me not to weep because he knew and understood, but, as only he could, he defused the tension.

To distract me he spoke a little of politics, making penetrating observations. As always he cut to the heart of our country's problems, yet he accepted everything that was happening as a natural course of events.

Time came for me to leave, and I asked him to pray. We held hands and lowered our heads, and he asked Nkulunkulu for blessings and understanding of our human frailty and guidance from the spirit on the path through this world. He spoke my name and told me not to be distressed, but I could not stop the tears from running down my cheeks. He looked at me kindly, and his bearing was firm and resolute. He knew that his time was coming soon, and he was prepared to meet the great God and his ancestors as a Zulu, unafraid and in the confidence that he had done his duty in life. "When my time is near," he said, "I will send for you and you will come. It is right that we should say goodbye to each other." I promised I would come when he called. In the distance I heard the coucal calling, the long liquid notes bubbling down the scale. It was his bird because it brought the rain, and he said it was one of the first bird calls he remembered from childhood when he grew up in the mist on the Ongeni hills. The coucal bird and the reedbuck whistling: these two sounds were his continuous link to his native land.

As we parted he took out and put on a raincoat I had bought him in London in 1987. He laughed and said if he wore it, rain would be sure to come, as it had in England. By the time I reached the Amatikulu River on my return journey, black clouds had filled the sky, and a blinding rainstorm swept in from the south.

Driving through the rain, I could smell the scent of the African earth and the faint scent of woodsmoke and maize-meal porridge from the huts near the road. Naked Zulu children danced in the falling rain, their little bodies shining as they stamped their feet and sang in adulation at the breaking of the drought. Soon the dust was washed off the nearby trees, and the sugarcane looked fresher, the African rainstorm carrying within it the amazing powers of transformation.

My car sped south into the darkening storm and more rain lashed down. I thought that the rain of political relief would come in God's good time too. I switched on the radio and, synchronistically, there was a news report of irreversible political moves that had been set in motion. The old South Africa was dying fast. During the rest of my journey through the rain squalls I thought about the political difficulties Magqubu and I had had to face under the apartheid regime. Our friendship was frowned upon, and there were many humiliating incidents. One of the worst was when the senior officials in the Parks Board refused to allow Magqubu to stay in the rest camps. He had given himself wholeheartedly in the service of wildlife conservation in Zululand, and now he was spurned by the very people for whom he had worked. Yet I think I was more ashamed and angry than he was. I railed and cursed while he sat stolidly and shrugged his shoulders. He had had to endure so much in his life, and this was just another incident. He knew he came from noble Zulu stock. His forefathers had been warriors and they had ruled the land, and he knew that the day would come when they would reassert themselves and once more impose their own kind of order. We used to joke about it. Once on an anti-poaching patrol he was digging a small hole to bury the fire ashes. I took the spade from him and carried on digging. "Why are you doing that?" he demanded. "Your back and your knee do not allow digging."

I said, "Magqubu, the day has come: it is the day of which we often speak. We are now equal, and because there are more of you, I dig the hole."

He laughed and laughed. "The day, the day," he repeated, smiling, his white teeth shining. Then he took two swift steps, snatched the spade out of my hands, and began digging again. "Tomorrow," he said. "Tomorrow is the day." He was always in command.

The rain came down in sheets on the bridge over the Thukela River. Up the hill the clouds lifted for a few brief moments, and on my left I saw the tall trees that marked the monuments and the gravestones of Fort Pearson, one of the invasion points in the Anglo-Zulu War. Down below the jutting hill, on the river bank, was the ultimatum tree, where the Zulu *indunas* had sat and listened to the impossible conditions the British imposed if Zululand were not to be invaded. Magqubu and I had often sat under that tree while he told the story of that dark and terrible time for the Zulu nation. By the 1980s it was obvious that the tree was dying, and for Magqubu this was symbolism of deep significance. He related it to the old order and the indignity his king, Cetshwayo, had had to endure. The ultimatum given to the king's *indunas* had been harsh, and the intent was clear to the grey-haired and bearded men with their *izicoco* (head rings) shining in the hot summer sun. The British wanted the destruction of the Zulu kingdom.

Now the tree was dying, and a younger one was growing near it. This to Magqubu and to me represented the beginning of the passing of the old white order and the emergence of a new and more representative government. The young tree with its strong trunk, firm branches, bright green leaves, and new fruit was a symbol of the future. We talked about it each time we passed and saluted the spirits in those small neat cemeteries. For Magqubu the spirits lived, and he sang out a praise song to all the men who had marched and fought across this landscape. As I approached Durban the clouds lifted and the sky turned a deep shade of grey with patches of blue between. An announcement on the radio was of another new government in the making.

In 1993 I travelled extensively to Australia and Tasmania, the United Kingdom, and finally Norway to attend the Fifth World Wilderness

Congress. I kept in touch with South Africa and had detailed reports of how Magqubu was faring. I remembered his statement: "When I send for you, you will come."

I returned from Norway and heard from a nursing friend in the Karkloof valley, where I live, that Magqubu had been in hospital in Empangeni, the nearest big town to his homestead. He had a biopsy for prostate problems, and as he was wheeled into the operating room he had the staff giggling and laughing over his imitations of animals and his stories. Wherever he went he had a captive audience. I had asked colleagues to monitor his progress, and he recovered well from the operation. Then he had a relapse, and I suspect had picked up jaundice. I was then in Botswana and stopped in Maun. There was an urgent fax from my secretary. The message was brief: "Magqubu very ill and he is asking for you." I had been expecting something to happen, because even in the central desert of Australia I had dreamed of him, and I knew he was sending a message in the telepathic language we so often used. I was in the Duck Inn having a cup of tea when the fax was handed to me by Nigel Cantle, whose father, Harry, I had known when he was a game ranger in the national parks service in Zimbabwe. Harry was one of the most experienced and bravest game rangers I had known. It seemed fitting that I should hear about Magqubu from Harry's son.

The friendship that existed between white game rangers and black game scouts in the former Rhodesia overcame racial differences and antagonisms. This was the case throughout Africa with most of the men who served in the field. They shared food from the same pot, slept on the ground together, faced charging elephants and armed poachers together, believing in a cause that few could ever fully describe. The colour of one's skin, one's race or creed was irrelevant once the Africa we carry within us was touched. It would be untrue to say that every white ranger and black scout had a firm friendship, particularly on the surface. This would be expecting too much. Yet I am sure that with all field men, there was a connection that many of them were not even consciously aware of. You only saw it in their actions and reactions in emergency situations. Africa is full of stories of black game scouts and white game rangers saving each other from crocodiles that had dragged them into rivers, or from being gored by rhino or trampled by elephant or shot by poachers – all outward manifestations of a link that most would find it difficult to articulate.

I read the fax and asked Nigel to ensure that I was on the next plane to South Africa. I was worried that I might be too late, yet I knew that Magqubu would never have waited until the last minute to warn me of his impending death. It was a pact that we would say goodbye to each other. He was always sure that he would go before I did. There was nothing morbid in this, only the matter-of-fact way as he lived his life. So I knew that my fears of not getting to his homestead at Macibini in time were not valid; intuition and telepathy told me this too, but consciously I was afraid.

I boarded a plane that day, relieved that I was on the move. The plane circled Maun before heading south, and I looked out toward the Okavango swamps. This is a part of Africa that still remains relatively wild, a remnant of a once greater area. I sat on the flight dozing and thinking with vivid mental pictures of experiences in our past. The incident with lions and his pot. The calm way he had awaited the attack of the lioness as he put his little pot down. He was making sure that the animal wanted to kill us before he fired a shot. Years of game control and then the terrible carnage in the *nagana* campaign had given him a feeling for a rifle that few other human beings except professional soldiers experience. The *nagana* killing in the 1940s was a profound psychic shock for him, which I am sure led to his interior journey after he had been bitten by the boomslang. His life had been dramatically changed by that experience, as mine had been by my encounter with Jungian psychology.

He had always accepted dreams as part of his life – I had to learn their importance. His intuition was so highly developed that he knew when to obey it and did so unhesitatingly. My grasp of the intuitive was a slow and often painful process because I doubted and for too long denied it. He was able to take in a situation at a glance. His superb tracking ability and his power to concentrate for hours on end while following an animal were just a few examples of what Jungian psychology would term a strong sensation function. I naturally projected my weak sensation onto him, but with insights gained from the study of Jung and my entry into analysis, I became more aware of the psychological aspects of our friendship.

I will always treasure a remark made by John Sanford, an American Episcopalian priest who left the church to become a Jungian analyst and writer of many books, including *Dreams: God's Forgotten Language*. We were on trail in the Mfolozi in 1984, and John Sanford said one evening, as we sat around the fire in the dark African night, that Magqubu was a man who had become whole without going through the analytical process. I came to realize how incredibly well-adjusted he was. His life had been a training ground of intense hardship interwoven with sound family and extended family relations, yet tinged with deep sadness at some wayward children and many infant deaths. His adopted English name was Moses, a name he bore with the pride of the old prophet himself.

To see Magqubu dressed in his white robes and carrying his long staff on his Saturday sabbath, striding out to the circle of erythrina trees to preach his sermon, was like witnessing a scene from the Old Testament. I remembered the many trails, patrols, and journeys we had been on together. At sunset Magqubu the game ranger, tracker, naturalist, Zulu warrior, and storyteller would emerge wearing his robes. He would kneel and pray aloud to Nkulunkulu, the great god. His respect for this divinity was awesome, yet it was a god to whom he spoke in everyday terms, a god he loved and respected yet knew was a friend who understood all his problems, his needs, and desires.

Before the great flood in Zululand in 1984, there was a tall sycamore fig tree well over a hundred years old growing on the banks of the Black Mfolozi below the cliffs of Amatshemnyama. When on trail it was to this tree that Magqubu went to kneel and pray. His voice was always firm and clear, and when sitting a few yards from the fire and with no intention of eavesdropping, I caught the echo of his conversation with God. I was impressed by the relationship. Never any pleading or begging, but a straightforward, deeply respectful conversation with a force that knew everything, was compassionate, but would allow no nonsense. At times it was like a report on what he had been doing and the goings-on in the *muzi*. Or it was asking for guidance or protection from danger for the trail party. I envied his openness and ability to converse in such a frank yet deeply respectful way. Magqubu knew this god, and he knew that he was known. There was no need for him to know the creed by rote: he lived it in his daily life. Yet, at the same time as Magqubu communicated with God, he lived in the community of his family and neighbours and sought to encourage them to talk with God as he did. He enjoyed, too, his relationship with the natural world. It was a creation of God, and everything lived and had a spirit, right from the tiniest flower to the trees, animals, and birds.

The plane climbed higher, and far on the western horizon over the green of the Okavango delta I caught a brief glimpse of the Tsodilo hills. We had visited them a few days before, enthralled by the mass of Bushman art there. I was reminded of Laurens van der Post, who had brought the plight of the Bushmen to the attention of the modern world with films and books. We had become friends over thirty years ago, and he had come to Mfolozi game reserve with a BBC television crew to make a documentary on a wilderness trail. He brought his granddaughter, Emma Crichton-Miller, and with Magqubu we spent two weeks filming.

When Magqubu and Laurens met there was an instantaneous recognition by each of the inner man in the other. I recalled a story I had read of two Englishmen meeting for the first time in some remote spot in the world.

They fell on their knees and embraced each other because they had seen the inner spirit. Magqubu and Laurens van der Post stared at each other, then clasped hands in a warm embrace that can only come when one recognizes the inner spirit. That first evening, as we gathered around the *umThombothi* fire and Laurens rocked backward and forward looking into the fire, his blue eyes reflecting the dancing flames, Magqubu looked at him and said to me that he had given him a name.

"What is it?" I asked.

"Inkunzimalanga," he said.

Literally translated it means The Bull of the Sun, but Magqubu explained that Laurens was a man who could push everything and everybody in front of himself, but so gently they would not know it was happening. Without having met or heard about him, Magqubu knew that this man had a special power of persuasion.

The plane landed in Johannesburg, and I took another to Durban, went to the farm to fetch Ann, and we were driven north by Jacob Nduli of the Wilderness Leadership School. Jacob, a former Natal Parks Board man, had known Magqubu for many years and respected and loved him as an elder of the Zulu people. He also understood Magqubu's devotion to Zulu history, Shembe, and the cause of wildlife conservation. Jacob was an important member of the Wilderness Leadership School staff and an excellent driver. It was a relief after all my travelling to hand over to him. Three and a half hours after leaving Durban we arrived at Magqubu's *muzi* in the Macibini area, east of the Mambeni gate leading into Mfolozi game reserve.

Ikonamangele, Magqubu's son, was driving the tractor and ploughing the rich black earth. His wife followed behind, sowing the mielies by hand from a reed bowl. She was framed by dark clouds coming up from the south, and she moved with ease and grace, a shawl over her head. In her long flowing dress she looked like a figure from the biblical past. We waited for the tractor to turn and come back, and Ikonamangele came to tell us what we already knew. Magqubu did not have long to live.

We went into his main hut, its peace and contents so familiar to me. Magqubu was on the floor being comforted by his wife Tabete. She was cradling Magqubu's head and weeping quietly. She whispered his name. "Mkulu, Mkulu [grandfather], Madolo has come," she said. I held his hand and wept uncontrollably. He was in a coma, but he came out of it and nodded his head when Tabete asked if he had seen me. He began retching bile, and the pain of it seemed to make him fully conscious. Bodily functions were a normal part of life, and he was not embarrassed by them. He lay back and gently squeezed my hand, comforting me as he had always done.

Outside, the clouds were louring over the landscape, bringing the promise of rain. The *uFukwe* bubbled down the scale, the soft notes rising and falling on the wind. Magqubu could perfectly whistle the notes of the call and always said that the bird brought rain. I remembered how we had often lain in our old army overcoats on damp cold mornings waiting for poachers while the coucals sang from clumps of bush in the open grasslands of the game reserves. When they grew silent we knew poachers were coming. Now, here on this darkening afternoon, the poacher that claims everyone in the end was approaching. All of us in the hut were weeping, but Magqubu was supported by a family and extended family system. Toddlers came into the room and sat near him, only dimly aware that Babamkulu was fading. The women did not allow them to make unnecessary noise, but they were not shielded from the oncoming death. A group of women in the adjoining room sat quietly, giving the weeping Tabete moral support. It is no wonder that Magqubu refused to return to hospital after his operation. Here he was with family, friends, and in familiar surroundings. He did not want the lonely white bed and the separation.

For a while he lapsed again into a coma, then suddenly and without effort he sat upright, pointing his index finger to the sky. He said firmly with his powerful voice, "Nkosi." In that moment I knew he had seen the divine light. His eyes were shining. The internal, or external, God had visited him in a blinding flash, validating him and his life's work, as though saying, "You good and faithful servant." Magqubu had served God, his family, the Zulu people, his fellow men, and the game reserves with unswerving dedication. This had been recognized by the living light force. He lay back sleeping and breathing gently.

We left him with a promise to Tabete that we would return with Malamba (Nick Steele) after we had attended the memorial service for the game-capture men drowned recently when crossing the flooded Black Mfolozi River. I was reminded of Magqubu's little song that he would sing when we approached the river. It was about the Black Mfolozi, which took away the people who crossed it and carried them like pumpkins to the sea.

We returned later, and Tabete said Malamba was in the room. Magqubu, now only a day from death, rolled over and recited Nick's praise names, not missing a single line. We were amazed at the seemingly never-ending reservoir of strength of this man. Nick and I held his hands, his skin still like a man's of forty.

We talked quietly about rhino-catching days, his expert tracking, and, even though we were half his age, how we could not keep up with him when walking. Magqubu lay back and nodded his head. I reminded Nick of the day we had tried to race him up the terribly steep winding path at Mdindini to Mpila. It was no contest.

"Do you remember, Baba?" I asked.

"Yebo," he said.

Even now, after months of illness his bare thighs were still powerful. Again outside the coucal was calling and more fine rain swept past the hut and dripped from the roof.

"They should take him outside to see and smell the rain," Nick whispered. After years of drought it would please him to know that as he was leaving this world rain was falling, but Magqubu was too weak. In this dry area, which was subjected to devastating droughts, rain was always a preoccupation, but on the hills of Ongeni, where Magqubu and his forefathers were born, rain and mist came with more ease.

How he had always longed to return, as he had been promised, after the tsetse-fly campaign. Nevertheless, he understood that what his people had so reluctantly given up was for the greater good of the world. My God, how we had both agonized over this. Now the graves of his forefathers are incorporated into the Mfolozi corridor and Hluhluwe game reserve, part of the rich history of the struggle and sacrifice for wildlife conservation in Zululand to which he had devoted his life. At the same time, Magqubu was adamant that all the people who had been removed with false promises should receive some financial compensation. He realized that it was impossible for everybody to return to their old *imizi*, which by now had become grazing grounds for wild animals. "But the government lied to us, and for this we must be paid," he said.

In the last few years of his life he would return again to the injustice of being lied to. His sense of association with the Ongeni hills was overwhelmingly powerful, and to go to the old hut sites and the graves and listen to him sing out to the spirits of his relatives affected me deeply. I had walked with him many times as he pointed out the stones he had played on, or the patch of forest where leopards had lived. He would always stop at his grandmother's grave site and talk to her as though she were alive. I imagine he would have been a favourite of hers, and to listen to the passion in his voice when he spoke to her, it was easy to imagine that she must have provided solace from the rigours of the harsh Zulu discipline. When he spoke to her spirit he was oblivious of me and anyone else nearby. He entered the world of the spirit and became part of what was going on in it, and he thanked his grandmother for her love and protection when he was a little boy. I saw Tabete do this with his grandchildren when he was after them for not looking after the goats or the cattle properly.

The next day we returned and sat in Magqubu's hut surrounded by women and children and some men who had come to see him. I thought again about the past. Apart from his own experience, Magqubu had learned well from his elders.

His father, uncles, and the other men who visited the *muzi* had sat around the fire at Ongeni telling stories. I often imagined him as a young boy, sitting within hearing distance and absorbing knowledge like a sponge. "My ears are my books and my lips are my pen," as he would say. His powers of observation were phenomenal, and he had eyes that could see better than my small binoculars, which he always disdained, yet he would talk with awe about Mali Mdhletshe, the *induna* of Vaughan Kirby and Captain Potter, under whom Mali and Magqubu worked. "That man Mali knew and could see everything," he said.

I remembered how when I was senior ranger at Mfolozi game reserve and Magqubu was the *induna* sergeant, he brought Mali Mdhletshe to the Mpila office. The love, respect, and veneration Magqubu had for the old game guard was most moving. He fussed around, bringing Mali tea and making sure he was comfortably seated in the sun. He insisted I take a photograph, which, thank God, I did, because I know of no other in existence. He spoke of Mali's bravery when he tackled white poachers, even when one of them shot his hat off. It was an experience to see Magqubu so concerned and so tender. To me at that time Magqubu was the tough no-nonsense sergeant of the guards. I have a photograph taken just before Mali's visit, and Magqubu's face is set unyieldingly. He took his responsibilities extremely seriously, and managing the guard force and all the family troubles of the men as well as the usual jealousies was no easy task. Yet there he was, responsive to every movement and gesture of old Mali.

He was so proud to have worked under him, and he told me later how Mali had imparted his knowledge in the true oral tradition. There was lots of time to learn, too, on the long patrols on foot and the interminable journeys to Mahlaba-tini, taking poachers to the police.

The police station commander would tell them when the court case would take place, and they made notches in a stick to mark the time. Men who had served Shaka when Mali was a boy were still alive to tell the history of the time. Magqubu absorbed every drop of it from Mali. When Mali left that afternoon I saw tears in Magqubu's eyes, a most remarkable sight, because he kept his emotions well controlled. I had never seen him weep until Mali came.

Women from the district sat on the floor in the room near to where Magqubu was lying. They were of the Shembe religion and wore white

Magqubu Ntombela and Mali Mdhletshe

dresses with black shawls over their heads. They were singing quietly, and the little children, two and three years old, clambered over Magqubu, holding his hands and stroking his face. I could sense that the children were a comfort to Magqubu. When they became too boisterous Tabete took them aside, but they were soon back clutching at Magqubu's beard or gripping his fingers. The Shembe women began to sing when we left the house. Their beautiful voices seemed to fill every space, and I could hear them from the car. I knew that as Magqubu would begin to drift down into his final long sleep, the women would be singing his spirit away to the next world. There could not have been a more gentle way to go.

Two days later I had a phone call at the farm to say that Magqubu had passed away. Although I knew it was coming, I was still shocked. It was a hard fact for me to accept. I took the long stick made from red ivory wood that he had given me and went for a walk. I went down the drive with its yellowwood trees to the one where our elder son Kenneth and I had buried my father's ashes in 1978. I never passed it without, in Zulu fashion, greeting my father and other family members. Today I added Magqubu to my family list. He was my other father, and I would never pass the tree again without adding my greetings to him. It was an overcast afternoon, and a dark sky was sweeping in from the south behind a steady drizzle. I walked around the farm, remembering many incidents when Magqubu lived here with us. He used to sing long hymns of praise to God, asking for our protection. His powerful voice could be heard as far as the main road, nearly a kilometre away. The farm had a special aura because of him. I passed the hut he used as a kitchen, and I remembered the times I sat with him beside the wattle-wood fire. Then, as I leaned against a stone wall I was suddenly aware of his presence, and I knew that he had come to say farewell before he went to the next world.

On Sunday, October 31, 1993, Magqubu was buried. The body lay in his bedroom while all the relatives shook his hand and said farewell. He was then brought into the marquee where we sat and other friends came to say goodbye. I knelt down to shake his cold hand before he was carried to the grave, wrapped in the skin of an ox killed the night before. The gift of the animal came from Laurens van der Post and Ronald Cohen in London. Some of the old game guards and companions of Magqubu stood weeping unashamedly. They were strong, tough men who had lived a hard life working in the game reserves, and I had never seen them so upset. They stood sobbing, speaking about Magqubu and the work they had done together. He had been their leader, counsellor, and friend, a man they could turn to whenever they had any trouble. He was always their intermediary with authority. He was the wise man, the judicious man, the sympathetic person who knew them and their families. To weep openly for such a man was no disgrace.

A young granddaughter, Lindiwe Ntombela, was in charge of the ceremonies for the funeral preliminaries. She conducted them with grace and diplomacy. She called my name and asked me to stand and speak. I dreaded the thought, because I had never been able to speak at funerals – I became too emotional. I knew that I would break down, and in my culture this is frowned upon. Men of my generation were taught from childhood never to show emotion. When I was beaten at school I could not cry; if a novel moved me I had to choke back the emotion when reading it aloud. Emotion had become a word of contempt and was used with devastating effect by our opponents against those of us in the conservation movement.

I have had to talk at functions in many parts of the world, but this was the hardest speech I have ever given, and I believe the best understood. To stand weeping in front of this crowd was no disgrace. The experience enabled me to make a personal breakthrough. I realized, while I stood there talking of my friendship with Magqubu and not holding back the tears, that even in death Magqubu had helped me.

Three Shembe priests took over for the burial. The women sang as the body was carried to the grave wrapped in the ox skin. A spear had been stuck into the ground at the head of the grave, and Ikonamangele began smashing the coffin and tearing up the sleeping mats made from *ncema* grass. Only the delicately embroidered borders of the mats were kept, and the nails from the coffin. The women continued to sing, joined now by the men, and the body was laid in the grave and other items were put next to it. Then the earth was shovelled in, rattling on the oxhide. Slowly I saw my old friend disappear under a mound of earth. Magqubu was buried as he always said he would be, like a Zulu, but I know of no man who so successfully bridged the gap between cultures.

We threw our handfuls of earth onto the grave, saying our goodbyes for the last time. A meal was prepared, and we ate with relatives and friends, a wake of which Magqubu would have approved.

Dark rain clouds were gathering on the distant hills when we left for Durban in the late afternoon. Soon rain would come and dampen the final resting place of this man around whom, as Nick Steele said, our lives had revolved.

I looked back at the *muzi*, framed now by the rain clouds, and said: "You're a better man than I am, Magqubu Ntombela. Hamba kahle, you old soul of the land." I made a mental vow that I would create a foundation in his name so that his great spirit would be remembered.

The rain began to come down in sheets, and thunder rolled over the Ongeni hills and vivid forked lightning lit the western sky. Then, above all the other sounds, I heard the liquid call of Burchell's coucal. It was Magqubu's bird and he knew it brought the rain, and he had at last gone home to join his ancestral spirits.